Contrastive Rhetoric

THE CAMBRIDGE APPLIED LINGUISTICS SERIES

Series editors: Michael H. Long and Jack C. Richards

This new series presents the findings of recent work in applied linguistics which are of direct relevance to language teaching and learning and of particular interest to applied linguists, researchers, language teachers, and teacher trainers.

In this series:

Interactive Approaches to Second Language Reading *edited by Patricia L. Carrell, Joanne Devine, and David E. Eskey*

Second Language Classrooms – Research on teaching and learning *by Craig Chaudron*

Language Learning and Deafness *edited by Michael Strong*

The Learner-Centred Curriculum *by David Nunan*

The Second Language Curriculum *edited by Robert Keith Johnson*

Language Transfer – Cross-linguistic influence in language learning *by Terence Odlin*

Linguistic Perspectives on Second Language Acquisition *edited by Susan M. Gass and Jaquelyn Schachter*

Learning Strategies in Second Language Acquisition *by J. Michael O'Malley and Anna Uhl Chamot*

The Development of Second Language Proficiency *edited by Birgit Harley, Patrick Allen, Jim Cummins and Merrill Swain*

Second Language Writing – Research insights for the classroom *edited by Barbara Kroll*

Genre Analysis – English in academic and research settings *by John M. Swales*

Evaluating Second Language Education *edited by J. Charles Alderson and Alan Beretta*

Perspectives on Pedagogical Grammar *edited by Terence Odlin*

Academic Listening *edited by John Flowerdew*

Power and Inequality in Language Education *edited by James W. Tollefson*

Language Program Evaluation – Theory and practice *by Brian K. Lynch*

Sociolinguistics and Language Teaching *edited by Sandra Lee McKay and Nancy H. Hornberger*

Contrastive Rhetoric – Cross-cultural aspects of second language writing *by Ulla Connor*

Contrastive Rhetoric

Cross-cultural aspects of second-language writing

Ulla Connor

Indiana University at Indianapolis

CAMBRIDGE UNIVERSITY PRESS

Published by the Press Syndicate of the University of Cambridge
The Pitt Building, Trumpington Street, Cambridge CB2 1RP
40 West 20th Street, New York, NY 10011-4211, USA
10 Stamford Road, Oakleigh, Melbourne 3166, Australia

First published 1996

Printed in the United States of America

Library of Congress Cataloging-in-Publication Data
Connor, Ulla, 1948–
Contrastic rhetoric : cross-cultural aspects of second-language
writing / Ulla Connor.
p.   cm. – (The Cambridge applied linguistic series)
Includes bibliographical references (p.) and index.
ISBN 0-521-44145-5. – ISBN 0-521-44688-0 (pbk.)
1. Language and languages – Study and teaching.   2. Rhetoric – Study
and teaching.   3. Contrastive linguistics.   I. Title.   II. Series.
P53.27.C66   1996
418'.007 – dc20   95-9965
                                                                  CIP

A catalog record for this book is available from the British Library

ISBN 0-521-44145-5 Hardback
ISBN 0-521-44688-0 Paperback

This book is dedicated to my mother, Esteri Niemelä, and to the memory of my father, Antti Niemelä.

Contents

Series editors' preface   ix
Preface   xi

I PRELIMINARIES; EARLY PHASES OF THE FIELD   1

1 Toward an extended definition of contrastive rhetoric   3
   Writing in a second language: anecdotal evidence about
   problems and solutions   3
   Study of second language writing: the emergence of
   contrastive rhetoric   5
   Aims, purposes, and outline of this book   6
   Building a comprehensive theory of contrastive rhetoric   8

2 Contrastive rhetoric studies in applied linguistics   12
   Contrastive analysis, error analysis, and analysis of
   interlanguage   12
   Development of contrastive rhetoric: parallel with contrastive
   analysis   14
   International Englishes   16
   New directions in contrastive rhetorical research in applied
   linguistics contexts   18
   Summary   26

3 Historical evolution of contrastive rhetoric: from Kaplan's
   1966 study to diversification in languages, genres, and
   authors   28
   Origins of contrastive rhetoric   28
   Arabic   34
   Chinese   37
   Japanese   41
   Korean, German, Finnish, Spanish, and Czech   45
   Summary   54

II   INTERFACES WITH OTHER DISCIPLINES   57

4   **Contrastive rhetoric and the field of rhetoric and composition**   59
The role of rhetoric and composition in college education in the United States   59
Classical rhetoric   62
The expressionist approach   71
Contrastive rhetoric and the expressionist approach   72
Writing as a cognitive approach   74
The social constructivist approach   76
Summary   79

5   **Contrastive rhetoric and text linguistics**   80
Brief overview of the history of text linguistics; definitions   80
Major schools of thought in text linguistics   81
Concepts and methods of text linguistics and their application to the study of writing   83
NORDTEXT and NORDWRITE text linguistic projects of student writing   89
Survey of contrastive rhetorical studies with a text linguistic emphasis   90
Summary   97

6   **Writing as an activity embedded in a culture**   100
Definition of "culture"   101
Psychological investigations of culture and literacy   101
Anthropological study of culture and literacy   105
Educational study of culture and literacy   107
Studies of culture and literacy conducted by applied linguists   113
Summary   115

7   **Contrastive rhetoric and translation studies**   117
Development of theories of translation studies   117
Transfer in contrastive rhetoric and translation theory   120
Issues in common: theories of "acceptability" and "adequacy" in translation   121
Summary   123

8   **Genre-specific studies in contrastive rhetoric**   126
The concept of genre   126
School writing   129

Academic writing   132
Professional writing   135
Learning academic writing in sociocognitive perspective as a
dynamic activity   145
Summary   149

III   IMPLICATIONS OF CONTRASTIVE RHETORIC   151

9   **Methods of research in contrastive rhetoric**   153
Guidance from studies of composition pedagogy   153
Methods of contrastive rhetorical research   155
Summary and implications   162

10   **Conclusion: Implications and research directions**   166
Implications from contrastive text studies   167
Implications from contrastive process-based writing   167
Implications from contrastive genre-specific research in EFL
settings   169
Testing ESL/EFL writing in a cross-cultural setting   170
Research directions   172

References   175
Author index   195
Subject index   199

Series editors' preface

The influence of the learner's first language on the acquisition and use of a second has long been a focus of interest within applied linguistics. Much of this work has been confined to the sentence or utterance level and has explored both the linguistic and psycholinguistic aspects of the processes involved. The field of contrastive rhetoric, by comparison, extends and broadens this area of inquiry to the levels of discourse and text. Its areas of focus are the role of first language conventions of discourse and rhetorical structure on second language usage, as well as cognitive and cultural dimensions of transfer, particularly in relation to writing. The expanding discipline of contrastive rhetoric studies is hence of considerable interest to the field of second language learning and teaching, particularly to those involved in teaching composition and English for Specific Purposes.

It is this approach to the study of second language literacy which is presented in Ulla Connor's comprehensive introduction to the field of contrastive rhetoric, as she defines the outer boundaries of the field. Drawing on a wide and interdisciplinary body of theory and research, Connor traces the history of contrastive approaches to the study of second language writing and explores the interfaces between contrastive rhetoric and other disciplines, including composition studies, translation, text linguistics, genre analysis, and cultural anthropology. She demonstrates, with examples from a wide variety of languages, how second language writers draw on a range of cross-linguistic and cross-cultural influences at both the sentence, paragraph, and textual level. Connor examines the effects of these influences on different aspects of textual organization, including cohesion, coherence, and schematic structure, and shows how both linguistically and culturally bound assumptions about the nature and purposes of written texts can transfer from one language to another. She reviews and assesses research methods and assumptions underlying research in contrastive rhetoric, examining both quantitative and qualitative approaches to research in contrastive rhetoric, and also demonstrates the practical applications of contrastive rhetoric research in applied linguistics and second language composition teaching.

This book therefore makes a valuable contribution to our understanding of second language learning and teaching. It will be an invaluable source of information and theory for scholars, composition specialists, and students of applied linguistics and will form a welcome addition to the Cambridge Applied Linguistics Series.

Michael H. Long
Jack C. Richards

Preface

During this book's gestation, I was influenced by several competing viewpoints of writing research. Along with many others in the profession, Robert B. Kaplan's 1966 seminal "doodles" article had a great impact on my teaching and L2 writing research. For five consecutive years, Bob Kaplan and I organized a session on contrastive rhetoric at the International TESOL Conference. During this period the late John Hinds transformed contrastive rhetorical research because of his rigorous text analysis combined with an acute understanding of the L1 languages and cultures. John Hinds was a forceful presence at our contrastive rhetoric colloquia at TESOL. The proceedings eventually resulted in a collection of essays that redirected contrastive rhetoric towards a more text analytic approach (Connor and Kaplan, 1987).

Since the mid 1980s, four notable experiences – outside the mainstream ESL/EFL teaching – have shaped my views about the teaching and research of writing. First, collaborating with the rhetorician Janice Lauer in research on persuasive writing cross-culturally proved a valuable link in connecting classical theories of rhetoric and composition for L1 writers in the United States with the study of second-language writing. Second, my association with the International Education Achievement Project, directed by Alan C. Purves, on the writing achievement of school students in 14 countries was an eye-opener about the need for carefully designed writing tasks, scoring scales, and systems of analyses in cross-cultural analyses of writing. Third, my involvement in the NORDTEXT writing group in the Nordic countries – initiated by Nils Erik Enkvist and later led by Lars Evensen – instructed me about the special needs of teachers and researchers of writing in EFL situations. Finally, as a member of the Antwerp-Indianapolis-Turku project (with Ken Davis, Teun De Rycker, Piet Verckens, and Meg Phillips), in which international business writing is taught to students in the three countries simultaneously, I have become more keenly tuned to the subtle interactions among language, culture, and writing for specific purposes in the international writing arena.

In the process of writing this book through discussions and correspondence, I am particularly indebted to the following individuals: Bob

Kaplan for his continued encouraging discussions clarifying my views about the role of contrastive rhetoric in applied linguistics; Nils Erik Enkvist for invaluable guidance in the interconnections among related fields having an impact on contrastive rhetoric such as translations studies; Sauli Takala for many insightful discussions and sharing his own writings about the reinterpretations of the Sapir-Whorf hypothesis and other crucial matters of this book; Ann Johns and John Swales for introducing me to genre analysis; Patricia Carrell, Joan Carson, Andrew Chesterman, Nils Erik Enkvist, Lars Evensen, Bill Grabe, Paula Kalaja, Janice Lauer, Ilona Leki, Alan Purves, and Ann Raimes for their helpful critiques of early drafts of certain chapters; Diane Belcher, Guanjun Cai, Sonja Tirkkonen Condit, Shoshana Folman, Tom Huckin, Anncha Lindeberg, Anna Mauranen, Paul Prior, Eija Ventola, and Hilkka Yli-Jokipii for generously sharing their work on writing across cultures.

I am grateful to my students throughout the years at Georgetown University, at Indiana University in Indianapolis, and at several Summer TESOL Institutes for their comments and observations concerning early pieces of this book, and in many cases for collaboration on related writing projects. Among the most memorable contributors are Dwight Atkinson, Linda Jacobsen, Susan Mayberry, Peter McCagg, Ildikó Melis, Miuyki Sasaki, and Robert Springer.

I wish to thank the Department of English and the School of Liberal Arts at Indiana University in Indianapolis for granting me a reduced teaching load one semester as well as providing clerical assistance. Paula Pace, Stuart Schleus, Bill Stuckey, and Susan Springer provided assistance in word processing and editing. Maggie Robillard worked faithfully and patiently during the last few months of manuscript revision even while she was finishing her own undergraduate studies. Ken Davis and Helen Schwartz, faculty colleagues, provided moral support and encouragement. I also owe thanks to the ESL faculty, Karen Asenavage, Mary Boyd, and Barbara Zimmer, for their continued support as well as to the ESL students for sharing their writing with me.

During final stages of preparation of the book, I have experienced the generous hospitality of two universities in Finland: Åbo Akademi University, where Roger Sell hosted my Donner Visiting Research professorship in the Fall of 1994 and where I collaborated with Håkan Ringbom on cross-cultural research; and the University of Jyväskylä where Kari Sajavaara provided me research facilities on two occasions during the completion of this book.

I would like to acknowledge the extremely helpful and stimulating reviews by the two anonymous readers recruited by Cambridge University Press. I wish to recognize the series co-editor Jack Richards for helping to focus the book at the initial stages as well as his continual counsel. Mary Vaughn, the Executive Editor, deserves thanks for her patience in communications related to the book, and Mary Carson for careful editing.

However large the constellation of supporters and friends connected with this book, there is one person who outshines them all. Ray Keller, professor emeritus, took tremendous trouble to read the many drafts of each chapter carefully, quickly, and with minute attention to the smallest detail. His comments not only improved the manuscript, but, more important, gave me an enthusiastic reader, making the writing process almost a joy. Ray is a linguist's linguist. I feel fortunate to have such a devoted former mentor – a role model of a linguist, scholar, teacher, and friend.

Finally, I thank John and Timo Connor, my husband and son, for their continued support and encouragement, for cheering me up by producing pleasant distractions of various kinds including gourmet meals and family trips. John, a competent writer of English himself and erstwhile collaborator, has been a tireless commentator on my research and writing throughout the years. Without his belief in me and my career, this book would have never been written.

Ulla Connor

PART I:
PRELIMINARIES; EARLY PHASES OF THE FIELD

1 *Toward an extended definition of contrastive rhetoric*

Writing in a second language: anecdotal evidence about problems and solutions

English as a second language (ESL) students often mention that when they write in English as a second language they translate, or attempt to translate, first language words, phrases, and organization into English. A Chinese ESL student describes his writing process as follows:

> While choosing Chinese words is a second nature for me, extracting the proper English word is much more difficult. In casual communication, my inner thoughts are like free river flowing directly from my mind to the paper. I can write whatever appears in my mind. When I write compositions, I come into trouble. There are many good sources I could get from the Chinese culture while I write in Chinese: such as literary quotations, famous old stories, and ancient word of wisdom. These rich sources definitely influence my paper quality in Chinese. Unfortunately examples like this are very hard to translate to English. Sometime I try to make a joke, but it loses its impact in translation. Finding the right English word to match what I am thinking in Chinese is very frustrating and often blocks my writing process. To continue my writing, I have two choices generally. One is to give up this sentence and try to express the same meaning in another way. The other alternative is to check a Chinese-English dictionary. However, translating like that usually leaves me with vague meanings and the impact is lost in the tattered pages of my dictionary. Writing like this is very choppy and does not flow.

This student is an advanced-level ESL student enrolled in a freshman English class. After attending several ESL courses at an American university, he still seeks to translate from Chinese into English in his ESL writing.

An ESL student from Iran ponders her writing process at the end of a freshman English class:

> Thinking in English rather than in Persian or in French was something that I had to take into consideration every time I started to write something. Many times I explained an idea the way I used to do in Iran and the reader could not understand my point. For example in my essay about "friendship," I used a Persian proverb and my writing group members did not really understand its

3

meaning so I had to change it. Gradually I learned to think in English but I still have to practice more.

This student recognizes the need to think in English just as she has learned to think in French, her first second language.

In her eloquent memoir, *Lost in Translation. Life in a New Language,* Eva Hoffman, editor of *The New York Times Book Review* and a native speaker of Polish, describes the feeling of not being able to find the right words in the new language:

But mostly, the problem is that the signifier has becomes severed from the signified. The words I learn now don't stand for things in the same unquestioned way they did in my native tongue. "River" in Polish was a vital sound, energized with the essence of riverhood, of my rivers, of my being immersed in rivers. "River" in English is cold – a word without an aura. It has no accumulated associations for me, and it does not give off the radiating haze of connotation. It does not evoke. (Hoffman 1989, 106)

Hoffman's description of the difficult decision about the language in which to write her adolescent diary is equally vivid in suggesting that bilinguals think differently in their two languages.

Because I have to choose something, I finally choose English. If I'm to write about the present, I have to write in the language of the present, even if it's not the language of the self. As a result, the diary becomes surely one of the more impersonal exercises of the sort produced by an adolescent girl. These are no sentimental reflections of rejected love, eruptions of familial anger, or consoling broodings about death. English is not the language of such emotions. Instead I set down my reflections on the ugliness of wrestling, on the elegance of Mozart, and on how Dostoyevsky puts me in mind of El Greco. I write down Thoughts. I Write. (Hoffman 1989, 121)

As a native of Finland, I can identify with some of the stages Hoffman went through. My first term papers in graduate courses were painfully hard to conceptualize and write because my English graduate studies in Finland had primarily tested knowledge through written examinations, not through writing term papers. I remember starting on papers early in the semester and involving native English-speaking roommates as editors. Twenty years later, after earning a Ph.D. and gaining several years of teaching and research experience in applied linguistics in the United States, I finally think that I am close to the final stage of second language development. This stage allows a learner to let ideas flow on paper without the interference of having to translate them or being overly conscious of the language. With this last stage comes confidence in oneself as a writer in English. This does not mean, of course, that I am unaware of some nonnativeness in my writing. For example, because Finnish uses neither articles nor prepositions, I tend to use them inappropriately.

Thus, it is not surprising that ESL teachers often comment that ESL students use patterns of language and stylistic conventions that they have learned in their native languages and cultures. This transfer is not just idiosyncratic variation but involves recurring patterns of organization and rhetorical conventions reminiscent of writing in the students' native language and culture. Acknowledgment of this aspect of second language acquisition led to the development of contrastive rhetoric in the United States, where rhetoric and the teaching of writing have been considered important aspects of both first and second language instruction for decades.

Study of second language writing: the emergence of contrastive rhetoric

Contrastive rhetoric is an area of research in second language acquisition that identifies problems in composition encountered by second language writers and, by referring to the rhetorical strategies of the first language, attempts to explain them. Initiated almost thirty years ago by the American applied linguist Robert Kaplan, contrastive rhetoric maintains that language and writing are cultural phenomena. As a direct consequence, each language has rhetorical conventions unique to it. Furthermore, Kaplan asserted, the linguistic and rhetorical conventions of the first language interfere with writing in the second language.

It is fair to say that contrastive rhetoric was the first serious attempt by applied linguists in the United States to explain second language writing. It is only within the past twenty years, however, that writing skills and the role of transfer in particular have been of interest to applied linguistic researchers. For decades, writing was neglected as an area of study because of the emphasis on teaching spoken language during the dominance of audiolingual methodology.

In the past two decades, the study of writing has become part of the mainstream in applied linguistics. Reasons for this change are many: the increased understanding of language learners' needs to read and write in the target language; the enhanced interdisciplinary approach to studying second language acquisition through educational, rhetorical, and anthropological methods; and new trends in linguistics. These new trends emphasize discourse analyses (analyses that extend beyond the sentence level) and include descriptions of sociolinguistic variations such as the different speech patterns of men and women and of speakers of different dialects of the same language.

In research on second language writing, contrastive studies have received more attention than perhaps any other single issue. The importance of contrastive studies for the understanding of cultural particulars as well as linguistic universals is summarized well by Marie-Paule Péry-Woodley:

Contrasting and comparing are basic to any form of anthropological investigation, and this includes of course linguistic investigation. It is the contrastive light which shows a particular practice as specific to a group; conversely, it is the contrastive approach which allows the identification of universals. Not only is a contrastive stance a superlative way of gaining precise descriptive knowledge about individual languages and cultures, it is invaluable in the quest for a general understanding of language-based communication, as it forces the researcher to relativise particular ways of doing things with language: it is the best antidote to "ethno/linguocentricity." (Péry-Woodley 1990, 143)

It is time, therefore, to analyze the achievements of contrastive analyses of composition in order to determine its universals as well as its cross-cultural particulars.

Aims, purposes, and outline of this book

This book has three purposes. It discusses the general value of contrastive rhetoric in the field of applied linguistics, and suggests practical implications for teachers and researchers. More important, it defines an emerging contrastive rhetoric discipline that draws on relevant interdisciplinary fields, particularly composition studies, rhetoric, text linguistics, and cultural anthropology.

For thirty years, contrastive rhetoric has been practiced within a ruling paradigm suggested by Kaplan's first research. However, as Thomas S. Kuhn has observed (Kuhn 1970, 104), all paradigms are corrigible under the impact of new emphases, new points of view. Accordingly, after assessing the principles of contrastive rhetoric, as well as its significant research, this book will explore the changing paradigm.

New designs for contrastive rhetoric studies will be suggested. There is an analogy with modern studies in rhetoric, which have proposed a "new rhetoric" as opposed to classical rhetoric. Classical rhetoric was concerned primarily with the logic of an argument and its persuasiveness: making a point and winning over an audience through a coherent, convincing presentation. The reader or auditor was considered a largely passive participant. The "new rhetoric," best explained by Perelman and Olbrechts-Tyteca (1969) in *The New Rhetoric. A Treatise on Argumentation,* focuses on the achievement of a particular effect on the audience. (Perelman and Olbrechts-Tyteca's "new rhetoric" is discussed in more detail in Chapter 4.)

Perelman and others who advocate the "new rhetoric" did not of course abandon classical rhetoric completely, but instead built on it. In the same way, the new extended paradigm of contrastive rhetoric builds on the foundation of the "traditional" contrastive rhetoric of Kaplan's model. This model was influenced by classical rhetoric and was developed as part of the applied linguistics of the 1960s. The extended contrastive rhetoric takes a broader, more communicative view of rhetoric, paralleling the developments in "new rhetoric"; it has been influenced by developments in applied linguistics in the 1970s and 1980s. In addition, it has expanded across interdisciplinary boundaries. No longer restricted to cross-cultural models of writing supplied by contemporary applied linguistics, contrastive rhetoric now includes models of writing developed in education, composition pedagogy, and translation studies.

The new perspective of contrastive rhetoric thus increasingly reflects the multicultural pluralism of these related disciplines even as it benefits from and continuously enriches its own point of view. Not surprisingly, such a perspective, especially in its interdisciplinary aspect, has been found to be helpful to teachers and insightful for researchers in applied linguistics. Hence the survey of research in contrastive rhetoric supplied in this book.

It is frequently said that contrastive rhetoric and contrastive rhetoric methodology are still in their formative stages (Purves 1988, 15). As a result, perhaps, contrastive rhetoric has been criticized because it lacks a single methodology and a single research program. But this multidimensionality is a positive feature because it allows for multiple analyses of the same issue. Consequently, contrastive rhetoric will be broadly defined in the context of English teaching. Research on writing in English as a second language (ESL) or in English as a foreign language (EFL) that takes a cross-linguistic perspective will be included. Thus, for example, we shall not be restricted to contrastive rhetoric conducted in or with relevance to traditional ESL writing courses, which in North America generally deal with prefreshman or freshman English writing. Instead, we will examine contrastive studies with relevance for English for specific purposes (ESP) instruction and practical use. Examining the importance of contrastive rhetoric at levels beyond basic and freshman English composition is necessary because of the expansion of ESL instruction to academic and content-area literacy.

Subsequent chapters fall into three sections: (1) Chapters 2 and 3 deal with the early phases of contrastive rhetoric (although the emphasis of this book is on recent approaches, it is important to review some earlier contrastive rhetoric research), (2) Chapters 4 through 8 deal with its interfaces with other fields, and (3) Chapters 9 and 10 consider practical applications and methodological concerns. Thus, Chapter 2 discusses the historical development of contrastive rhetoric in applied linguistics as well as its future directions, whereas Chapter 3 provides an evaluation of contrastive rhetoric studies beginning with Kaplan's 1966 study. Specific studies are categorized by the language in question, and generalizations are provided about language contrasts.

In Part 2, (dealing with the interfaces of contrastive rhetoric with other related fields), Chapter 4 provides an overview of theories of first language (L1) rhetoric and composition instruction from the mid 1970s to the mid 1990s and their effects on second language (L2) composition instruction and contrastive rhetoric. Foci in L1 composition in the 1980s have been on the examination of writers' cognitive processes in the act of writing and, in the early 1990s, on the context and situation of writing and their effects on the creation of meaning in writing.

Chapter 5 surveys a new area of contrastive investigation, text linguistic studies. There are still very few studies in this area, and they deal with contrasts between English and a number of languages: Swedish, Finnish, Norwegian, and English; Hebrew and English; Farsi and English; Chinese and English; Japanese and English; and Czech and English. Although most of the research deals with analyzing a specific grammatical phenomenon in a discourse, some of it provides analytical tools to discover how full texts work as functional wholes with multiple interacting levels. A great deal of the research has been conducted in Europe and Asia as well as in North America.

Chapter 6 discusses contrastive research, the main focus of which is the acquisition and development of literacy skills in the first language and their effect on L2 writing. The effect of the educational and cultural atmosphere on L1 writing, as well as in some cases on L2 (e.g., Chinese-speaking students in China, English-speaking students in the United States), is described. Chapter 7 discusses the field of translation studies and its influence on contrastive rhetoric. Chapter 8 reviews an increasingly important new area of study, contrastive writing in English for specific purposes, settings, and different genres. Studies in this area examine advanced second language writing in such varied fields as business, economics, and science. Here, again, American developments are somewhat paralled by European efforts.

Chapter 9 reviews the research methodologies of contrastive rhetoric. Chapter 10 describes the implications of contrastive rhetoric for the teaching and testing of second language writing and discusses future research directions that contrastive rhetoric needs to or is likely to take. The chapter also indicates possible areas of future research.

Building a comprehensive theory of contrastive rhetoric

Kaplan's first study of contrastive rhetoric provided a model of writing for a theory of second language teaching that is more useful in some applications than in others. For example, the model is not particularly relevant for the theory of translation, since it refers to second language texts only when speculating about first language influence. A model for translation needs to compare texts in both first languages, the source

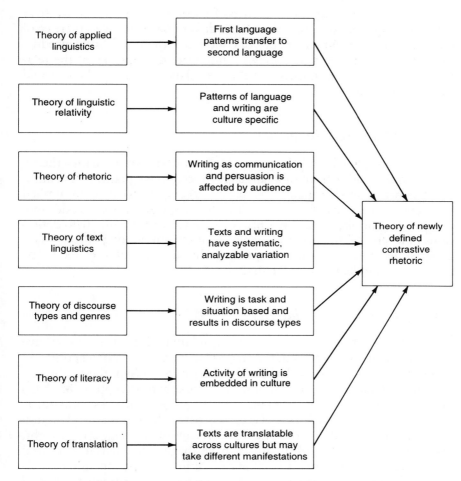

Figure 1   Influences on newly defined contrastive rhetoric.

language (in which the text was originally written) and the target language (into which the text was translated.) But Kaplan's model is indeed useful in evaluating second language written products, even though a different model is needed to describe differences in composing processes across cultures. Finally, his model helps to describe essays written by college students for school purposes. However, I will argue in this book that a different contrastive model is needed for the description of cross-cultural writing in academic and professional situations. Moreover, the concept of contrastive rhetoric adopted is more inclusive than the concept that the early researchers in the field would have employed.

Figure 1 summarizes the influence of various theories on contrastive rhetoric. Although the figure shows one-directional influences, there is, of course, bidirectionality. A theory of contrastive rhetoric is influenced by many theories, as the figure shows. Only brief descriptions of the relationships follow here; subsequent chapters elaborate on the theories and the relationships.

Theory of applied linguistics

A theory of applied linguistics provides contrastive rhetoric with a theory of language transfer from first language to second language. It also influences contrastive rhetorical research by keeping it oriented to applied problems – problems of learners in foreign language classes. In addition, the theory of applied linguistics provides contrastive rhetoric with definitions of levels of language proficiency, relationships among different language skills, measurement of language skills, and variables related to the acquisition and learning of languages.

Theory of linguistic relativity

The Sapir-Whorf hypothesis of linguistic relativity is basic to contrastive rhetoric because it suggests that different languages affect perception and thought in different ways. The strong version of the hypothesis, the version that insists that language controls thought and perception, has been disproven; but the weak version, that language influences thought, is regaining acceptability in linguistics and psychology (Hunt and Agnoli 1991). Hence, instead of focusing on universals of language and thought, many psychologists and linguists have begun to identify cultural differences. A similar trend is taking place in composition studies; cultural and linguistic backgrounds are shown to affect writing activity and written products. A more thorough discussion of linguistic relativity is given in Chapter 3.

Theory of rhetoric

A theory of rhetoric is obviously fundamental to contrastive rhetoric. It is interested in assessing the direct or indirect effect of communication on the hearer or reader. Kaplan's first model of contrastive rhetoric was based on Aristotelean rhetoric and logic. Naturally, rhetoric, and especially modern rhetoric, is interested in the situational relativity of communicative effectiveness. These issues will be explored more thoroughly in Chapter 4.

Theory of text linguistics

A theory of text linguistics provides a descriptive apparatus for describing textual cohesion, structures of texts, theme dynamics, and metatextual features. Hence it is basic to contrastive rhetoric procedures. Text linguistics is here treated synonymously with text analysis, discourse analysis, and discourse linguistics of texts. Most recent publications treat text linguistics as an analysis of written texts that extends beyond the sentence level and considers the communicative constraints of the context (van Dijk 1985b). See Chapter 5 for a full discussion of these issues.

Theory of discourse types and genres

Constrastive rhetoric is applicable to many different kinds of texts. Hence a theory of text types and genres is needed to establish the comparability of texts. Three definitions will be used: (1) discourse type, selected according to the aim of the discourse, such as argumentative prose, (2) text type, selected according to the mode of discourse, such as narrative passage in an argumentative text, and (3) genre, which refers to texts formed according to cultural and traditional expectations as required by specific purposes and tasks such as a research report in biology. The first two distinctions follow Kinneavy's (1971) theories of aims and modes as well as Virtanen's (1990; 1992) review of text types; the third definition, genre, follows Swales's (1990b) theory of genre, which defines genre as a text type that is ultimately determined by the task and situation and is immediately defined by communicative purpose.

Theory of literacy

A comprehensive theory of contrastive rhetoric deals with the development of literacies, not merely written products. Recent theories of literacy are beneficial in documenting why certain styles of writing are valued in certain cultures as well as in giving information about the teaching and learning of literacy cross-culturally.

Theory of translation

The field of translation studies has much in common with contrastive rhetoric. Both areas stem from linguistics and, in the past decade, have expanded their scopes beyond structural analyses and literal translations. Theories of translation have a great deal to offer to contrastive rhetoric. These issues will be discussed in Chapter 7.

2 Contrastive rhetoric studies in applied linguistics

In applied linguistics, contrastive rhetoric has been influenced by such major movements as contrastive analysis and research on international Englishes. These influences are discussed in this chapter, followed by sections on current forces affecting contrastive rhetoric research in applied linguistics contexts.

Contrastive analysis, error analysis, and analysis of interlanguage

In the 1950s and 1960s, the theory of second language learning suggested that L1 interfered with L2 acquisition. The dominant model of the contrastive analysis hypothesis emphasized the negative, interfering effects of the first language on second language acquisition, which were considered harmful.

By the late 1960s, however, second language learning was being compared to the first language acquisition process, in which language learners are intelligent beings creating rules and systems based on the rule systems of language they hear and use. Among influences in this "creative construction" of language are such sources as a limited knowledge of the L2, knowledge of L1, and knowledge of communication, the world, and other human communicators. New models of second language acquisition and learning emerged, which emphasized the importance of "interlanguage" (a system of language that is structurally between L1 and L2, Corder 1967; the term was coined by Selinker in 1972). These models, such as Krashen's monitor model (1977), suggested that neither L1 nor L2 is a "bad" influence on second language acquisition.

Teachers of ESL and foreign languages have always been familiar with the negative effects of transfer; they recognize that their students speak the target language with an accent that reflects phonemic characteristics of the student's native language. For example, ESL students whose first language is Finnish, a non-Indo-European language, experience difficulty in distinguishing and pronouncing English voiced stops (/b/, /d/, /g/) because Finnish does not have many voiced stops. It is therefore not surprising that transfer from the native language has been studied by applied linguists in great detail. In fact, in the teaching of spoken language, the role of transfer from the native language, or cross-linguistic influence, took center stage for some thirty years, from the 1950s to the 1980s.

Three approaches concerning transfer have dominated: contrastive analysis; error analysis; and its later development, an analysis of the transitional system called "interlanguage." However, as Odlin (1989) observes in a recent book reviewing the research on the subject, thinking about the role of transfer has changed significantly since the beginning of transfer studies. In earlier contrastive analysis studies of the phenomenon, the influence of the native language was considered an interference in the acquisition and learning of the target language. Later research, involving error analysis and analyses of "interlanguage" systems of learners' actual performance, suggests that the influence of transfer on the acquisition of the target language is more complex. Other factors now considered include knowledge about the target language itself, the learner's communicative strategies, the instructional situation, and the combined effects of these factors.

Contrastive analysis, the first of the three approaches to transfer, originally developed by Fries (1945) and expanded by Lado (1957), maintained that mistakes made by L2 learners were caused by the native language. Dissatisfied with the ability of this approach to predict the difficulty levels among target language structures, error analysts attempted to study systematic errors in the performance of second language learners. Well known studies dealing with the order of morpheme acquisition of ESL learners by Dulay and Burt (1974) and by Bailey, Madden, and Krashen (1974) showed a similar order of acquisition of certain English morphemes between ESL learners and children acquiring English as a first language. For example, Dulay, Burt, and Krashen (1982, 214) report that the acquisition order for the five bound morphemes (e.g., the *-s* in "eats" or the *-ing* in "smiling") "have been found to be similarly ordered for L2 and L1 learners." They report that rank order correlations have ranged from 80 to 90 percent.

Error analysis later evolved into the study of "interlanguage." Interlanguage was defined by Selinker, Swain, and Dumas (1975) as a "system" that is "distinct from both the native language and the target language." Corder (1967) referred to it as "the transitional competence of the L2 learner." A learner is seen as an active participant in the learning process, one who is forming and testing hypotheses in the process of creating an internalized system of how the target language works. More recently, interlanguage research has been criticized for looking at syntax in an exclusively syntactic framework, excluding semantics, phonology, and pragmatics. Hence Rutherford (1982) called for interlanguage research on functional perspectives in language in the light of pragmatics and discourse linguistics.

These, then, are the three approaches to second language acquisition: contrastive analysis, error analysis, and interlanguage research. The orientation and training of the applied linguists involved in these three approaches varies. Those who contributed to contrastive analysis considered themselves applied linguists who worked in the structuralist tradition of linguistics and whose purpose was to improve language teaching. Those in error analysis saw themselves much more as students of psycholinguistics. The Finnish applied linguists Sajavaara and Lehtonen (1980), whose large-scale Finnish–English contrastive project was psycholinguistically oriented, endorse the importance of a communicative approach and the role of scholars with interdisciplinary orientation to the study of language acquisition:

Cross-language communication analysis cannot rely on linguistics alone. Since it works with similarities and differences in human verbal and non-verbal codes and with the clash of the two codes in the language-behaviour of a foreign language student, it will have to absorb both theoretical perspectives and practical methodology from various branches of the disciplines which deal with language and speech or human behavior in general. The theory and methodology of linguistics used must inevitably be supplemented by disciplines such as sociology, psychology, neurology, and applied mathematics, as concerns the analysis and description of pragmatic patterning, cognitive mechanisms, perception, and information-processing systems in man. (1980, 8)

Sajavaara and Lehtonen also criticize the traditional contrastive analysis approach because it involves a static view of interlingual contrasts. The learner's position in relation to the target language is considered stable. Adding to the static picture of interlingual contrasts is the neglect of the nonstatic nature of human interaction. From the point of view of Sajavaara and Lehtonen, language acquisition should be seen as a communicative process in which both the speaker and the listener have complex and interdependent roles.

Development of contrastive rhetoric: parallel with contrastive analysis

A similar shift of emphasis from earlier to later research is evident in the development of contrastive studies of writing. The first such studies were concerned with beginning-level ESL students' writing. They had a pedagogic rationale, and combined the contrastive and error analysis approaches. Contrastive rhetoric, like contrastive analysis, began as an effort to improve pedagogy, and its adherents believed that interference from L1 was the biggest problem in L2 acquisition. It was initially founded on error analysis; "errors" in beginning-level students' paragraph organization were examined and reasons for them were hypothesized based on the language background from which the student came. However, contrastive rhetoric never entered the next stage, interlanguage analysis. As a result, contrastive rhetoric researchers of ESL have not tried to describe stages in learners' L2 writing acquisition and to explain errors as evidence of the language learning process to the extent that researchers of spoken language did. Nor has contrastive rhetoric developed a large enough body of ESL data to compare stages of acquisition of linguistic and rhetorical structures. Because contrastive rhetoricians have used a number of different analyses, and because a unified methodology has not yet been developed, it has been hard to build a large set of acquisition data. Spoken language research, in contrast, often examined a small number of easily identifiable surface structures such as the individual morphemes analyzed in the Dulay and Burt studies (e.g., *-ing, -s,* regular past tense, irregular past tense, copula). It has also established clear acquisition sequences.

In a way, the lack of studies on structures in contrastive rhetoric may have been a blessing. Instead of spending its energies on syntactic issues in writing, contrastive rhetoric moved ahead to compare discourse structures across cultures and genres. It has dealt with issues such as the orientation that places interpretative responsibility on the reader, as contrasted with that which places responsibility on the writer, in Japanese and American newspaper articles, respectively (Hinds 1987); or organization of information in research papers and dissertations written by nonnative English speakers with a variety of language and disciplinary backgrounds (Swales 1990a; 1990b).

Kaplan's pioneering study (1966) analyzed the organization of paragraphs in ESL student essays. Kaplan identified five types of paragraph development for five groups, as indicated in his frequently reproduced diagram (Figure 1), showing that L1 rhetorical structures were evident in the L2 writing of his sample students.

Kaplan's work suggested that Anglo-European expository essays follow a linear development. In contrast, paragraph development in Semitic languages is based on a series of parallel coordinate clauses. Essays written in Oriental languages use an indirect approach and come to the point only at the end. In Romance languages and in Russian, essays are permitted a degree of digressiveness and extraneous material that would seem excessive to a writer of English.

Culture-specific patterns of organization were considered negative influences in ESL writing. To combat them, Kaplan recommended that ESL students learning to write essays in an Anglo-American style study model compositions constructed with the straight line of development thought

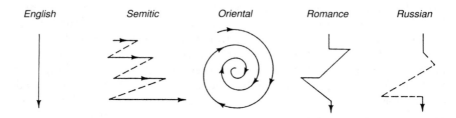

Figure 1   Diagram on cross-cultural differences in paragraph organization in Kaplan's (1966) study on cultural thought patterns in intercultural education.

typical of that style. A variety of exercises in which students were asked to reorganize sentences in paragraphs were also recommended.

Kaplan's "traditional" contrastive rhetoric has been criticized for several reasons: for being too ethnocentric and privileging the writing of native English speakers (Matalene 1985); for examining only L2 products and ignoring educational and developmental process variables (Mohan and Au-Yeung Lo 1985); for dismissing linguistic and cultural differences in writing among related languages, that is, for including Chinese, Thai, and Korean speakers in one "Oriental" group (Hinds 1983a); and for considering transfer from a first language a negative influence on second language writing (Raimes 1991a). Kaplan has modified his earlier position in a number of recent publications (e.g., Kaplan 1987; 1988), calling his 1966 article his "doodles" article and suggesting that rhetorical differences do not necessarily reflect different patterns of thinking. Instead, differences may reflect different writing conventions that are learned in a culture.

International Englishes

Another shift of emphasis may be seen in the Englishes that constitute the basis of contrastive rhetoric research. Typically, contrastive rhetoric considers Anglo-American English rhetorical patterns as the norm. Linguistic research, however, points to numerous differences between spoken and written modes of American and British English (Biber 1988, for example). Hence, contrastive rhetoric is beginning to consider the variation in American, British, and other "native" Englishes (e.g., Canadian, Australian, and New Zealand English) as well as nonnative varieties of English as norms.

Although "English is used by more people than any other language on earth, its mother-tongue speakers make up only a quarter or a fifth of the total" (Strevens 1987, 56). Strevens estimates that the number of native speakers of Englishes is around 350 million, but as many as 700 to 750 million people use English as a national, second or foreign language, or as a language for commerce, industry, science, or other purposes.

Singapore is an example of a society where native speakers of several languages (Mandarin, Tamil, and Malay) use a local variety of English, "Singapore English," as the lingua franca. According to Altehenger-Smith (1987), approximately 85 percent of the pupils attending school in Singapore are taught in a language that is not spoken at home; the language for court transactions is English; and a knowledge of English is necessary for civil service appointments. English has been designated as the language for interethnic communication and is becoming the ethnic mother tongue for intraethnic communication.

In discussing the situation in Singapore, Hong Chua and Chew (1993) advocate the teaching of non-Anglo-American English as an international language. Non-Anglo-American English as an international language encourages tolerance for nonnative norms of English. According to the above authors, the majority of learners of English around the world are being taught by nonnative speakers of English; accordingly, it is unrealistic to think that these teachers could teach a single standard correct model of English, such as Anglo-American English. The models accepted in Singapore are approved by the ministry of education and are all varieties of English spoken by educated members of the society such as newsreaders, academics, and teachers. The language adheres to standard English norms, but diversity is found in phonological patterns, vocabulary, and the structuring of information, according to the authors (53). Since intelligibility is not jeopardized, the authors recommend the recognition of nonnative English norms.

Linguist Braj Kachru, in *The Other Tongue: English Across Cultures* (1984), examines the linguistic and sociolinguistic bases for international Englishes and discusses a variety of situations involving differences among "native" speakers as well as English bilinguals or nonnative speakers. With the increased interest in contrastive rhetoric of advanced-level writers in many settings, including economic and political interactions, the knowledge to be gained from the impressive body of work by Kachru and others in the area of international Englishes will increase in importance. For example, in Europe, because of the European Union, there is increasing talk about "Eurospeak" or "Euro-English." No published studies exist yet about its definitions and characteristics. Kachru's research on international Englishes will be useful for researchers describing Euro-English.

New directions in contrastive rhetorical research in applied linguistics contexts

Despite many past attacks on contrastive rhetoric, the time has not yet come to dismiss it as a viable theory of second language writing. In fact, thanks to the celebration of cultural diversity in the United States and the increasing recognition of differing speech patterns owing to cultural and regional contexts in sociolinguistics, the 1990s have seen a renewed interest in the study of writing across cultures. In 1991, for example, two leading ESL composition experts, Ann Raimes and Ilona Leki, each wrote about the importance of contrastive rhetoric as a means of raising awareness among teachers of different L1 backgrounds and the effects of these backgrounds on L2 writing. Raimes (1991a) calls for a broader definition of contrastive rhetoric in which students' L1 is shown to be an important resource rather than a hindrance in writing. Leki (1991) focuses on the benefits of contrastive rhetoric for ESL teaching.

In the 1990s, significant changes have taken place in contrastive rhetorical research. Contrastive rhetoric seems almost to have experienced a revolution in the Kuhnian sense, a paradigm shift. The traditional contrastive rhetoric framework is no longer able to account for all the data, and an expanded framework is needed. A broader definition that considers cognitive and sociocultural variables of writing in addition to linguistic variables has been substituted for a purely linguistic framework interested in structural analyses of products.

Both internal and external forces have necessitated this new framework. Internal criticisms such as those mentioned earlier have forced contrastive rhetoricians to go beyond the traditional, linguistic parameters of analysis and consider discourse-level features as well as processes of writing. Equally important have been two major external forces: changing foci in L1 composition research and new developments in the area of discourse analysis and text linguistics.

In L1 composition research, cognitive models of writing describe writing as a discursive process of generating, organizing, and translating ideas into text (Flower and Hayes 1981). Increasingly, also, the nature of writing is viewed as inherently interactive and social. It involves more than the generation, organization, and translation of ideas (Nystrand 1982; 1986; 1989). Writing is seen as interaction within a particular discipline or scholarly community. The writers' own purposes are not considered sufficient to explain the decisions that writers make. The context, situation, and the reader also need to be considered.

Both the cognitive and the social-cultural emphasis in composition studies has influenced the study of cross-cultural rhetoric in applied linguistics contexts. Contrastive rhetoric has moved from examining only products to studying processes in a variety of writing situations. In addition, another external force, discourse analysis and text linguistics, allows for analyses that consider whole texts as dynamic entities (Enkvist 1987; Brown and Yule 1983; Connor 1987b).

Contrastive rhetoric in the context of applied linguistics is taking new directions in five domains: contrastive text linguistics (comparison of discourse features across languages); the study of writing as a cultural activity (comparing the process of learning to write in different cultures); contrastive studies of the classroom dynamics of L2 writing; contrastive rhetoric studies conducted in a variety of genres in a variety of situations for a variety of purposes (e.g., journal articles, school essays, and business reports); and contrastive rhetoric studies dealing with the inculcation of culturally different intellectual traditions and ideologies. A short description of each trend follows; subsequent chapters elaborate on the topics.

Contrastive text linguistics

Text linguistics is often spoken of synonymously with text analysis and written analysis. Text linguistics is written discourse analysis, an analysis of texts that goes beyond the sentence level. However, a distinction between discourse analysis and text linguistics is made by European text linguists such as the Finnish text linguist, Nils Enkvist (1984). Enkvist notes that the term "text" can refer to both spoken and written language, but some linguists maintain a distinction between "text" as discourse without context and "discourse" as text and its situational context. The distinction between "text" and "discourse," in which "discourse" includes "text," is found in a great deal of influential literature (Brown and Yule 1983; Edmondson 1981; Hoey 1991).

But the distinction between "text" and "discourse" is not always so clear-cut. Virtanen (1990) provides a comprehensive historical and synchronic review of the terms and notes that "text" formerly referred to the structural qualities of discourse, whereas today "text" is increasingly seen through the processes of text production and comprehension, bringing the term "text" closer to the connotation of "discourse." According to this perspective, which is also adopted in this book, text linguistics is concerned with the processes that readers and writers go through in their attempts to comprehend and produce texts.

Several text linguistic studies have contrasted coherence and discourse patterns of various kinds in different languages. Perhaps the most influential has been the work of applied linguist John Hinds. He has shown that certain text structures are used to achieve coherence, which guides the reader in making the right inference; and that textual patterns used to express coherence vary among languages and cultures.

Hinds (1990) has described how writing in Japanese, Chinese, Thai, and Korean favors a "quasi-inductive" rather than an inductive or a deductive style of presentation, or what Hinds calls a "delayed introduction of purpose" (p. 98). This delayed introduction of purpose makes the writing appear incoherent to the English-speaking reader (although not to the native reader). (Hinds's work is discussed in more detail in Chapter 3.)

In addition to achieving coherence through textual structures such as an inductive or deductive organization, writers need to be sensitive to the different expectations of readers and writers across cultures. In proposing a new typology of language based on "speaker and/or writer responsibility as opposed to listener and/or reader responsibility," Hinds has shown that, with respect to coherence, Japanese writing demands more of the reader, whereas the rhetorical form preferred in the West places the expository burden chiefly on the writer (Hinds 1987, 143, 146). English readers expect and require landmarks of coherence and unity as they read. The writer needs to provide transitional statements. In Japanese, on the other hand, transitions may be lacking. The reader is expected to piece sections together to make a coherent text.

Text linguistic studies that compare texts and their production in many other languages in addition to Japanese, Chinese, Thai, and Korean have been conducted. Clyne's research has been on German (1987); Eggington's (1987) work deals with contrasts between English and Korean; Söter (1988) focuses on English–Vietnamese and English-Arabic contrasts; and Connor has compared English, Finnish, and German texts (1987a).

Clearly, developments in text linguistics in the past couple of decades have had far-reaching consequences for contrastive rhetoric. In fact, some authors want to frame contrastive rhetoric in purely textual terms. Martin's (1992) book, *Towards a Theory of Text for Contrastive Rhetoric,* proposes de Beaugrande and Dressler's seven-feature text model (1981) as "the conceptual anchor of an interactive approach to text with direct relevance to research in contrastive rhetoric" (p. 64). The textual features are cohesion, coherence, intentionality, acceptability, informationality, situationality, and intertextuality. Although the book offers a highly formalistic approach, it is an important contribution to theory building in contrastive rhetoric.

Study of writing as a cultural activity

The 1980s saw a proliferation of research examining the processes of becoming literate in one's native language and culture. Anthropologists, psychologists, and researchers in education are among those who have particularly investigated the processes of learning literacy and the effects of literacy on learners' thinking as well as social behavior. Although this research is still just beginning, at least in its contemporary form, important discoveries have been made about the embeddedness of discourse and writing in culture and about the roles that schooling and instruction play in this embeddedness. Most significantly, research points to the fact that written texts and the ways they are used vary according to cultural group.

Empirical research examining the relationship between culture and discourse falls into three categories. The first type of research is conducted in the domain of anthropology and psychology and focuses on the social functions of writing. Scribner and Cole (1981) investigated the various kinds of literacy among the West African Vai, and Heath (1983) researched the varying oral traditions and their effects on subsequent literacy development among African-American and white Appalachians.

The second major research direction is educational and deals with the role of instruction on writing in a given language and culture. The International Study of Written Composition, planned and carried out during the 1980s as part of the International Association for the Evaluation of Educational Achievement (IEA), examined the relationships among culture, writing, and the curriculum in schools in fourteen countries (Gorman, Purves, and Degenhart 1988; Purves 1988). Although the findings point to some universal characteristics of the conventions and uses of writing, they also confirm culture-specific uses and conventions in school writing. The IEA study is directly relevant for contrastive rhetoric in that it examined essay writing, the long-preferred domain of traditional contrastive rhetoric.

The influence of research on the development of literacy in L1 is clearly evident in the third area of investigation, which comprises studies of ESL students' backgrounds and the effect of background on their literacy in L2. A beneficial direction of research in ESL related to this general area is the one charted by Carson (1992) and by Folman and Sarig (1990). Each originated research that will provide valuable knowledge for the teaching of ESL literacy. Each study used a different type of theoretical, quantitative, and qualitative analysis.

In a discussion of the development of literacy in L1 and L2, Carson (1992) examines how Chinese and Japanese speakers learn to read and write in L1 and how that learning affects their expectations and strategies in learning to read and write in L2. Carson is concerned about the influences of social context, particularly the educational system, and she emphasizes cognitive considerations such as problems pertaining to orthography in learning to read and write in L1 and later L2. She begins by describing how Japanese children learn to read and write in a society that values "the importance of education (and of literacy), the need to work hard to succeed, the inherent values of the group, and the primacy of shared social purpose" (1992, 42). Japanese children learn to understand the value of language in this context as expressing social cohesion, not as primarily a medium for individual expression.

In China, the situation is a little different. Carson writes:

To summarize, becoming literate in China involves learning to read and write in a society that values education, but that has only recently been able to develop positive attitudes among the masses towards literacy. Schools reflect the traditional function of Chinese education, which is to teach moral principles reflecting basic societal values: patriotism, the collective good, group loyalty, and respect for authority. In this context, schools are controlled and regimented, with a focus on maintaining order and authority. As in Japan, language is not thought of as primarily a medium for expressing individual meaning, although in China clear public expression is valued as a tool for successful communication. These, then, are the values and attitudes that define the social context of schooling in which literacy is acquired in China. (1992, 44)

Carson also discusses strategies of learning required to master literacy in four different systems in Japan: two syllabaries (*katagana* and *hiragana*), one system consisting of Chinese characters (*kanji*), and the Roman alphabet and Arabic numerals. She notes that in Japan, traditional methods of memorization, repetition, drill, and testing are used to teach the thousands of different signs and symbols of the written language. In China, which has a logographic writing system, memorization of symbols and passages is a large part of literacy instruction. "Still, there is a strong belief that the path to lively and creative writing styles lies in internalizing others' styles," writes Carson (53).

Folman and Sarig (1990) conducted a quantitative study to find out whether and to what extent rhetorical structures preferred by native Hebrew speakers differ from those preferred by U.S. native English speakers when constructing meaning in reading and writing in their native languages. Folman and Sarig found differences in the rhetorical patterns used by the two groups of subjects. They then compared American English with Israeli writing instructional norms using a taxonomy for cross-cultural comparison of writing instruction developed in the IEA study discussed earlier. They concluded that although there is considerable similarity between the two systems concerning norms for written expression, the rhetorical differences found in their contrastive studies:

. . . do not seem to lie only within the realm of "different thought patterns," but more – [we] would like to suggest within the realm of the professed and implemented syllabuses of language arts and educational linguistics of each of the instructional systems, the formal agents of each of the cultures. (1990, 73)

Folman and Connor (1992) continued this cross-cultural investigation of the effects of educational emphases on students' literacy skills. They examined the ways in which senior high school English papers differ in Israel and the United States. The findings showed that although there are similarities (students in both countries have difficulty synthesizing source material readings in written reports), some differences exist in the types and amount of source readings used and in the length of papers. They concluded by asserting that the differences reflect the norms set for senior papers in the two settings, a school in Israel and a school in the United States.

Classroom-based contrastive studies

Research on writing as a social construction of meaning has shown the value of examining perceptions and beliefs about literacy and learning in writing classrooms (Hull et al. 1991). Cultural mismatches in classrooms manifest themselves in a number of situations such as classroom conversation, collaborative groups, and teacher-student conferences.

Hull et al. have shown that competence in writing classrooms means "interactional competence as well as competence with written language: knowledge when and how and with whom to speak and act in order to create and display knowledge" (1991, 301). Classroom talk is deeply embedded in culture. In Western culture, Hull et al. continue, classroom conversations consist of a tripartite series of turns in which a teacher initiates, a student replies, and the teacher evaluates the response. As shown by examples from linguistic minority groups in the United States, students from linguistically diverse backgrounds may not function well in this type of conversation.

Research by sociolinguists on the style and patterns of oral interaction also show interethnic and cross-cultural differences that often impede communication. Scollon and Scollon (1981) studied cross-cultural interaction between Athabascan Native Americans and native English-speaking North Americans, noting frequent conflicts in communication. They found differences in the amount of talk (Athabascans talk little; other Americans talk a great deal) as well as in the expected role of the speaker and the listener (Athabascans expect the dominant person to do the talking, such as a teacher or an interviewer, for example), and they observe that these cultural differences are consequential for the educational achievement of Athabascan children.

Although the research of both the writing experts (Hull et al.) and the sociolinguists (Scollons) points to the importance of understanding cultural variation in classroom behavior and conversational patterns, little published research in ESL investigates this issue. However, cross-cultural influences are beginning to be addressed in collaborative writing groups in ESL and other writing classes. This research also relies on sociolinguistic analyses of cross-cultural interaction during writing groups when students give peer responses about each other's writing. Cultural differences emerge in the quality and quantity of these responses. Allaei and Connor (1990) offer suggestions for classroom practice in handling some of the problems of international student collaboration and peer response. Carson and Nelson (1994) warn against different assumptions about "group good" versus "individual good" between Chinese and Japanese students on the one hand and American students on the other.

Another related area of research is teacher–student conferencing, where cultural differences may also hinder smooth and productive communication. Goldstein and Conrad (1990) conducted a study that examined the degree to which active participation and negotiation were present in teacher–student conferences and what the effect was on revision and final written products. Large differences were found in the students' participation and negotiation of meaning in the conferences. Although there were only three students in the study, Goldstein and Conrad were able to speculate about the effects of culturally different role designations: "In our study, it is possible that the variation we have seen across the three students may result, at least in part, from these students using culturally diverse rules for how much teachers and students control the discourse when interacting with each other" (1990, 456). The study of conferencing seems another important direction of contrastive research with implications for the classroom as well as for the writing center.

Contrastive rhetoric and genre analysis

As has been pointed out (Connor and Lauer 1988), most contrastive rhetorical studies have dealt with expository prose. Only recently have other genres such as persuasion and argumentation been studied in contrastive studies. With the increased interest in writing for many purposes and in many contexts for ESL learners, the specification of genre is important. A useful model for defining genres and discourse communities in contrastive rhetoric analysis is provided by Swales (1990b). He criticizes Ostler's research (1987), for example, because it compared student essays written by Arabic-native ESL learners with published Arabic texts. According to Swales, contrastive text analyses need to compare texts written for similar purposes in similar contexts.

In fact, genre-specific research in specific discourse communities is already underway in Mauranen's investigation of Finnish and English economists' metalanguage strategies in economic reports (1993), in Connor's study of a Japanese manager's and an American manager's negotiation styles in written business correspondence (1988), and in Connor and Kramer's comparison of ESL and American business graduate students writing business case reports (1995). Research like this helps to untangle the combined effects of culture, the writer's own background, and the specific situation. The research conducted so far shows that some characteristics of processes and products in specific genres can be explained by traditional contrastive rhetoric findings (Japanese and Chinese tend to be more indirect than Americans; Finns have different coherence conventions than English speakers – they leave unsaid things that they consider obvious, whereas English speakers expect them as clarification; Korean students do not want to take strong positions in defending business case decisions). Future research needs to continue addressing the interactions among the various variables – L1 culture, genre, situation, and students' individual backgrounds.

Contrastive rhetoric and the teaching of an ideology

It has been pointed out that in emphasizing Anglo-American patterns of writing, contrastive rhetoric may encourage students to look down upon their first language writing styles. Kubota's work (discussed in Chapter 3) addresses the issue of Japanese native speakers' preference for the linear pattern of English after their introduction to it, and Eggington writes about Korean academics transporting the American way of writing to their native country (also in Chapter 3).

Advocates of the theory of the social construction of meaning through writing (see Chapter 4) insist on the importance of helping writers see themselves in reference to their audience and social context. In addition to emphasizing the personal growth and integration inherent in such self-evaluation, social constructionist theory in L1 composition has allied itself with an anti-authoritarian ideology. Students are encouraged to take charge of their own lives:

Students must be taught to identify the ways in which the control over their own lives has been denied them, and denied in such a way that they have blamed themselves for their powerlessness. (Berlin 1988, 490)

In a similar vein, Trimbur (1989) recommends a pedagogy that encourages the development of individualism in students while lessening the authority of teachers.

Such a critical pedagogy, prevalent in many composition classes in L1 instruction in the United States, has not been embraced by ESL teachers and researchers, despite the many studies on writing as a social construction of meaning discussed above. Santos (1992) provides an excellent discussion of the lack of a desirable ideology in ESL writing classes, a trend she laments. According to her, there are several reasons for this missing ideology. First, ESL teachers have been trained in linguistics – a supposedly objective science that discourages speculation. The thinking is that teachers teach the language; they do not dwell on feelings. Second, ESL teachers in the United States have been pragmatists; they want to help students write according to the expectations of members of their chosen academic discourse communities. Third, a great deal of EFL teaching is conducted outside the United States where the power structures do not follow the U.S. pattern. In other words, teaching at the international level makes the critical pedagogy of L1 composition in the United States somewhat meaningless when extended beyond the United States.

McKay (1993a; 1993b), however, gives a more optimistic view of the role of sociopolitically minded teaching in ESL and EFL. Extending second language writing to include literacy development – a view espoused in this book – McKay writes about the importance of understanding various social practices that inform academic discourses and create negative power relations in the classroom:

Power in many classrooms resides to a great extent in the teacher. Freire (1970) terms such an approach a *banking model of education,* in which the role of the teacher is to transmit to students a particular body of knowledge. In many L2 composition classes, this body of knowledge includes the social conventions that govern writing in a Western academic discourse setting. Certainly such a transmission model of education is ideal if the goal of writing classes is to initiate students into the academic discourse of Western universities. But if the goal is not for a one-way initiation but rather for an understanding and validation of other intellectual traditions that can inform academic discourses, relationships in L2 classrooms will need to change. (1993a, 76–77)

McKay points out that many L2 writers bring to the classroom ways of structuring discourse, interacting with audiences, and valuing knowledge that they have learned in their first language, employing some of these social practices as they write in English. ESL teachers of writing need to learn about these different traditions by studying traditions of writing in other cultures as well as learning through think-aloud protocols and interviews with other student writers. McKay urges a "dialogue across differences" in which teachers and students together seek to understand different assumptions regarding texts, writers, audiences, and the knowledge writers can have about writing.

This view of writing is highly relevant for contrastive rhetoric and its implications for the teaching of writing. It emphasizes individual and cultural-societal contributions of writers. It helps celebrate diversity and explains that nonnativeness in writing derives from social and cultural traditions imprinted upon each individual whose writing practices contribute variety to the norm.

Summary

The role of contrastive rhetoric in applied linguistics is significant and reflects the enhanced role of teaching writing in ESL, EFL, and FL instruction. Contrastive rhetoric research is interdisciplinary; it draws on several related fields of study such as text linguistics, composition pedagogy, and literacy development. These influences enrich the scope and depth of contrastive rhetoric research, enabling recommendations for teaching L2 writing in several ways: evaluating written products of ESL and EFL students based on textlinguistic insights, understanding cultural differences in writing processes, appreciating influences of L1 literacy acquisition on L2 writing, understanding writing cross-culturally in academic and professional situations, and being sensitive to societal-cultural differences in intellectual traditions and ideologies.

3 Historical evolution of contrastive rhetoric: from Kaplan's 1966 study to diversification of languages, genres, and authors

This chapter has five sections. The first section begins with a discussion of the theory of linguistic relativity, the cornerstone of contrastive rhetoric, and then reviews Kaplan's seminal works on contrastive rhetoric – an article (1966) and a book (1972). The next four sections provide reviews of contrastive rhetorical research conducted by several other ESL researchers. These reviews provide the reader with references to the most significant research. The research is categorized by the first language of the ESL students whose writing was studied: Arabic, Chinese, Japanese, Korean, German, Finnish, Spanish, and Czech.

Origins of contrastive rhetoric

The theory of linguistic relativity

The Sapir-Whorf hypothesis of linguistic relativity, also called the Whorfian hypothesis, suggests that different languages affect perception and thought in different ways. Anthropologist Edward Sapir wrote:

It is highly important to realize that once the form of a language is established it can discover meanings for its speakers which are not simply traceable to the given quality of experience itself but must be explained to a large extent as the projection of potential meaning into the raw material of experience.

Language is heuristic, not merely in the simple sense which this example suggests, but in the much more far-reaching sense that its forms predetermine for us certain modes of observation and interpretation. (Mandelbaum, 1951)

Benjamin Whorf, a student of Sapir's, elaborated on the ideas of Sapir, as the following quotation shows:

This study shows that the forms of a person's thoughts are controlled by inexorable laws of patterns of which he is unconscious. These patterns are the unperceived intricate systematizations of his own language – shown readily enough by a candid comparison and contrast with other languages, especially those of a different linguistic family. This thinking itself is in a language – in English, in Sanskrit, in Chinese. And every language is a vast pattern-system, different from others, in which are culturally ordained the forms and categories by which the personality not only communicates, but also analyzes nature, notices or neglects types of relationship and phenomena, channels his reasoning, and builds the house of his consciousness. (Carroll, 1956)

The Whorfian hypothesis thus asserts that one's native language influences and controls thought, consequently barring fluent second language acquisition. However, it has been criticized frequently by linguists and psychologists. Joshua Fishman, a sociologist of language, discredits (1977) the hypothesis, citing the large number of bilinguals who in most cases have no problem switching between the grammars and lexica of their languages. Psychologists, too, have maintained that the strongest version of the hypothesis, which states that language controls both thought and perception, has been proven false. Even the weaker form, which states that language merely influences thought, has been considered vague and unprovable (Clark and Clark 1977, 557). A similar critical stance about both the strong and weak forms of the Sapir-Whorf hypothesis is expressed by cognitive scientist Steven Pinker (1994).

Recently, however, a new argument for the defense of the weaker form of the hypothesis has been gaining ground. Psychologists Hunt and Agnoli (1991), through careful review of theories and experiments in linguistics and psychology, claim that the Whorfian hypothesis should be considered a hypothesis about language performance rather than a linguistic hypothesis about language competence (the native speaker's conscious knowledge of language and its grammar). According to Hunt and Agnoli, every language is translatable, but there is often a loss involved – an utterance that is completely natural in one language may be completely unmanageable in another. This supports the weaker version of the Whorfian hypothesis, that language influences thought.

Hunt and Agnoli maintain, for example, that it is not because counterfactuals do not appear in Chinese that they are seldom used. (A counterfactual is the "if/then" construction in English, such as "If I were rich, I would buy a sailboat.") Instead, the Chinese seldom use counterfactuals because the Chinese language does not have the subjunctive mood. Thus, in order to make a counterfactual statement the Chinese need to resort to a circumlocution that is elaborate and time consuming both to reason out and to speak. Consider an English sentence uttered by a judge: "If you weren't leaving tomorrow, you would be deported." The Chinese translation would read: "I know you are leaving tomorrow, but if you do not leave, you will be deported" (Bloom 1981, 18). For the Chinese speaker, the sentence is awkward to form and difficult to understand. For this utterance, the relative cost of reasoning is greater in Chinese than in English. Here we see the plausibility of the weaker version of the Whorfian hypothesis, a thesis that is regaining respectability in linguistics and psychology.

Robert Kaplan's model of contrastive rhetoric

In 1966, Kaplan, reinforcing the Whorfian view that each language imposes a world view on its users, claimed that not only spoken language but also logic and rhetoric are culture specific. Kaplan wrote:

Logic (in the popular rather than the logician's sense of the word) which is the basis of rhetoric, is evolved out of culture; it is not universal. Rhetoric, then, is not universal either, but varies from culture to culture and even from time to time within a given culture. It is affected by canons of taste within a given culture at a given time. (1966, 2)

Kaplan's article, "Cultural Thought Patterns in Intercultural Education," began the discipline of contrastive rhetoric in the field of applied linguistics. Originally published in *Language Learning* (1966) and reprinted in several ESL anthologies (e.g., Croft 1972), the article explains Kaplan's contrastive rhetoric hypothesis and tests it with ESL student essays. In addition to being neo-Whorfian, Kaplan's 1966 theoretical position held that one cannot use a purely linguistic analysis to analyze texts. Kaplan saw American theoretical linguistics (particularly Chomskyan linguistics) as essentially atextual (letter to the author, July 1993).

Kaplan's article was the first in a new field of ESL that focused on the rhetoric of writing, thus extending analysis beyond the sentence level. Sentence-level linguistic analyses of structures had hitherto been the interest of other ESL researchers. This pioneering article and his book (1972) reflected Kaplan's interest in and knowledge of rhetoric and logic, which typically are still outside the interest of ESL experts whose training is frequently primarily in linguistics.

Kaplan maintained that logic and rhetoric are interdependent as well as culture specific. He viewed the relationship between language and thought in the same way: "Sequence of thought and grammar are related in a given language" (1966, 4). In addition to the underlying premise that each language or culture has rhetorical conventions that are unique to it, Kaplan maintained that the rhetorical conventions of students' L1 interfered with their ESL writing, as was discussed in Chapter 2.

According to Kaplan, ESL students needed to be made aware of rhetorical conventions in English as in other languages. At that time Kaplan described the structure of English exposition as linear, because a paragraph in English typically begins with a topic statement supported by examples that are related to the central theme. Paragraphs in other languages have different typical structures, as shown in Kaplan's famous diagram summarizing five types of paragraph formation (Figure 1 in Chapter 2). This diagram had an immense impact in part because it is intuitively appealing and easily remembered. Reproduced in many first-language writing textbooks in the United States, it has alerted thousands of first language students and teachers to differences in writing styles across cultures.

Unfortunately, Kaplan's diagram and his hypothesis have been interpreted too simplistically and too literally. Novices reading the article assume that all writers of a particular language compose all their writings in the organizational pattern described by Kaplan. It is even more unfortunate that Kaplan's diagram is taken to mean that a writing pattern reflects a thinking pattern. In other words, the Chinese write in circles; therefore, they must think in circles. Moreover, as the research reviewed will show, many researchers have shown forcefully that the diagram is too simple a model for the representation of a theory of contrastive rhetoric. Contrastive rhetoric is a large and complex discipline, which is influenced by and influences numerous other theories. It merits many models.

THEORETICAL PREMISES OF KAPLAN'S WORK

Kaplan's book on contrastive rhetoric, *The Anatomy of Rhetoric: Prolegomena to a Functional Theory of Rhetoric,* presented the development of his theory "over a period of some eight years" (1972, ix). In the book, Kaplan discussed what he considered to be the fallacies of linguistic and rhetorical analyses of the 1950s and 1960s. He argued against both the linguistic premises of Bloomfield's 1933 linguistic theory, which considered a sentence as the basic unit of syntax, and the Aristotelian concept of discourse, "in which the word itself was the basic unit" (Kaplan 1972, 2). These positions, according to Kaplan, resulted in static analyses in rhetoric and sentence-based analyses of linguistics. As an alternative, Kaplan proposed that the paragraph be considered a unit of analysis. In this, he was ahead of his time. Few would now disagree that he was right on target when he called for analyses of texts that extend beyond the sentence level, even though adequate tools were not then available.

Kaplan's early treatment of rhetoric, however, has been criticized. According to Liebman (1992), Aristotelean rhetoric traditionally involved five elements: invention, memory, arrangement, style, and delivery. Liebman points out that Kaplan's (1966; 1972) approach reduced them to one – arrangement or organization. Furthermore, in his 1972 volume, Kaplan adopted a popular, but limited, view of rhetoric as understood in the English-speaking countries in the last century or more. This rhetoric classified discourse into description, narration, argumentation, and exposition. Absent from this classification was persuasion, the major component of classical rhetoric, which had been replaced by argumentation. Argumentation focused exclusively on the rational, logical appeal and emphasized instruction in deductive and inductive reasoning. The result was that a concern for the other two appeals – for credibility and the appeal to the emotions – was lost from the analysis and formal instruction of rhetoric for a century. Only in 1971 was persuasion distinguished from exposition with the publication of Kinneavy's book, *A Theory of Discourse,* which included persuasion as one of the four major aims of discourse. (See Chapter 4 for discussion of Kinneavy's theory.)

TEXT ANALYSIS USED BY KAPLAN

Kaplan introduced a text analysis based on the theories of the rhetoricians Christensen (1963) and Pitkin (1969), central to which are the discourse bloc and the discourse unit. The former denotes the central idea and the latter its supporting ideas. Kaplan argued that language is understood in a context larger than a sentence; that discourse units, the supporting ideas of a discourse bloc, "constitute those units within a discourse bloc which are related to each other by either coordination, subordination, or superordination" (1972, 27). Such units may normally consist of one or more paragraphs. In order to describe the communicative dynamism among sentences, Kaplan found useful Pitkin's discourse bloc, which denotes the central idea of a text. A discourse bloc "may or may not coincide with units marked by initial indentation/capitalization and terminal punctuation period" (27).

A sample essay with its accompanying "discourse bloc-discourse unit" analysis is given in Figure 1 (from a paper on Arabic writing by Shirley Ostler, one of Kaplan's students, in Connor and Kaplan 1987, 169–170, 179). In examining the diagram, one notices that the analysis represents a linearly constructed outline of the essay. The outline includes the main idea or the discourse bloc: "We face two serious problems in my country." The supporting ideas are diagrammed as discourse units. The essay has five discourse units: The first two explain the problems; the next two offer solutions and the last includes a conclusion. Each contains supporting details. It is worth noting that the diagram lists each idea in the essay in the same sequence as it appears in the essay itself. Some may think that the analysis, based on discourse blocs and discourse units, is a somewhat subjective sentence-by-sentence analysis of semantic linkages across a sentence. It does not allow one to judge the passage for its cohesion and communicative strength or other features considered to be important goals of modern textual analysis.

Nonetheless, Kaplan's model of contrastive rhetoric gave impetus to the serious study of ESL student writing. Guided by the Whorfian hypothesis, it introduced a discourse-based analysis to the study of second language writing. It encouraged the development of tools for describing and evaluating texts. Finally, as the following survey shows, Kaplan introduced testable hypotheses about writing patterns in many cultures and languages.

DB.* We face two serious problems in my country.
DU I.* The first problem is that
  A. 1. we import many things from other countries and
     2. we cannot depend on ourselves in producing the things we need.
  B. We import different kinds of food, electric materials, cars and clothes [sic].
DU II. The second problem is that
  A. 1. we depend on one source of income and
     2. that is the oil.
  B. Our national economy depends on it.
  C. 1. We have a lot of revenues each year from oil export
     2. that come to us from selling this material.
  D. 1. It is not good for our country to depend on one source and
     2. it has to vary its resources.
DU III. We can solve the first problem by building many factories and
  A. we have to develop our soil to be useful to agriculture.
  B. We have to form educated people to serve and to develop their country.
DU IV. We can solve the second problem
  A. by seeking for other resources that we have in my country
  B. not to depend on one source like oil.
DU V. A. Finally we will become a developed country and
  B. we can insure our future and our life.

---

*DB = Discourse Bloc; DU = Discourse Unit

We face two serious problems in my country. The first problem is that we import many things from other countries and we cannot depend on ourselves in producing the things we need. We import different kinds of food, electric materials, cars and clothes [sic].

The second problem is that we depend on one source of income and that is the oil. Our national economy depends on it. We have a lot of revenues each year from oil export that come to us from selling this material. It is not good for our country to depend only on one source and it has to vary its resources. We can't insure that the oil will be enough forever.

We can solve the first problem by building many factories and we have to develop our soil to be useful to agriculture. We have to form educated people to serve and to develop their country. We can solve the second problem by seeking for other resources that we have in my country not to depend on one source like oil. Finally we will become a developed country and can insure our future and our life.

Figure 1 *Sample essay analysis using discourse blocs and discourse units.* (From Writing Across Languages: Analysis of L2 Text, *edited by Ulla Connor and Robert Kaplan,* © *Addison-Wesley, 1987, pp. 169–170, 179.* Reprinted by permission.)

CONTRASTIVE RHETORICAL STUDIES BY LANGUAGE

In the following sections, contrastive rhetorical studies are reviewed by language. Generalizations about rhetorical patterns of languages based on the results of the studies will be highlighted. This review is not intended to include every study ever conducted; instead, it is selective and focuses on works that are most significant for contrastive rhetoric theory and its future directions. For a more exhaustive bibliographic listing of ESL and native English speaker writing, Silva (1993) includes seventy-three research reports involving twenty-seven different languages. Silva's review lists a large number of unpublished dissertations and research reports, a useful resource for teachers and researchers interested in the writing of predominately undergraduate college students of a specific language.[1]

Arabic

Kaplan (1966; 1972) and Ostler (1987) have claimed that Arabic writing is characterized by a series of parallel constructions. They suggest that this style is influenced by the forms of classical Arabic, as found in the Koran, which was written in the seventh century c.e. In English, subordination is preferred in many situations and is taught to students through sentence combining and other syntactic methods, whereas coordination is preferred in Arabic. Therefore, using Kaplan's (1972) examples, in English a coordinated sentence, "The boy was here, and he drank the milk," could be changed to a subordinated sentence through semantic subordination, "The boy was here. He drank the milk," or grammatical subordination, "Milk was drunk by the boy who was here." In Arabic, the coordinated form is preferred.

Kaplan argues that not only are sentences coordinated in Arabic, but paragraph development also adheres to principles of coordination through parallel constructions. Instead of developing paragraphs in the manner of English (a general statement followed by a series of specific examples), Arabic develops paragraphs through a series of parallel constructions, both positive and negative. Kaplan relates the parallelism of

---

1 It is curious that 58 percent of the references in Silva's (1993) review article on ESL and native speaker contrasts are in the form of dissertations and research reports, unpublished in major books and journals. Does the large number of unpublished research hint at problems getting contrastive work published? Or does it reflect the fact that many dissertations in the United States on rhetorical contrasts are written by international students, who often move back to their native countries and may not find suitable outlets for their work? Could it also be that these internationals find acceptance by U.S.-based language journals in particular rather difficult because of their nonnativeness? Ventola and Mauranen (1991) argue the latter point in the case of scientific disciplines they have studied.

Arabic prose to parallel constructions used in the King James version of the Old Testament, most of which was translated into English from Hebrew, which, like Arabic, is a Semitic language whose coordinating structure favors rhetorical parallelism.

According to Kaplan, parallel construction as illustrated by four types of parallelism occurring at the sentence level also prevails in Arabic prose at the passage level, as shown by examples of writing from Arabic-speaking ESL students. Ostler (1987) provided examples by comparing English essays written by Saudi Arabian students with ten English paragraphs selected at random from books. The results showed that the essays written by the Saudi Arabians had a significantly higher number of coordinated sentences than the English passages. In addition, the two languages differed in the use of discourse blocs and discourse units. The essays by Arabic-speaking students contained more discourse units (supporting ideas) than the English passages, frequently began with a superordinate, universal statement, and ended with some type of formulaic or proverbial statement.

A useful volume dealing with the learning of English by speakers of Arabic, Swales and Mustafa's *English for Specific Purposes in the Arab World* (1984) includes several chapters on contrasts between Arabic and English. Especially noteworthy are the contributions by Al-Jubouri, Williams, and Holes. Al-Jubouri discusses the role of repetition in Arabic argumentative texts at three levels: the morphological level, word level, and "chunk" (that is, phrases, clauses, and larger discourse sequences). A careful analysis of Arabic newspaper texts demonstrates that Arabic argumentative texts manifest repetition as an argumentative strategy at all three levels.

Williams provides a much-needed contrastive analysis of English and Arabic theme-rheme progressions in the development of the coherence of texts, attempting to explain patterns of repetition and parallelism. According to Williams, Arabic texts contain exact coreference of the theme in sentence after sentence as well as repetitions of lexical items for esthetic or cohesive reasons.

Finally, Holes examines linguistic and stylistic differences between a research report written in English by a Yemeni graduate student and the expected native English-speaker norm. Using four different versions of an introduction to a research report, Holes provides an excellent discussion of language and textual problems that Arabic-speaking ESL students have in writing academic English. The first version is the original written by the Yemeni student; the second version contains an English teacher's corrections of grammatical and lexical mistakes, some of which are attributed to Arabic influence related to different relative clause formations. The third version adds text cohesion through, for example, lexical "chunking" of information by sections; and, finally, the fourth version develops the text tone by making fewer direct references to the author. This makes the text less like spoken language and more like an academic text in English. Holes's work is a valuable step-by-step analysis of academic writing by an Arabic-speaking English writer.

Many researchers agree that Arabic writing is characterized by parallelism but object to the explanation that it stems from the influence of classical Arabic texts. Bar-Lev (1986) contends that "fluidity" rather than parallelism characterizes Semitic languages and is achieved by the use of "so" and "and," whereas Sa'adeddin (1989) claims that Arabic has two styles of text development, "aural" and "visual." Aural style is characterized by repetition, a limited and imprecise lexicon, and overreliance on abstract generalizations; visual style has linear development, varied lexis, and complex syntax. Because the social function of text determines the style, the visual rather than the aural style is prefered in scholarly writing.

In summary, research on writing in Arabic has focused on syntactic constructions. The findings suggest a preference for parallel constructions, which often translates into similar patterns in ESL writing. However, there is no agreement about reasons for the preference for parallel constructions. Some claim that the preference is explained by an adherence to classical texts, particularly the Koran. Other researchers explain the preference primarily through sociocultural and situational factors rather than the linguistic influence (Bar-Lev 1986; Sa'adeddin 1989).

In the future, contrasts between Arabic and other languages will probably focus on discoursal and pragmatic functions of texts. Valuable insights for future research come from the work of the sociolinguist Barbara Johnstone (1986), who compared a Middle Eastern argument with a Western argument. Johnstone studied the famous 1979 interview between the Italian journalist Oriana Fallaci and Iran's Ayatollah Khomeini, which turned into an abusive argument. Johnstone showed how Fallaci and Khomeini used completely different persuasive styles. Fallaci used a quasi-logical, Western style of argumentation in which statements are supported with evidence and data. For example, an assertion may be, "There is no freedom in Iran," and evidence would come from observable or verifiable facts: "We have seen many people imprisoned and executed for speaking out." Often left unstated is the ground or the basic presumption of the argument. The ground for the above statement would be something like, "Freedom means being to be able to speak out freely."

The Ayatollah, on the other hand, chose to persuade through parables from the Koran and through analogies such as: "Just as a finger with gangrene should be cut off so that it will not destroy the whole body, so should people who corrupt others be pulled out like weeds so that they will not infect the whole field." As the ground of all his arguments, Khomeini invoked the authority of Islam, through statements such as "because Islam says so." It would be worthwhile to examine cross-cultural patterns of argument in writing, thus extending the contrastive rhetoric analysis of Arabic beyond the level of syntax.

Chinese

Kaplan (1966) argued that Chinese as well as other "Oriental" writing is indirect. A subject is not discussed directly but is approached from a variety of indirectly related views. In his book (1972), he explained the indirectness by the influence of the "eight-legged essay," an essay form that became the standard device of the civil service examination in the middle of the fifteenth century and survived as an accepted literary form until the early twentieth century. It constituted the principal framework for Chinese expository and persuasive writing in China, Taiwan, Hong Kong, and Singapore.

Other writers corroborate the importance of the eight-legged essay for Chinese writers (cf. Cai 1993 and in press). The length, organization, and topics for eight-legged essays were derived from classic Chinese books such as the *Four Books* and the *Five Classics,* which convey the teachings of Confucius and set the moral standards for society. Two principles are basic in Confucian thinking: *ren,* or benevolence; and *li,* or propriety of behavior and loyalty to the social traditions. Individuals were to maintain social harmony. Government officers needed to prove their skills in social harmony through the writing of the eight-legged essay, which did not allow for much individual self-expression, considered socially harmful. Guanjun Cai, a Chinese scholar working in the United States, refers to an old Chinese expression in discussing the importance of not offending the higher officers and the societal rule: "For the sake of safety, do not speak about policies when you are not in the position to make them." (Cai 1993, 6).

According to Cai, the designated eight parts were *poti, chengti, qijiang, qigu, xugu, zhonggu, hougu,* and *dajie* literally meaning the opening-up, amplification, preliminary exposition, first argument, second argument, third argument, final argument, and conclusion. The most important part was *chengti,* usually consisting of two or three sentences, in which the writer introduced the chosen topic and expressed the intended thesis of the essay. In the next five parts the writer elaborated on the topic for ten to twenty sentences by drawing anything from the required Chinese classics. Then, the writer concluded the essay in two to four sentences.

Mohan and Lo (1985) dispute Kaplan's claim of the importance of indirectness in Chinese and the influence of the eight-legged essay. They claim that the eight-legged essay was only one of the variations allowed under the *wen-yan* style, a pattern that was used by government officers for centuries. Furthermore, according to Mohan and Lo, the *bai-hua* style (based on spoken language) replaced the *wen-yan* pattern in the early twentieth century. Additionally, they argue that both classical and modern Chinese styles taught at schools today favor a direct rather than an indirect expressive mode. After surveying teachers of native Chinese-speaking ESL students in both Hong Kong and in British Columbia, the authors claim that the organizational pattern of Chinese writing does not differ markedly from that of English and that the instruction students receive in English classes in Hong Kong influences their organizational patterns in writing. Future research should continue examining educational and literacy experiences of second language learners, as the discussion in Chapter 6 suggests.

On the other hand, other researchers, such as linguist Ron Scollon (1991) and writing expert Carolyn Matalene (1985), support the Kaplan hypothesis of indirectness in Chinese writing, although they do not explain it merely as an influence of the organizational pattern of the eight-legged essay. Scollon attributes the indirectness in Chinese writing to a different view of self in Chinese culture from the Western image of selfness. He observes that the process theory of writing in the West emphasizes the experience and voice of the individual. Along with the focus on the individual comes the stance of sincerity to one's true self. This leads to directness; when you know yourself and want to express your belief or feelings, you are expected to express it in specific, nonambiguous sentences.

Scollon argues that the Chinese concept of self makes it difficult for Chinese writers to be direct, to express a point of view in a thesis statement at the beginning of a piece of writing. The Confucian self on which the Chinese self is based relies on four core relationships: affection between parent and child, righteousness between ruler and ruled, differentiation between elder and younger, and trust between friend and friend. It is realized as it participates in these relationships. Individualism is seen as problematic.

Matalene (1985) shows in sample essays written by Chinese ESL students in China that arguments are often delayed, include narration, and use statements that seem unconnected in the eyes of the Western reader. To such a reader, Chinese rhetoric lacks argumentative coherence because of its reliance on appeals to history, tradition, and authority and its frequent references to historical and religious texts as well as proverbs. According to Matalene, these phrases, sayings, and allusions are used to ornament and enliven discourse, but to the Western reader they are distractions.

Cai encourages a cultural and sociopolitical explanation of these cross-cultural differences. He provides a comprehensive, historical description of the teaching of writing and models of good writing in China and supports a contrastive hypothesis similar to Kaplan's: "[t]he rhetorical patterns of discourse strategies of a first language exert an overwhelming influence over students' writing habits in a second language. This influence extends the syntactical and grammatical levels to the rhetorical and ideological levels of discourse" (1993, 11). According to Cai, this is true of Chinese students writing in English:

> Specifically, English compositions by Chinese ESL students have consistently shown evidence of use of either the eight-legged or the four-part or the three-foot organizational patterns, a restricted expression of personal feelings and views, an indirect approach to the chosen topic, and a preference for pre-scribed, formulaic language, all of which are so unfamiliar to native English-speaking instructors that they mistakenly perceive these students as "poor writers." (1993, 11)

Cai maintains that teachers need to be familiar with the sociocultural sources of the problems encountered by Chinese students when writing in English as a second language. Cai's position may be summarized as follows:

1. The eight-legged essay is still a powerful organizing principle for many Chinese students. In addition, the application of the more recent four-part model of *qi-cheng-jun-he* to organize paragraphs is very common (*qi* prepares the reader for the topic, *cheng* introduces and develops the topic, *jun* turns to a seemingly unrelated subject, and *he* sums up the essay). Fagan and Cheong (1987), for example, analyzed sixty English compositions written by Chinese ESL ninth graders in Singapore and found that as many as 50.9 percent of the students wrote their English compositions following the Chinese four-part model instead of the English pattern in which a topic sentence is supported by other sentences. A sample paragraph given by Cai is shown below.

> [*qi*] We are dependent, for understanding and for consolation and hope, upon what we learn of ourselves from songs and stories. [*cheng*] From this statement, we can know that through songs and stories, people realize themselves, humanity, and their societies. The literacy – mastery of language and knowledge of books – is the essential factor that enlarges people's knowledge, and improves mutual realization of people, and then creates the smooth society. [*jun*] From kindergartens to colleges, from homes to offices, we learn how to interact with someone and how to realize ourselves and our societies. The literacy helps us to accustom and realize them. [*he*] Hence, "literacy is not an ornament, but a necessity." (1993, 12)

2. Chinese students seem to avoid free expression of personal views and feelings, as shown by Matalene, Kaplan, and Tsao, for example. Instead they resort to poetry, quotations, and references to the past. According to Cai, quoting from old, even ancient, texts is considered cultured as well as respectful of authorities. To accept traditional values and social norms is considered polite behavior. Matalene's example displays Chinese writers' fondness for using quotations and allusion:

> Confucius, the ancient Chinese philosopher, maintains that whatever your calling, "The first thing to do is to give everything a true and proper name."

Now, we have got a name, "tractor," it is true, "A motor vehicle that pulls farm machinery," according to my Longman's dictionary. What we should do now is to give every tractor a chance to live up to its expectations. I am nothing of a philosopher, but I have a dream that everyone of us is aware of this simple, pragmatical idea: Call a spade a spade. Use a tractor as it should be used. (1985, 804–805)

3. Chinese writers tend to "suggest" or be indirect. They use rhetorical questions, analogies, and anecdotes to reveal intentions. Matalene provides a good example of the indirect approach in an essay in which the writer intends to criticize the inefficiency of the Chinese Department of Agriculture:

I am not an economic policy maker, but I have a dream of tractors singing in the fields and trucks roaring effortlessly on roads. I am not an agricultural technical program planner, but I have a dream of seeing farmers studying science and technology and working comfortably with machinery. (1985, 804)

Thus researchers of Chinese writing reject the overly simplistic explanation offered by Kaplan in his early writings about the effect of the eight-legged essay on Chinese ESL writers. Recent discussions about contrasts between Chinese and English are characterized by agreement about the complexity of the issue. Taylor and Chen (1991), for example, studied the relationships among "culturo-linguistic" systems, discourse structures, and disciplinary conventions in article introductions by three groups of physical scientists: Anglo-Americans writing in English, Chinese writing in English, and Chinese writing in Chinese. Their research is worth highlighting because it shows the methodological problems in contrastive studies resulting from the complex interactions of variations in both regional and disciplinary cultures.

Altogether Taylor and Chen analyzed thirty-one papers in the related fields of geophysics, metallurgy, and mineral processing; materials science and materials engineering. Swales's four moves were examined in the introductions of these papers (Swales's moves are explained in Chapter 8). The papers were published in the English-speaking world as well as in the People's Republic of China: eleven in English from English-speaking countries; ten in English by Chinese native speakers; and ten in Chinese by Chinese speakers. The analysis of the four move structures (establishing the field, summarizing the relevant previous research, preparing for present research by showing a gap, and introducing the present project by stating its purpose or objectives) showed that each of the four moves was employed by all three groups. Yet some variation was found among the groups, and a fairly consistent pattern of difference was found between the Anglo-American-English group on one hand and the two Chinese groups on the other. The Chinese scientists were less likely to elaborate the moves, wrote at less length, and cited fewer references. The major difference was in the second move: The Chinese scientists paid less attention to summarizing the literature in their fields of study.

Explanations for the findings are speculative, and two alternatives are offered. First, for a long time disputation was absent in the Chinese scientific tradition, whereas the western scientific exposition involves debate; and, second, rather prosaically, Chinese scientists do not have access to the bibliographic sources available in Western laboratories. Furthermore, differences were found in the use of the move structures across disciplinary lines. Geologists treated the four-moves paradigm in a more cavalier fashion than did scientists in metallurgy and mineral processing and in materials sciences.

Taylor and Chen's conclusion, related to the complexity of contrastive rhetorical research, is an appropriate summary of the state of contrastive rhetorical research between Chinese and English:

> Our conclusion must therefore be that there is an internationalization of scientific discourse that is nevertheless heavily qualified by significant variations in both regional and disciplinary cultures. It is in the study of these interactions, rather than in broad generalizations about national rhetorical styles or about universals, that we can best approach how to help students of English as a second or foreign language to deal with the requirements of writing for "academic purposes." (1991, 332–333)

In summary, contrastive rhetoric studies have discovered differences between Chinese and English writing. These differences are explained by a number of sociopolitical and cultural reasons. It is believed that the organization of the eight-legged essay by itself is not the reason for the seeming indirect writing of Chinese writers. Instead, explanations that consider cultural orientations toward self, others, society, and social interaction are brought into the interpretation.

Japanese

The most extensive research on Japanese–English contrasts has been conducted by Hinds. His studies are frequently cited and have influenced contrastive rhetorical research dealing with Japanese, Chinese, Korean, and Thai (1980; 1983a; 1983b; 1984; 1987; 1990). Three of the most influential of Hinds's articles are discussed here.

Japanese compositions are characterized by the *ki-shoo-ten-ketsu* or four-unit pattern, which is equivalent to the Chinese *qi-cheng-jun-he* pattern. The introduction of the *ten* part – material that has a connection but not a direct association to the rest of the text – causes Japanese expository prose to seem incoherent to a reader who is not used to the organization. Hinds (1984) shows how this principle works by using an article written for a Japanese newspaper column, "Tensei Jingo," translated into English in the *Asahi Evening News* as "Vox Populi, Vox Dei." Japanese and English-speaking readers were asked to evaluate several "Tensei Jingo" essays for "unity," "focus," and "coherence." English-speaking readers were negatively affected by the organization and gave the essays consistently lower marks than the Japanese readers did.

In 1987 Hinds continued the study of the *ki-shoo-ten-ketsu* pattern and proposed a new typology of language based on speaker and/or writer responsibility as opposed to listener and/or reader responsibility. He showed that, with respect to coherence, Japanese writing demands more of the reader than the Western pattern, resulting in reader–responsible prose. His sample passage was again a column from "Tensei Jingo"; the English translation came from the English translation of the same column.

In 1990 Hinds demonstrates how writing in Japanese, Chinese, Thai, and Korean follows an organizational pattern which he terms "quasi-inductive." Hinds's argument is that English-speaking writers and readers are familiar with strictly deductive and inductive organizational patterns: "inductive writing is characterized as having the thesis statement in the final position whereas deductive writing has the thesis statement in the initial position" (p. 89). Hinds writes: "English-speaking readers typically expect that an essay will be organized according to the deductive style. If they find that it is not, they naturally assume that the essay is arranged in the inductive style." (Hinds 1990, 90).

Showing examples from each of the four languages, Hinds argues that there is an Oriental writing style, though not the only style in those languages, which cannot be classified as either deductive or inductive. Instead, the thesis statement is often buried in the passage. This style involves "delayed introduction of purpose" (Hinds's term), with the topic implied, not stated.

Hinds's argument for a quasi-inductive style is related to his (1987) assertion that Japanese is a reader-responsible language. Readers are expected to fill information and transitions in the four Oriental languages; writing that is too explicit is not valued. Hinds writes:

Seen in this light, we must recognize that the traditional distinction that English-speaking readers make between deductive and inductive writing styles is inappropriate to the writing of some nonnative authors. We may more appropriately characterize this writing as quasi-inductive, recognizing that this technique has as its purpose the task of getting readers to think for themselves, to consider the observations made, and to draw their own conclusions. The task of the writer, then is not necessarily to convince, although it is clear that such authors have their own opinions. Rather, the task is to stimulate the reader into contemplating an issue or issues that might not have been previously considered. (Hinds 1990, 99–100)

Hinds was the first to point out limitations in Kaplan's first study (Hinds 1983a). His research takes a new direction. Instead of considering English prose the starting point of comparison, Hinds views Japanese rhetoric as equally developed and systematic. Significantly, Hinds does not attribute to Japanese rhetoric the shaping influence of the language. Thus, Hinds implicitly disregards the Whorfian hypothesis. Having lived in Japan and knowing the Japanese language and culture, Hinds, a native English speaker, is in an excellent position to make these cross-cultural comparisons and explain cross-cultural differences.

Despite the respect that Hinds's work enjoys among applied linguists and contrastive rhetoricians, some critics have pointed out that Hinds bases his generalizations about Japanese expository prose on analyses only of articles from one newspaper in Japan. Critics assert that different genres may require different styles. This may be true, but Hinds's point is that there is a difference in the perceived coherence of Japanese and Anglo-American texts. His approach is linguistic reflection, not empirical experimentation with a number of texts.

Studies of Japanese–English contrasts are being initiated by native speakers of Japanese. Kobayashi (1984) reports a study that compared U.S. and Japanese students' use of general statements in essays. Altogether, 676 writing samples were obtained from 226 students from four groups: U.S. college students, Japanese advanced ESL students in the United States, English-major Japanese students in Japan, and non-English-major Japanese students in Japan. Each student wrote three compositions involving narration and exposition. The first three groups wrote in English, whereas the non-English-major Japanese students in Japan wrote in Japanese.

The results showed intergroup differences. U.S. students favored the general-to-specific pattern, placing the general statement at the beginning. Japanese students writing in Japanese favored the specific-to-general pattern, placing the general statement at the end. The two Japanese groups writing in English differed from each other: the Japanese students in the United States wrote more like the U.S. students, whereas the Japanese students in Japan wrote more like the non-English-major Japanese students in Japan. Kobayshi's study is noteworthy because of its design, which included writers of L1 and L2 both in the native language and the second language settings. The results confirmed the prevalence of cross-cultural rhetorical patterns and reinforce the importance of the setting of writing.

An important contribution is Kubota's (1992) doctoral dissertation, which compared expository and persuasive essays of both American and Japanese students in their first languages and investigated the transfer of first language patterns into second language writing in the Japanese students' writing. Although the findings of her study suggest some interesting patterns about the organization and use of discourse structures by each group, the most significant aspect of the dissertation is its thought-provoking discussion of the results.

Kubota found that the Japanese students indeed tended to place the main idea at the end of paragraphs (i.e., Hinds's inductive style), but when asked to evaluate styles, they claimed to prefer the deductive style. About half of the Japanese students, when asked about their perceptions about differences between English and Japanese, pointed out a difference between Japanese and English and offered judgments such as the following: "Japanese text is indirect, ambiguous, roundabout, illogical, digressive, has the main idea at the end, and contains a long introductory remark and long, complex sentences; English is direct, clear, logical, has the main idea stated at the beginning and has unity in the paragraph and little digression."

Such judgments frequently appear in books and articles on Japanese and English published in Japan, according to Kubota, who cites as examples Saisho (1975) and Nozaki (1988). Saisho claims that Japanese excels in expressing the writer's emotions, whereas English surpasses Japanese in logic, analytic ability, and succinctness. Nozaki maintains that the English used by Japanese is often unclear to native speakers of English. Thus the view held by some students in the study by Nozaki about the difference between Japanese and English and about the need to teach the Japanese to write in the American English manner is widely held in Japan. Contrary to the implications of the labels, however, Kubota asserts that a Japanese text can indeed be described as logical, analytical, direct, and succinct; and it can even express the main point at the beginning. She concludes that a more positive view of Japanese writing should be adopted by the Japanese as well as by Westerners. Clearly, the issue is complex. Kubota, acknowledging this complexity, provides an insightful discussion of the roles of the political and economic histories in Japan and the West.

Finally, concerning Japanese – English writing research conducted by native speakers of Japanese, two recent research projects are extremely promising: the research of Hirose and Sasaki on one hand, and the research of Oi and Sato on the other. The research of Hirose and Sasaki (1994) examines the relationship between Japanese students' English L2 expository writing and several factors that might influence the quality of the writing product, including L1 writing proficiency. For contrastive rhetoric research, one of the most significant contributions of the Hirose and Sasaki research is the potential development of comparable tests of writing ability for both English and Japanese. The research by Oi and Sato (1990) deals with argumentative strategies used by Japanese and Americans in letters of application and refusal. Working in the contrastive rhetoric framework, Oi and Sato more recently have examined the effects of teaching Anglo-American argumentative writing patterns on Japanese students' school essays.

In summary, contrastive rhetorical research on Japanese and English is receiving a great deal of attention. The impact of the globalization of business, Japan's eminence in world trade, and the role of English as the emerging lingua franca of business have helped change the direction of contrastive rhetoric from examining essays written by ESL students to looking at writing for business and other purposes. Studies dealing with international business writing, including English–Japanese contrasts (Jenkins and Hinds 1987; Connor 1988), will be discussed in Chapter 8.

Korean, German, Finnish, Spanish, and Czech

Korean

Korean texts have been analyzed by applied linguist William Eggington. He shows (1987) that Korean texts are characterized by indirectness and nonlinear development. A four-part pattern, *ki-sung-chon-kyul,* typical of Korean prose, contributes to the nonlinearity. This pattern corresponds to the Japanese *ki-shoo-ten-ketsu* and the Chinese *qi-cheng-jun-he* styles. Thus, in Korean texts, there is an introduction, the development of a topic, a turning to a somewhat unrelated topic, and a conclusion. Indirectness is caused by the placement of the thesis statement at the end of a text. In his discussion of this placement, Hinds (1990) includes Korean in the category of languages with "delayed introduction of purpose"; the other languages are Chinese, Japanese, and Thai.

Eggington's 1987 work was innovative in that it introduced a rigorous text linguistic analysis of Korean texts. Another highly significant contribution was that it posed a question about the impact of American academic education on Korean students' subsequent academic writing. Eggington reports a study that tested newly arrived Korean students' reading recall of two Korean passages: one written in the nonlinear, Korean pattern, the other written in the linear, American English pattern. The results showed that although there was no significant difference in the recalls betweeen the two conditions under the immediate recall condition, there was a difference in the delayed recall. The Koreans "do have more difficulty recalling information after a period of time when that information is presented in a linear rhetorical style" (166). Eggington points out that a significant portion of Korean academic prose is written in a Western-influenced linear style. A large number of Korean academics, however, may not be able to process academic writing with Western organizational patterns as efficiently as desired. As a result, bilingual Western-educated Korean academics may have an advantage over their Korean-educated colleagues after they return to their native country.

A good example of contrastive research on Korean–English contrasts was conducted by Choi, a native speaker of Korean (1988). Choi studied the argumentative text structure of native speakers' writing in English. The text structure of eleven essays on three argumentative topics, given to three American and six Korean graduate students of linguistics at the

University of Illinois at Urbana-Champaign, was analyzed using a multi-level linguistic analysis of argumentative structures following the work of Tirkkonen-Condit (1985) and Connor (1984; 1987a). Choi found that the dominant structure of English essays of native speakers is claim + justification + conclusion, but it was present in only one Korean essay and two English essays of Korean speakers.

In summary, published research reveals Korean texts tend to be non-linear and to place the main topic at the end of a text.

German

Relatively few studies have examined German–English contrasts in an applied linguistics context. Clyne, in the 1983 *Annual Review of Applied Linguistics* volume on contrastive rhetoric, laments the lack of contrastive studies of German and other languages at the discoursal level, noting that until the 1980s, no contrastive studies of texts – except insofar as they affected word order – had been undertaken. In the *Annual Review* article, Clyne contemplates the seemingly different expectations on the part of academics and the education system in general in English-speaking and German-speaking countries. Based on textbook comparisons and comparisons of high school essays, Clyne asserts that form is of greater importance in educational discourse in English-speaking countries than in German-speaking countries, where content seems more important. Clyne (1987) compared the linear organization of academic papers and articles written by English-speaking and German-speaking linguists and sociologists, and examined the hierarchical development of superstructures of texts, the development of arguments, the symmetry of text segments, and the uniformity of formal structures. He found that writing by English speakers favored a linear development, in contrast to writing by German speakers, which favored digression. Thus, in the German texts, there was both more textual and more propositional asymmetry, as well as discontinuity in argument – that is, a new argument was begun before a previous one had been developed. English papers had "advance organizers" to clarify the organization of the paper, whereas German papers scattered the organizers, if they used them at all. However, papers written in English by German writers used more advance organizers than their papers in German.

Clyne explains the differences as a result of different attitudes about the readability of texts in different cultures. English-speaking writers strive to make their texts readable, whereas German writers emphasize content over form. The German reader is expected to make the connections. (One notes a similarity with Hinds's analyses of English and Japanese.)

In summary, relatively few studies have examined German texts from an applied contrastive point of view. The significance of German, however, in the European context will most likely increase in the next years as English, French and German become the major languages in the European community.

Finnish

Finland in the 1980s experienced a rapid growth in the sciences including applied linguistics. Because Finnish is a non-Indo-European language with only 5 million speakers in Finland, Finns recognize the need for good language learning and teaching. Finnish children learn several languages at school: Swedish is required; English, German, Latin, French, Russian, and Spanish are also taught. About 95 percent of all students choose to study English. Because differences between Finnish and languages such as English are vast, Finnish applied linguists are keenly aware of contrasts between Finnish and the Germanic languages. Teacher training focuses on these contrasts.

Three schools of applied linguistics involved in contrastive rhetorical research emerged at the Finnish universities of Jyväskylä and Helsinki, and Åbo Akademi University during the 1970s.[2] At Jyväskylä, several cross-cultural studies involving Finnish have been conducted in the past twenty years under the auspices of Jyväskylä Cross-Language Studies (earlier, Jyväskylä Contrastive Studies), directed by Kari Sajavaara and Jaakko Lehtonen. Although the project has involved analyses of both spoken and written language, the following discussion includes only research on written texts.

A joint cross-cultural study between a Finn (Raija Markkanen) and two Americans (Avon Crismore and Margaret Steffensen) analyzed persuasive student writing of Finnish and American college student writers (Markkanen, Steffensen, and Crismore 1993; Crismore, Markkanen, and Steffensen 1993). The research is ground breaking because it compared the writing in the native languages of the two groups. The Finnish researcher, Markkanen, identified metadiscoursal markers in Finnish that correspond with such markers first identified in English. The use of metadiscoursal strategies, which signal the writer's own presence, was compared via a sample of persuasive essays written by fifty students from each country. Of the fifty essays written, twenty were selected for closer

2 A survey of Finnish studies may seem irrelevant to some readers of this book. After all, most languages are spoken by many more people than is Finnish. The Finnish studies are included primarily because they, like most of the research reviewed in this book, provide contrastive rhetoric with fresh new concepts, methods, and interpretations. Also they reflect the urgent needs of a small nation to communicate internationally without undue stigmatization for poor linguistic manners.

analysis (ten male and ten female students). Following previous definitions of metadiscourse, primarily Vande Kopple's (1985; 1986), the research examined linguistic material in the essays that does not add to the propositional information but allows the writer either to organize what is being said or express personal feelings and attitudes and interact with the reader.

As indicators of metadiscoursal strategies in English, the research, built on Vande Kopple's classification, includes the following categories. Under "textual metadiscourse" are "textual connectives" that help readers with the organization of the text (such as "first" and "next"); "code glosses" that help readers to interpret meanings of words and phrases ("x means y"); "illocution markers" that indicate the speech act ("to sum up" and "to give an example"); and "narrators" that let readers know who said what ("according to"). Under "interpersonal metadiscourse," Vande Kopple includes the following markers: "validity markers" that assess the truth of the content and show the author's commitment such as "hedges" (such as "might" or "perhaps"), "emphatics" ("clearly" and "obviously"), and "attributors" ("according to"); "attitude markers" that reveal the writer's attitude toward the content ("surprisingly," and "it is fortunate that"); and "commentaries" that draw readers into implicit dialogues with the author ("you may not agree that," "you may wish to read the last section first"). A summary of the categories is shown in Figure 2. The figure shows that the classification of Crismore et al. differed slightly from that of Vande Kopple's, shown in the same figure.

The results of the study showed that students in the United States and Finland used both textual and interpersonal metadiscourse in their persuasive writing. Both sets of students used more interpersonal than textual metadiscourse. There were differences, however, between the students: "Finnish students considered hedging the propositional content and expressing their attitudes about it more important than the U.S. students. On the other hand, these data suggest that the U.S. students considered expressing certainty and attributing ideas to sources more important than the Finnish students" (Crismore et al. 1993, 63).

The differences are explained by sociocultural reasons. Crismore and associates speculate that Finns may use more hedges and be more cautious about expressing their true feelings because of their long history of living next to and under the domination of two powerful countries, Sweden and Russia. The higher percentage of certainty markers used by the U.S. students may reflect the view in the United States that certainty of expression is a sign of strength, whereas hedging is a sign of weakness.

At the Language Centers of the University of Helsinki and Jyväskylä, a great deal of contrastive writing research has begun to focus on genre-specific texts. In particular, the language of Finnish academics writing in their specific disciplines has been compared with the writing of native

Classification system for metadiscourse

Textual metadiscourse
1. Text connectives, which help readers recognize how texts are organized, and how different parts of the text are connected to each other functionally or semantically (e.g., *first, next, however, but*)
2. Code glosses, which help readers grasp and interpret the meanings of words and phrases (e.g., *X means Y*)
3. Illocution markers, which make explicit what speech act is being performed at certain points in texts (e.g., *to sum up, to give an example*)
4. Narrators, which let readers know who said or wrote something (e.g., *according to X*)

Interpersonal metadiscourse
1. Validity markers, which assess the truth-value of the propositional content and show the author's degree of commitment to that assessment, that is, hedges (e.g., *might, perhaps*), emphatics (e.g., *clearly, obviously*), attributors (e.g., *according to X*), which are used to guide readers to judge or respect the truth-value of the propositional content as the author wishes.
2. Attitude markers, which are used to reveal the writer's attitude toward the propositional content (e.g., *surprisingly, it is fortunate that*)
3. Commentaries, which draw readers into an implicit dialogue with the author (e.g., *you may not agree that, dear reader, you might wish to read the last section first*)

(Vande Kopple 1985, as it appeared in Crismore et al. p. 46)

Revised classification system for metadiscourse categories

I. Textual metadiscourse (used for logical and ethical appeals)
  1. Textual markers
    – Logical connectives
    – Sequencers
    – Reminders
    – Topicalizers
  2. Interpretive markers
    – Code glosses
    – Illocution markers
    – Announcements
II. Interpersonal metadiscourse (used for emotional and ethical appeals)
  3. Hedges (epistemic certainty markers)
  4. Certainty markers (epistemic emphatics)
  5. Attributors
  6. Attitude markers
  7. Commentary

(Crismore 1993, 47)

Figure 2 Metadiscoursal features (From Crismore, et al., "Metadiscourse in Persuasive Writing," in Written Communication *10, 1, © Sage Publishers, 1993, pp. 46–47. Reprinted by permission.)*

English-speaking academics in the same field. Most of this research is being conducted under the direction of applied linguists Eija Ventola and Anna Mauranen.

Ventola and Mauranen (1991) describe preliminary results of a research project in which they analyzed scientific articles written by Finnish- or Swedish-speaking employees of Helsinki University. The scientific articles had been revised by a native speaker of English, a language editor, at the Language Center of the university. The data included analyses of articles written by Finns as well as by native speakers of English. In addition, the writers in the study were interviewed on their experiences writing in a foreign language. The authors describe the inadequacy of the editor's work, which concentrated on mechanics and lexical matters, and urged editors to correct text features related to theme, rheme, connectors, and other global features. In particular, they found that Finnish writers used too few connectors, did not handle thematic variation well, and had problems with the use of pronouns and articles as reference.

Working from a contrastive rhetoric perspective, Mauranen in a subsequent publication writes:

There is ample evidence that all writing is strongly anchored in the values of the writing cultures that people get socialized into as they learn to write (for example, Kaplan 1988). It can therefore be assumed that two sets of values are simultaneously at work in the writing of a scientific report: those common to the academic community and those held in esteem in the writer's national culture. Both sets of values can be expected to leave their traces on texts. (1992, 239)

In the paper, "Reference in Academic Rhetoric: A Contrastive Study of Finnish and English Writing" (1992), Mauranen analyzed the use of Halliday and Hasan's reference cohesion in scientific texts by Finnish and native-English-speaking writers. In addition, she tested a hypothesis that Finnish writers tend to write inductively when compared to native English speakers, who write deductively. The fourteen texts used in this study were texts written by Finnish scientists in English, texts written by scientists who are native speakers of English, and texts written by Finnish scientists in Finnish. All were medical papers. The Ll texts had been published in medical journals, and the L2 texts were intended for publication, but had been sent for advance language revision to native speakers of English.

Mauranen reports differences between Finnish and native English-speaking science writers' styles. First, differences were observed in the use of reference items: Finnish writers employed fewer selective demonstrative references than native English speakers. According to Mauranen, this results in less persuasive text by disinviting solidarity from the reader through not appearing to present issues from a perspective shared by both the writer and the reader. Another difference was the relatively late introduction of the central referents in the text written by the Finnish in comparison to texts written by native speakers of English. The excessive use of this strategy, according to Mauranen, contributes to an effect of vagueness and indirectness in a reader "expecting to know sooner what the key elements are in the text" (1992, 249).

In a subsequent publication, "Contrastive ESP Rhetoric: Metatext in Finnish-English Economics Texts" (1993), which compared Finnish and

English academic texts from the same data source, Mauranen examines a variety of other textual features, including findings from cross-cultural comparisons of the use of metatextual features in the English writing of the economists from the two cultures. Mauranen follows theories of metatext discussed earlier in the case of Markkanen's studies. Mauranen chose a system adapted from Vande Koppel by Crismore and Farnsworth (1990) with four types of metatext to be analyzed: connectors, reviews, previews, and illocution markers.[3]

The results showed that Finnish economists employed relatively little metalanguage for organizing the text and orienting the reader. These features, according to Mauranen, indicated implicitness. In contrast, native English speakers in the sample used plenty of devices for orienting the reader in terms of what is to follow in the text and how the reader should understand the different sections in the text.

Mauranen discusses at length the implications of these differing strategies and the cultural reasons for them. In sum, it seems that Finnish academic prose is reader-responsible, whereas English academic prose is writer-responsible. Some might consider Finnish prose aloof and uncaring toward the reader. But Mauranen thinks that the Finnish style could be interpreted as polite and not patronizing to the reader (what is obvious is left unsaid). Mauranen asserts that, after all, Finnish students at school are taught in their L1 writing to address an intelligent, knowledgeable, and patient reader. Considering previous contrastive rhetoric work and the interpretation of indirectness and directness in writing across cultures, it is interesting to note that Mauranen considers Finnish indirectness as a positive trait and one that can be understood well in its cultural setting.

At Åbo Akademi, Finland's Swedish-language university, contrastive rhetorical research confirms results of studies described earlier. For example, Lindeberg conducted a study of Finnish speakers' essay writing in English and examined text linguistic features such as topic development and functions of verbs. She found differences between Finnish and English, and claims that Finnish writing is closer to German writing. According to Lindeberg, one reason for certain similarities between Finnish/Finland-Swedish and German discourse patterns may be that "academic learning traditions in Finland have to a great extent been influenced by German academic traditions" (1988, 33). Essay article writers in Finland, in Lindeberg's words, "let the facts speak for themselves," and "seem

3 Connectors are conjunctions, adverbials, and prepositional phrases that indicate relationships ("however," "for example," "as a result"). Reviews contain indicators that an earlier text is being repeated or summarized ("so far we have assumed"). Previews contain explicit indicators that a later stage of text is being anticipated ("we show below"). Illocution markers indicate discourse markers being performed ("to illustrate the size of this distortion").

reluctant to hammer home their points in too obvious a manner, perhaps out of fear to seem to underestimate or to intrude upon their readers" (1988, 33). The unique structure of the Finnish language itself does not obviously contribute to Finnish rhetoric; here again, as in Japanese, the Whorfian hypothesis is insufficiently explanatory.

In summary, various studies using a number of research approaches show that Finnish texts can be characterized as being organized inductively, the main point being made at the end. In addition, Finnish texts suggest things rather than spell them out directly. Much is left for the reader to infer. If we accept Hinds's definitions, Finnish texts could be called reader-responsible as opposed to writer-responsible. On the other hand, the Finnish researchers who initiated the research have pointed out that being reader-responsible is being reader respectful.

Spanish

Some of the first empirical investigations of contrastive rhetoric were dissertations dealing with Spanish (Santiago 1970; Santana-Seda 1970). Surprisingly, anthologies on contrastive rhetoric have not included studies of Spanish (cf. Kaplan 1983b; Connor and Kaplan 1987; and Purves 1988).

Several recent studies, involving large numbers of subjects and extensive quantitative text analyses, provide consistently uniform results about the characteristics of Spanish writing. Each study suggests that native Spanish-speaking writers prefer elaborate and ornate language, with perhaps a leaning toward the loose association of clauses. Reid's (1988) dissertation compared the English writing of 184 native Spanish-speakers with the English writing of native Arabic, Chinese, and English speakers in a study that involved an essay-writing task on the Test of English as a Foreign Language's (TOEFL's) Test of Written English. She found that the Spanish L1 writers used longer sentences and used more pronouns than the native English speakers, demonstrating a preference for "loose coordination."

Montaño-Harmon (1988; 1991) examined variation among four groups of students: Mexican secondary students writing in Spanish, recently arrived immigrant Mexican-American secondary students in the United States, Spanish L1 students who grew up in the United States, and native English-speaking U.S. students. The first group wrote in Spanish and the latter three groups wrote in English. All students wrote a 30-minute personal-opinion essay on their views about their own education. Because of the uniqueness of the data involving L1 writing by the two groups, of special interest are the findings comparing the writing of Mexican students writing in Spanish and U.S. native English-speaking students writing in English. According to Montaño-Harmon, Spanish students, when compared to the Anglo students, wrote significantly longer sentences, had more run-on sentences, used fewer simple sentences, used more synonyms, and used more additive and causal conjunctions. The use of longer sentences and fewer simple sentences, according to Montaño-Harmon, contributed to the Spanish writers' style as elaborated; the greater use of additive and causal conjunctions agrees with Reid's characterization of Spanish style as preferring "loose coordination." The native English-speaking American students, on the other hand, "used simple vocabulary, few synonyms, and no flowery language" (1991, 424).

The findings about the elaborate style of Spanish writers are corroborated by research presented in a dissertation by Lux (1991), who compared university-level Ecuadorian Spanish writers and university English L1 students in the United States. The students wrote for 50 minutes on a task asking them to give an opinion on the role of testing in higher education.

Finally, Reppen and Grabe (1993) offer further convincing evidence about the different writing styles of Spanish and native English-speaking writers. They investigated L1 Spanish and L1 English elementary students' writing in English in the United States. An impressive total of 545 texts (311 English L1 and 234 Spanish L1) were analyzed for a variety of lexicosyntactic features. The findings confirm earlier assertions of studies with adult writers, described above, and point to Spanish L1 transfer effects for students when writing in English, "particularly with regard to the use of elaborate style." Reppen and Grabe's study is noteworthy in the thoroughness of its research as well as its insightful discussion of previous and future contrastive rhetoric research involving Spanish and English.

In summary, after a 20-year lapse of research on Spanish–English rhetoric, recent research is vigorously addressing the topic. The new effort is impressive in its approach owing to the diversification of genres (university as well as school-level writing) and its inclusion of both Spanish and English L1 and L2 writing.

Czech

Czech-English contrasts are discussed briefly as an example of the growing interest in the teaching of writing in English in Eastern and Central Europe. The Czech Republic, as part of Czechoslovakia under the influence of the Soviet Union from 1948 to 1990, experienced several different cultural emphases evident in its educational and scientific practices. Czech linguist Svetla Čmejrková discusses the resulting changes on the teaching of writing to native Czech speakers in a paper, "Academic Writing in Czech and English" (1994a). (See also Čmejrková 1994b.)

According to Čmejrková, Czech scholarship developed through direct contact with German thinking, or "Teutonic" style, more recently transmitted via the Russian intellectual tradition. The German style affected Czech scholarly writing by adding to its syntactic complexity a large number of nominalizations, overloaded phrases, and agentless passives. Characteristic of Czech writing are also delayed purpose, "baroqueness, associativeness, and multiplicity of standpoints," (1994a, 13) making Czech a reader-responsible language.

Čmejrková's comparisons of Czech and English academic writing reveal many differences: Czech journal articles typically lack an abstract; the purpose and goals of articles are not strongly expressed at the beginning; and the formal macrostructures of articles such as section divisions are not marked explicitly.

It is interesting to note that Čmejrková, like the Finnish text linguists Ventola and Mauranen, considers the reader responsibility of Czech texts as an asset rather than a disadvantage, as shown by the following quotations of Czech linguists she interviewed as to why they are reluctant to state the purpose of their writing in the beginning of their articles:

"I do not feel like stating at the beginning what I want to reach in the end."
"The article should read like a detective story, it has analogic principles. I wish my reader to follow the course of my thought."
"If I were to formulate the purpose of my article, I would have to repeat my exposition word by word." (1994a, 18)

The interest in written discourse in the Czech Republic is keen, perhaps owing to the strong text linguistic tradition of the Prague school, a dominant European school of linguistics before the Soviet invasion in 1968 and active again beginning in 1990 in the international arena of linguistics. The research on written contrasts in the Czech Republic is likely to be followed in other Central and Eastern European countries such as Hungary and Poland.[4] Research on contrastive rhetoric in these countries will be fascinating owing to their crossroad positions in Central Europe and their eagerness "to enter Europe" (Čmejrková's phrase) and its discourse communities.

Summary

Since Kaplan's first study, a wealth of research has compared writing patterns and styles in many languages and cultures. Kaplan's study con-

---

4 Poland has, of course, been on the frontlines of contrastive linguistic research with the contrastive project at Poznan University, headed by linguist Jacek Fisiak. However, as the volume *Contrastive Linguistics and the Language Teacher* (Fisiak 1981) shows, the emphasis of these contrastive studies has been on linguistic rather than textual features.

trasted English essay writing with the ESL essay writing of international students with the largest concentrations in the United States in the 1960s, namely students from Asia, the Middle East, and Europe. Subsequent studies, such as the great many studies focusing on Chinese, Japanese, and Arabic, echo similar contexts and goals. Yet significant changes in emphases of research are obvious. Although committed to the general goal of better understanding ESL writing, research has not been limited to analyzing L2 student writing. Instead, writing patterns and styles in a variety of first languages have been addressed both by ESL experts working in the United States and by EFL experts in many other countries. The initiatives of contrastive rhetoricians working in many countries and languages have reduced the Anglo-American bias in the earliest contrastive rhetoric.

Other changes, apart from a tacit and gradual modification of the Whorfian hypothesis on which contrastive rhetoric was originally based, include a diversification of types of writing studied: newspaper writing, both news stories and editorials; academic writing; and professional writing of all sorts, particularly business correspondence and facsimiles. This change reflects the realization that English is now the international language of science and commerce, and the consequent need for English for specific purposes in both the United States and other countries.

PART II:
INTERFACES WITH OTHER DISCIPLINES

4 Contrastive rhetoric and the field of rhetoric and composition

In addition to discussing reasons for the importance of writing at the college level in the United States, this chapter describes four major approaches in the teaching of writing: approaches based on rhetorical theories, the expressionist approach, the cognitive approach, and the social constructivist approach. Their influences on contrastive rhetoric in second language writing are assessed.

Contrastive rhetoric research owes much of its current revival to the important role that the teaching of writing plays in undergraduate education in colleges and universities in the United States.

The role of rhetoric and composition in college education in the United States

Historians of composition theory and practice (e.g., Berlin 1987; North 1987) note that the rise of interest in the formal teaching of writing in the United States can be traced back to 1873, when Harvard University first added an English composition requirement to its list of admission standards. The Conference on College Composition and Communication was formed in 1949. Together with other English teachers' organizations, such as the Modern Language Association and the National Council of Teachers of English, this group has brought composition into a central position of interest among English educators.

Beginning in the 1960s, the study of student composing and of written products became a respectable object of academic inquiry. Faculty involved in the research and teaching of writing have gained legitimacy in English departments; writing courses are often taught by tenure-track faculty members, not just by part-time instructors or teaching assistants. Numerous journals are devoted to the research and teaching of writing, among them *College Composition and Communication, Written Communication, Rhetoric Review, Journal of Basic Writing, Journal of Teaching Writing,* and *Journal of Second Language Writing.*[1]

1 The importance of teaching writing, or even its mere existence, at the college level in

Rhetorician James Berlin provides a comprehensive history of the composition field in his two-volume work, *Writing Instruction in Nineteenth-Century American Colleges* (1984) and *Rhetoric and Reality: Writing Instruction in American Colleges, 1900–1985* (1987). In discussing the recent rise of composition as a legitimate area of teaching and research, he mentions two important influences: the increased emphasis on communication during the decades of 1940–1960, and the importance of educational reforms in the 1950s and 1960s. The 1940s saw a mushrooming of general education courses with emphasis on communication skills leading to the establishment of communication courses designed to provide "a sense of cultural inheritance and citizenship" (Berlin 1987, 92). The threat and fears of World War II had affected thinking about curriculum. Instead of a narrow focus on vocation and specialization, students were considered to need strong bases in citizenship and democratic values. Courses emphasized writing, reading, and speaking skills as well as subject matter. Such courses, taught in English departments, were precursors of a required course, focused solely on composition, which was instituted a couple of decades later.

In the 1950s and 1960s, Berlin observes, educational reforms in the United States came about as a result of the reaction of the U.S. government to the threat from the Soviets' launching of the Sputnik satellite. Increased numbers of young people went to college, and writing became a required subject at most colleges.

Today, colleges test students' writing skills upon entrance; if students do not pass the test, they are assigned to either a remedial writing class to prepare them for a "freshman English writing" class, or directly to freshman English writing. Freshman English writing classes typically focus exclusively on composing and other writing skills rather than on the study of literature or the English language. The objectives at my institution are fairly typical of beginning-level writing courses. Figure 1 shows the overall goals of the course.

Berlin describes how the renaissance of composition since the 1960s produced many competing "rhetorics" – approaches to teaching writing. He categorizes the major rhetorical approaches during 1960–1975 as follows: objective rhetoric, subjective rhetoric, and transactional rhetoric. Figure 2 summarizes the major principles and advocates related to each approach.

the United States is surprising to colleagues outside the United States. Writing skills are not taught as separate courses in most other countries. Instead, students are expected to master basic skills of writing in high school, *lycée*, or *gymnasium*. Proponents of the American way argue that high schools cannot possibly prepare students for the complexities of academic literacy expected at college. It is also said that the research conducted on writing skills at colleges helps improve teaching practice at the public school level, too.

Students successfully completing W131 should:
— Demonstrate the ability to recognize rhetorical situations and to apply varied strategies to meet them appropriately.
— Demonstrate the use of various organizational plans based on purpose.
— Demonstrate the ability to use varied stylistic devices and structures based on rhetorical situation.
— Demonstrate the ability to synthesize materials drawn from varied sources with their own ideas and experiences.
— Demonstrate knowledge about writing as an activity by analyzing and discussing their own work.

Figure 1   General goals for W131 (freshman English writing) at Indiana University in Indianapolis, 1993–1994.

Approach	Principles	Major advocates
Objective rhetoric	— behavioristic — uses model essays — includes process and product	Bloom and Bloom 1967
Subjective rhetoric	— writing is art — writing is a solitary act — writing is discovering oneself	Elbow 1968 Murray 1970
Transactional rhetoric 1. Classical rhetoric	— classical rhetoric provides for invention and for teaching appeals	Corbett 1965
2. Rhetoric of cognitive psychology	— cognitive process of writing can be taught — writing is creative problem solving	Emig 1971
3. Epistemic rhetoric	— writing is a social phenomenon — writing is dialectic and takes place in a discourse community	Bruffee 1973

Figure 2   Summary of early approaches to composition and rhetoric, 1960–1975.

Now, after some 20 years of active research in composition instruction, four major approaches have been advanced: approaches based on classical rhetoric, expressionist approaches, cognitively based approaches, and the social constructivist approach, which emphasizes the role of language and discourse communities in forming knowledge. Although the four terms are commonly used in the field and the taxonomy cannot be attributed to any single person, it is easy to see that some approaches are derived directly from the rhetorics discussed by Berlin. For example, Berlin's "subjective rhetoric" shows clear links to the expressionist approach, whereas Berlin's "epistemic" has influenced the fourth approach. Berlin's first category, "objective rhetoric," is no longer considered a separate school of thought, whereas "rhetoric of cognitive psychology" has since the 1970s become a major approach of its own.

Each of these modes has had a role in transforming contrastive rhetoric, although some (particularly the expressionist and cognitive approaches) initially affected contrastive rhetoric negatively. Others (especially the rhetorical and social constructivist) have consistently influenced the development of contrastive rhetoric positively. A discussion of each category and the influence of each on contrastive rhetoric follows. However, classical rhetoric will receive more extensive treatment because it provided the impetus for development of contrastive rhetoric and it is discussed only minimally in previous texts on ESL writing such as the recent works by Leki (1992) and Reid (1993).

Classical rhetoric

This section begins with definitions and a brief historical overview of classical rhetoric in Western cultures, particularly in North America. Discussions of the roles of Aristotelean rhetoric and the "new" rhetoric in today's composition research follow. Finally, the impact of classical rhetoric on contrastive rhetoric is described.

Changing definitions of "rhetoric"

The term "rhetoric" has had different meanings throughout its long history. Ong (1983) discusses these changes in the use of the term. In the past, rhetoric in the West, Ong writes, referred to "one of the most consequential and serious of all academic subjects and of all human activities. Rhetoric affected the entire range of human actions as nothing else in theory or practice quite did. The study and use of rhetoric enabled one to move others, to get things done" (p. 1).

According to Ong, among the ancient Greeks, rhetoric referred to public speaking, not writing. "Rhetor" in Greek means orator, public speaker, and "rheto-rike" means primarily public speaking. Persuasion in written form was a much later development. Yet it must be remembered, Ong points out, that speeches in Aristotle's time were no longer purely oral but were affected by writing and literacy.

For Aristotle, rhetoric was positive, as his major work on the topic, *Rhetoric,* shows. Yet, rhetoric also gained negative attitudes because of views that a good rhetor can win any argument with a set of skills rather than concern for beauty or truth. Therefore today, Ong writes, "rhetoric" to many suggests "verbal profusion calculated to manipulate an audience, an operation whose aims are suspect and whose typical procedures are most trivializing" (Ong, 1983, 1).

In the recent past, for many linguists, rhetoric has had a negative connotation, suggesting unscrupulous persuasion and coercion. Other linguists may have considered rhetoric in a more positive light but still typically have ruled it outside the domain of sound linguistic inquiry.

Today, however, many linguists studying writing are finding the notion of rhetoric useful. This new research views rhetoric as persuasive discourse without its negative connotations. The Finnish linguist Anna Mauranen's research on academic writing is a good example of the benefits of a rhetorical approach. True to the new wave, Mauranen, in her recent book *Cultural Differences in Academic Writing* (1993), writes: "The study of rhetoric has been rediscovered not only as a means of improving efficiency in verbal presentation, but as an analytical tool that can be used by different disciplines for uncovering certain aspects of discourse." (20) Her work provides an insightful discussion about the linguistic and non-linguistic (sociological and philosophical) approaches to rhetoric in today's scientific research.

Thus, with the expanded definitions of rhetorical studies of writing, rhetoric is becoming an integral part of contrastive writing research.

Classical rhetoric in the West

Rhetoric flourished in the West throughout the Middle Ages and Renaissance. The writings of Cicero and Quintilian particularly influenced philosophic thought and helped to shape the establishment of church and government. The eighteenth century was a turning point in the history of rhetoric. Rhetoric declined in proportion to the gain in prominence of other disciplines such as logic, philosophy, and literary criticism. Horner (1983) suggests two reasons for this: a shift in interest from oral to written language because of the separation of poetry and rhetoric, and a shift from rhetoric's emphasis on speakers to an emphasis on readers and their interpretations of texts.

According to Connors, Ede, and Lunsford (1984), the comparative decline of rhetoric in America in the late eighteenth century was closely linked to the belles-lettres movement and the establishment of teaching literature in the new English departments. The first professors in the discipline of English insisted on including English literature in the curriculum. Writing as opposed to oral language was emphasized. Instead of relying on rhetoric, however, writing in colleges emphasized style in writing.

In America in the early twentieth century, scholars of rhetoric and public speaking broke away and formed departments of public speaking. Connors et al. note that in the 1920s and 1930s, "scholarship in classical rhetoric began in earnest in speech departments" (1984, 7). English departments, on the other hand, grew further away from the theory of classical rhetoric.

There was a rebirth of interest in rhetoric in English departments in the 1930s and 1940s owing to the communication movement referred to earlier in the context of Berlin's assessment of the rise of the teaching of writing at U.S. colleges and universities. Composition studies were revived, and the influence of classical rhetoric was reconfirmed. A real interest began in the 1960s when English faculties began the serious study of written discourse.

Aristotelean rhetoric

Aristotle's *Rhetoric* was unknown in the West during the Middle Ages, but then became the paradigm for European rhetorical study and practice until well into the modern period. Rather than the historically important works of Quintilian and Cicero – studied in the Middle Ages and Renaissance – Aristotle's text is the major influence upon American composition scholars of today.

For Aristotle, rhetoric existed primarily to persuade. "It is clear, then," he writes in *Rhetoric*, "that the technical study of rhetoric is concerned with the modes of persuasion" (1984, 2153). There need to be different modes of persuasion, he writes, depending on three major components in the communication: the speaker, the audience, and the content of the argument. In Aristotle's times the audience was likely to be a judge and members of the assembly, or jurymen. The type of audience determined the three Aristotelean divisions of oratory: judicial or political in the forum, legal or deliberative in the court, and ceremonial or panegyrical on state occasions.

In order to make an argument, one had to study three points: the means or sources of persuasion, the language, and the arrangement of the various parts of the treatment. The means or sources of persuasion are inventional strategies for making three appeals, those of *ethos, pathos,* and *logos:* "The first kind depends on the personal character of the speaker, the second on putting the audience into a certain frame of mind, the third on the proof, or apparent proof, provided by the words of the speech itself" (2155).

The language of the argument had to be carefully crafted; word choice was important, and the use of appropriate *topoi,* or themes, and metaphors, or *tropes,* was encouraged. Finally, the arrangement was also important: "A speech has two parts. You must state your case, and you must prove it" (2257). A well-organized or properly arranged speech had three parts: introduction, argument and counterargument, and epilogue. "What you *should* do in your introduction is to state your subjects, in order that the point to be judged may be quite plain; in the epilogue you should summarize the argument by which your case has been proved" (2268).

Aristotelean rhetoric in modern composition studies

Some leaders in the composition field, such as rhetoricians Janice Lauer at Purdue University and Edward Corbett at Ohio State University, have pioneered the revival of classical rhetorical theories as a basis for the teaching of composition. Aristotle's rhetoric is the major influence for others as well, such as rhetoricians Richard Young at Carnegie Mellon and Andrea Lundsford at Ohio State University. All have adopted Aristotle's rhetoric for the teaching of any kind of writing, even though Aristotle's rhetoric concerned only three kinds of eloquence, judicial, deliberative, and panegyric oratory. Since the overriding theme in the adoption of Aristotelean rhetoric is the need to develop arts or strategies to guide phases of writing, from invention to editing, major components of Aristotle's rhetoric have been applied in composition instruction and textbooks. Persuasive appeals are taught: *ethos* (the personal appeal of the sender), *pathos* (appeals to the emotions or values of the receiver), and *logos* (appeals to reason). The intended targets of the appeals (sender, receiver, and content, "Aristotle's triangle" of communication) help organize many textbooks of writing.

Connor and Lauer (1988) provide a helpful discussion of the application of Aristotle's rhetoric for the teaching and evaluating of persuasive writing. According to them, from Greek times through the Renaissance, the education of a communicator was synonymous with instruction in persuasion. In the eighteenth century, England and the United States came under the domination of a four-component model of discourse: description, narration, argumentation, and exposition. Persuasion was replaced by argumentation in the writing curriculum. Connor and Lauer mention two influential theoreticians of the time, Campbell (1776) and, much later, Bain (1866), as instigators of the new classification. Argumentation, their emphasis, focused on logic, and the two other appeals, the appeal to credibility and the affective appeal, were dropped from teaching. According to Connor and Lauer, the neglect of persuasion continued until Kinneavy's classification (1971), which again distinguished persuasion from exposition. James Kinneavy, a rhetorician at the University of Texas, included persuasion in his classification of discourse as one of the four major aims of communication: referential, persuasive, literary, and expressive. As major features of persuasion, Kinneavy distinguished rational, ethical, and emotional appeals as different strategies. The three appeals were adapted for composition research by Connor and Lauer (1985; 1988), who developed a scale and rubrics for evaluating the quality of persuasive appeals in student essays, shown in Figure 3.

The "new rhetoric"

In addition to those rhetoricians who look principally to classical rhetoric for answers, other rhetoricians have developed new theories that help keep rhetoric viable in the modern world. Daniel Fogarty's *Roots for a New Rhetoric* (1959) outlines a "new" rhetoric as follows:

[The new rhetoric] will need to broaden its aim until it no longer confines itself to teaching the art of formal persuasion but includes formation in every kind of symbol-using . . . ; it will need to adjust itself to the recent studies in the psychology and sociology of communication; and, finally, it will need to make considerable provision for a new kind of speaker-listener situation. (1959, 130)

The "new" rhetorics are especially relevant for those interested in second language writing: Toulmin's model of argumentative writing and

Rational
0 No use of the rational appeal*
1 Use of some rational appeals* minimally developed or use of some inappropriate (in terms of major point) rational appeals
2 Use of a single rational appeal* or a series of rational appeals* with at least two points of development
3 Exceptionally well developed and appropriate single extended rational appeal* or a coherent set of rational appeals*

Credibility
0 No use of credibility appeals
1 No writer credibility but some awareness of audience's values or
  Some writer credibility (other than general knowledge) but no awareness of audience's values
2 Some writer credibility (other than general knowledge) and some awareness of audience's values
3 Strong writer credibility (personal experience) and sensitivity to audience's values (specific audience for the solution)

Affective
0 No use of the affective appeal
1 Minimal use of concreteness or charged language
2 Adequate use of either picture, charged language, or metaphor to evoke emotion
3 Strong use of either vivid picture, charged language, or metaphor to evoke emotion

*Rational appeals were categorized as quasi-logical, realistic structure, example, analog.

Figure 3   Scales for judging persuasive appeals (From "Cross-Cultural Variation in Persuasive Student Writing," by Connor and Lauer, in Writing Across Languages and Cultures, *edited by Alan C. Purves, © Sage Publishers, 1988, p. 147. Reprinted by permission.)*

Perelman's "new rhetoric." Toulmin (1958) designed his theory of argumentation to reproduce the structure of arguments in the practice of law. Toulmin's model, therefore, defines argumentation as an attempt to justify statements. The first step in argumentation is to express an opinion in the form of an assertion, preference, view, or judgment. The statement put forward to be upheld is called the "claim." The second feature in an argument is the "data," designed to support the claim and to counter any possible challenge to the claim. The data can be in the form of experience, facts, statistics, or occurrences. The accuracy and appropriateness of the data may be challenged, however, so the arguer must be prepared to provide further support for the claim by showing the relation of claim and data by means of the justification, or "warrant." The warrant serves as a bridge from the data to the claim. Warrants are "rules, principles, inference-licenses or what you will instead of additional items of information" (Toulmin 1958, 98). They are typically general, hypothetical statements that authorize the relationship between the data and the claim.

Claim, data, and warrant are obligatory in every argument, according to Toulmin. In his extended model three other elements of argument – "*backing*," "*rebuttal*," and "*qualifier*" – are optional. Backing means "generalizations making explicit the body of experience relied on to establish the trustworthiness of the way of arguing in any particular case (Toulmin, Rieke, and Janik 1979, 57). Conclusions often need to be accomplished with rebuttals, that is, "the extraordinary circumstances that might undermine the force of supporting arguments" (Toulmin et al. 1979, 75). Qualifiers refer to the "strength or weakness, conditions, and/ or limitations with which a claim is advanced" (Toulmin et al. 1979, 70). These qualifiers often take the form of modal qualifiers, such as "necessarily," "certainly," "very likely," and "maybe." The six features in the model do not have to appear in any particular sequence in a good argument.

Toulmin's model was used in a cross-cultural study of writing, which compared argumentative writing in students' essays from three English-speaking countries (Connor and Lauer 1985; 1988; Connor 1990a) and in a study of international students' essay writing (Connor 1991). Connor and Lauer operationalized Toulmin's model for a quantifiable, reliable analysis in order to evaluate the level of argumentative strength of the essays. Figure 4 shows the scale and rubrics developed for judging the quality of claim, data, and warrant. In the series of studies, they found that Toulmin's model was a powerful predictor of writing quality in the sample essays.

Toulmin's model of argumentation is particularly relevant in today's writing research, which emphasizes the diversity of purposes and tasks. Toulmin et al. (1979) describe analyses of arguments in the special fields of law, science, the arts, and business management, showing how

Claim
1. No specific problem stated and/or no consistent point of view. May have one subclaim. No solution offered, or if offered, nonfeasible, unoriginal, and inconsistent with claim.
2. Specific, explicitly stated problem. Somewhat consistent point of view. Relevant to the task. Has two or more subclaims that have been developed. Solution offered with some feasibility with major claim.
3. Specific, explicitly stated problem with consistent point of view. Several well-developed subclaims, explicitly tied to the major claim. Highly relevant to the task. Solution offered that is feasible, original, and consistent with major claim.

Data
1. Minimal use of data. Data of the "everyone knows" type, with little reliance on personal experience or authority. Not directly related to major claim.
2. Some use of data with reliance on personal experience or authority. Some variety in use of data. Data generally related to major claim.
3. Extensive use of specific, well-developed data of a variety of types. Data explicitly connected to major claim.

Warrant
1. Minimal use of warrants. Warrants only minimally reliable and relevant to the case. Warrants may include logical fallacies.
2. Some use of warrants. Though warrants allow the writer to make the bridge between data and claim, some distortion and informal fallacies are evident.
3. Extensive use of warrants. Reliable and trustworthy allowing rater to accept the bridge from data to claim. Highly relevant. Evidence of some backing.

Figure 4   Criteria for judging the quality of claim, data, and warrant (From "Cross-Cultural Variation in Persuasive Student Writing," by Connor and Lauer, in Writing Across Languages and Cultures, *edited by Alan C. Purves,* © *Sage Publishers, 1988, p. 145. Reprinted by permission.)*

warrants – shared values or premises – determine the development of an argument.

Toulmin's model has been applied in writing pedagogy for native English speakers for a number of years. The model can be found in at least fifteen different textbooks on writing and argumentation, the best known being Toulmin et al.'s *An Introduction to Reasoning* (1979) and Rottenberg's *Elements of Argument: A Text and Reader* (1985), which presents the model through a variety of readings. Toulmin's model also appears in two articles in the *Journal of Teaching Writing*. Karbach (1987) explains how the basic model is a useful heuristic both for teachers and students in college. Stygall (1987) focuses on a need for different warrants for different argument fields. She shows how students' critical thinking skills can be challenged when they construct arguments on the same subject for different argument fields or audiences. One of her examples deals with the differing argument developments in the United States between "language purists" and "linguists" regarding the issue of "English only as the official language."

Evidence from L1 instructional practice points to the potential usefulness of Toulmin's model in L2 writing classes. It is appropriate for L2 situations because it recognizes field-invariant aspects of argument (structure and development of argument) but allows for field-independent evaluations of argument. Therefore, as Karbach and Stygall have shown, writing classes benefit from the Toulmin model because it encourages the development of arguments for different purposes. In undergraduate L2 classes, students can benefit from learning the structure and sequence of argument development. In advanced, graduate-level classes, L2 students can learn to master the writing and argumentation of their specific disciplines. They can explore acceptable warrants of their discipline in order to build valid arguments with claims that are worth making and with data that are accurate.

Another popular model is Perelman's "new rhetoric." Perelman's (1982) and Perelman and Olbrechts-Tyteca's (1969) new rhetoric is more concerned with informal argument as it is practised in the modern world. They do draw on classical rhetorical theory, however, especially Aristotle's *Rhetoric*. The focus is on the achievement of a particular effect on the audience: on "the adherence of the members of an audience to theses that are presented for their consent" (Perelman 1982, 9). Perelman and Olbrechts-Tyteca introduced their discussion of argument and audience when no other researchers were concerned about audience. They tried to articulate for the modern world what can be the starting points of arguments by cataloging modern values and the types of arguments used in the modern world.

Perelman's greatest contribution was his emphasis on audience. He distinguishes among three audiences: those the speaker expressly addresses; the speaker himself, "reflecting privately about how to respond to a delicate situation"; and the "universal audience," which consists of all of humanity or "at least all those who are competent and reasonable" (1982, 14).

The strategies used in an argument are determined by the type of audience, and the speaker chooses "as his points of departure only the theses accepted by those he addresses" (1982, 21). The universal audience provides a norm for objective argumentation. However, understanding a universal audience can be difficult. Perelman suggests that we need to consider as our universal audience the image, the mental construct, that each speaker holds of the universal audience she is trying to win over. The notion of the universal audience as an image created by our experiences and beliefs is important when cross-cultural argumentation is discussed. Perelman and Olbrechts-Tyteca admit that:

Everyone constitutes the universal audience from what he knows of his fellow men, in such a way as to transcend the few oppositions he is aware of. Each individual, each culture, has thus its own conception of the universal audience. The study of these variations would be very instructive, as we would learn from it what men, at different times in history, have regarded as *real, true, and objectively valid.* (1969, 33)

In Perelman's theory, the strategies used in argument are determined by the nature and knowledge of the audience as well as the purpose of the argument – whether the person wants to refute the opponent's thesis or seeks to win him to his cause (1982, 145). Perelman and Olbrechts-Tyteca provide a number of argument-related schemata and techniques attuned to the audience from which approval is sought. Among the categories they describe are quasi-logical arguments (arguments by comparison); arguments based on the structure of reality (e.g., argument from authority); and relations establishing the structure of reality (e.g., analogy, metaphor).

The effect of rhetorical theories on contrastive rhetoric

Naturally, the effect of classical rhetoric on contrastive rhetoric has been significant. In fact, contrastive rhetoric would not exist had Kaplan not gone beyond linguistic analyses to describe the writing performance of ESL learners, focusing on the rhetoric – or "logic," as he called it – of the ESL essays he analyzed. His 1966 article focuses on rhetorical differences and associates the writing of Anglo-Americans with the traditions of Western rhetoric as represented in the theories of Aristotle. Despite the focus on rhetoric, Kaplan's interpretation of Aristotelean rhetoric was narrow. He spoke only of the organization of writing, in Aristotle's term its "arrangement" – one of the three major components in Aristotle's rhetoric. The two other components of Aristotle's rhetoric, rhetorical appeals and persuasive language, were ignored.

Recent contrastive rhetorical research reflects trends in the rhetorical research of L1 composition researchers. Two major influences of classical rhetoric on contrastive rhetoric are obvious. First, the work of Kinneavy and other rhetoricians who have helped explicate differences between the aims and modes of discourse has forced contrastive rhetoricians to re-evaluate the types of texts used in cross-cultural contrasts. For example, early contrastive rhetoric examined only expository student essays. More recent contrastive rhetoric has included narrative student essays (e.g., Söter 1988) and persuasive student essays (Connor 1987a; Connor and Lauer 1988). Recent work has included collaborative research between rhetoricians and linguists. Connor and Lauer (1985; 1988), for example, analyzed persuasive essays cross-culturally. For their analyses, they developed a linguistic/rhetorical system that helped quantify linguistic features in essays (such as cohesion, coherence, or discourse organization) and rhetorical features (such as adaptation to the audience; strength of claim, data, and warrant; and persuasive appeals). A summary of the features in their system is shown in Figure 5.

Variable	Measures
1. Syntactic	Computerized analysis of twelve syntactic features; two underlying dimensions: interactive vs. edited text and abstract vs. situated style (Connor and Biber 1988)
2. Coherence	Scale including three different variables related to topic development in texts, based on topical structure analysis, a linguistically grounded theory (Connor and Farmer 1990)
3. Persuasiveness a. Superstructure	Frequency of four different argument slots (Connor and Lauer 1985; 1988)
b. Reasoning	Scale measuring Toulmin's categories of claim, data, and warrant (Connor and Lauer 1988)
c. Persuasive appeals	Scale measuring three appeals: rational, affective, and credibility (Connor and Lauer (1988)
d. Persuasive adaptiveness	Scale measuring levels of audience awareness and persuasive adaptiveness (Connor and Takala 1987)

Figure 5   Summary of variables and measures for evaluating persuasive essays across cultures. (From "Linguistic/rhetorical measures for international persuasive student writing," by Ulla Connor, in Research in the Teaching of English, 24, 1, © *National Council of Teachers of English, 1990, p. 70. Reprinted by permission.)*

The second major influence of rhetorical theories has been the increased emphasis on audience in contrastive rhetoric research. As was discussed earlier, the concept of audience is important in all theories of rhetoric from Aristotle's rather fixed audiences to Perelman's multiple audiences – the expressed audience, the writer as audience, and the universal audience. Contrastive rhetoricians have begun to define universal audiences in different cultures. For example, Hinds's research on reader-responsible vs. writer-responsible prose in different cultures proposes a new dimension for contrastive rhetorical research, one that has been embraced eagerly by many researchers.

The expressionist approach

The expressionist approach emphasizes writing as a solitary activity and as an opportunity to explore one's inner feelings. Leading expressionists of the 1960s and 1970s were Donald Murray (Murray 1970) and Peter Elbow (Elbow 1981). According to the expressionist approach, teachers need to provide environments for students to explore and write about. Free writing, brainstorming, and peer review are some of the practices of the approach. Writers are not supposed to interact with the rest of the world through their writing; instead, through their writing they are expected to learn about themselves.

Advocates of the process approach in ESL in the 1980s, the most prominent of them being Ann Raimes (Raimes 1985; 1987; 1991a; 1991b), Ruth Spack (Spack 1984), and Vivian Zamel (Zamel 1976; 1984; 1987), embraced many of the practices of the expressionist approach. Writing was seen as a creative set of behaviors in which the writer was the center of attention engaged in the discovery of meaning.

It is important, however, to make clear the distinction between the expressionist approach and the process approach. The expressionist approach deals with the type of writing produced, whereas the process approach pays attention to the development of any type of writing. Thus an expressionist approach might always involve a process approach, but the reverse is not necessarily true.

Raimes (1991b) discusses how an overemphasis on the writer's role at the expense of the other elements has sometimes given rise to an unbalanced "therapist's" stance. Textbooks following an expressionist approach often ask students to write about personal experiences and make no mention of grammatical accuracy. According to Raimes, "critics of a process approach often mistakenly label this extreme position as 'the process approach'" (242).

A useful distinction is to consider the level of students when one makes recommendations about instructional approaches. Raimes maintains (letter to the author, March 16, 1994) that beginning-level ESL students need ESL as a language course, and more advanced students benefit from ESL as an academic writing course with some language development. Concerning the expressionist approach, she writes: "[T]he college ESL textbooks that emphasize inner feelings usually are using that for language production purposes, not for teaching academic writing."

Contrastive rhetoric and the expressionist approach

In the pure expressionist approach, a process-oriented approach, there seems to be little place for contrastive rhetoric. All students, regardless of their L1 backgrounds, are expected to have similar problems in generating meaning, revising, and learning about themselves. There has been a great debate about the advantages and disadvantages of process-oriented composition instruction, particularly of the expressionist approach. As has been pointed out by many ESL experts (Reid 1984a; 1984b; Horowitz 1986a; 1986b), the expressionist approach may not be appropriate even for beginning-level ESL students. ESL students differ from their native English-speaking counterparts in many respects, chief of which is the fact that many of them think and write in their L1 and do not have to learn to discover their inner feelings through writing. In many of their cultures, too, as for many American undergraduates who need to learn to write to fulfill general requirements, writing about oneself is often an alien concept.

The strangeness of the concept of self in the expressionist approach for Chinese students from Taiwan has been discussed by Scollon, who taught and studied ESL writing in Taiwan. Scollon (1991) discovered that the expressionist approach in Elbow's *Writing with Power* (1981) did not go over well with Scollon's Taiwanese students. Scollon points out that Elbow's self-expression evokes the Western individualist sense of self, which is alien to Chinese writers. In the Confucian sense of self, one is more a self in human relationships, and less a self in isolation. As a result, writing about their inner feelings to themselves is difficult for Chinese ESL students. Scollon writes:

> The Chinese student is not writing primarily to express himself or herself but for the purposes of becoming integrated into a scholarly community. The purpose of student writing is to learn to take on a scholarly voice in the role of commentator on the classics and on the scholarship of others. One is writing to pass on what one has received. (1991, 7)

A personal experience of a Chinese student learning English writing is related by Fan Shen. Fan Shen describes how, in order to learn to write acceptable English in a composition class at a U.S. university, she had to "reconcile (her) Chinese identity with an English identity dictated by the rules of English composition" (1989, 459). Her Chinese identity emphasized "we," her English identity emphasizes "I." Fan Shen writes:

> Rule number one in English composition is: Be yourself. (More than one composition instructor has told me, "Just write what *you* think.") The values behind this rule, it seems to me, are based on the principle of protecting and promoting individuality (and private property) in this country. The instruction was probably crystal clear to students raised on these values, but, as a guideline of composition, it was not very clear or useful to me when I first heard it. First of all, the image or meaning that I attached to the word "I" or "myself" was, as I found out, different from that of my English teacher. In China, "I" is always subordinated to "We" – be it the working class, the Party, the country, or some other collective body. Both political pressure and literary tradition require that "I" be somewhat hidden or buried in writings – and speeches; presenting the "self" too obviously would give people the impression of being disrespectful of the Communist Party in political writings and boastful in scholarly writings. (1989, 460)

The writer continues:

> Now, in America, I had to learn to accept the words "I" and "self" as something glorious (as Whitman did), or at least something not to be ashamed of or embarassed about. It was the first and probably biggest step I took into English composition and critical writing. (1989, 460)

The notion of self in other cultures besides Chinese has not been compared with the Anglo-American self in contrastive rhetoric literature.

From personal experience as a native speaker of Finnish, I conclude that there are differences in the way Americans and Finns talk about themselves. Finns tend to be quiet; talking about oneself, one's thoughts, and one's accomplishments is considered boasting. Being boastful is considered a negative characteristic (Lehtonen and Sajavaara 1985). In addition, Finns tend to be indirect in their social interactions and writing (Mauranen 1993). Indirectness in writing is in conflict with the expressionist approach, which emphasizes the truth and directness of one's convictions.

Based on anecdotal evidence from Chinese speakers of ESL and on sociolinguistic notions about cultural differences about self, it seems safe to say that the expressionist approach to writing about oneself is not fruitful by itself. This is especially true when one considers that expressive writing may be practised in undergraduate classes among North American students, but certainly in upper level undergraduate and graduate classes, genres other than expressionist narratives are required: book reports and term papers, for example.

Related to the previous discussion in this section about the difference between the expressionist and process approaches, one needs to keep in mind that a process approach in college courses deals with ideas and academic topics and not just "writing about oneself" in terms of feelings and personal experience. Clearly, contrastive rhetoric has a place in process pedagogy.

Writing as a cognitive approach

The third major approach in composition studies considers writing as a complex cognitive process requiring appropriate strategies. In the past two decades, a great deal has been learned about these processes. Both L1 and L2 researchers have examined the mental states of writers, their problem-solving strategies and decisions about focus, audience, and language use; their stylistic decisions as well as composing processes – planning, decisions during writing, and revising – in order to determine what is involved in the act of writing and what skills are required.

For example, researchers have studied student writers while they are writing. In first language writing, Emig's (1971) pioneering research, *The Composing Processes of Twelfth Graders,* was the first to shift the emphasis from product to process and to establish a case-study approach using audiotaped think-aloud protocols as data. Emig analyzed the writing processes of eight high school seniors, audiotaping their composing aloud, observing the students while they wrote, and interviewing them afterwards.

One of the most powerful cognitive models of composing is that developed by Flower and Hayes (1981) based on their studies of think-aloud protocols collected from mature, college-level writers while in the act of writing. Flower and Hayes's cognitive process model represents writing as consisting of four interactive components: task, environment, the writer's long-term memory, and the composing processes themselves. The task environment consists of the writing topic, the audience, the degree of urgency of the task, and the text produced so far. The writer's long-term memory retains definitions of the topic, the identity of the audience, and possible writing plans. The writing processes include planning, translating, and reviewing. Planning involves generating ideas, goals, and procedures. Translating involves expressing ideas and goals in verbal forms, and reviewing includes evaluating and revising.

Using this theoretical model to explain data from numerous empirical studies, Flower and Hayes have identified composing as an exceedingly complex problem-solving activity responding to a rhetorical situation in the form of a text. Most important, their research has determined that writing ordinarily is not a linear process where a writer moves from planning to translating and to reviewing in an orderly sequence. Instead, most writers have been found to write recursively, not knowing what the written outcome will be when they start. This research on the composing process contradicts the assumptions of traditional pedagogy, which required that students find a topic, construct an outline, and then write in an orderly, linear sequence. It has also discovered differences between the strategies of skilled and novice writers. Skilled writers pay greater attention to matters of content and organization, whereas weaker writers are preoccupied with mechanics. (See Hillocks 1986 for a comprehensive review of L1 writing process research.)

Second-language writing research imitates L1 writing process research. (See Krapels 1990 for a review of the ESL writing process research.) Raimes's (1987) case study is a good example; it includes only one writing task, and data are gathered from both process- and product-oriented sources. Think-alouds are analyzed with regard to process model components: students' planning, translating, and reviewing are charted; strategies to address the audience are assessed; and procedures to address the writing task in general are explained. With regard to product-oriented data, students' written essays are analyzed and evaluated according to their length, use of various syntactic measures, coherence, development, and other features contributing to essay quality.

Krapels (1990) points out that the findings from the 100 or so studies on L2 composing are sometimes contradictory, because of the limited number of subjects and tasks in the case studies. The results tend, however, to lead to the following major conclusions:

1. Composing competence is more important in ESL writing than language competence.
2. The composing processes of expert L2 writers are similar to the composing processes of expert L1 writers; likewise, the composing processes of novice L2 writers are similar to the composing processes of novice L1 writers.
3. Composing processes in L1 are transferrable to L2.
4. Composing processes in L2 are somewhat different from those in L1 (a contradiction of #2, Krapels points out).

At this time, it seems too early to generalize about L2 writing processes because the studies have been conducted with few students in different settings. Typically, the subjects have written an essay on a prescribed topic. The research has focused on one aspect, composing processes, and has not controlled for other variables that, according to the communicative model, enter into the writing situation – for example, knowledge of the audience, the context, and the purpose. However, the influence of process-orientation research on contrastive rhetoric has been significant. Some applied linguists working on contrastive rhetoric have learned that studying written products without analyzing the context, situation, audience knowledge, and purpose of the writing task is not enough, while others are making a contribution by looking at the processes of writing from a cross-cultural point of view.

The social constructivist approach

The 1970s have been said to be the decade that discovered the composing process and the 1980s the decade that discovered the role of social context in composing (Nystrand, 1986, 1989). In the 1980s, researchers turned to examining writers and writing in particular settings, what Witte (1992) calls "situated writing." Some of the pioneering work contributing to this new movement were Nystrand's (1982) essay on "speech community," Bizzell's (1982a; 1982b) essays on "discourse community," Odell and Goswami's (1985) study of nonacademic writing, and Heath's (1983) ethnographic study of two communities and their literacy practices. These studies showed that writers' plans, goals, and other process-based strategies are dependent on the particular purpose, setting, and audience of writing.

Context and situation being important for the "social constructivist" writing theorists, the concept of "discourse community" has become an integral part of social models of writing. The concept of "discourse community" assumes that "discourse operates within conventions defined by communities, be they academic disciplines or social groups" (Herzberg 1986). According to Swales, "discourse community" is "nothing more than composition specialists' convenient translation of the long-established concept of 'speech community' common to sociolinguistics and central to the ethnography of communication" (Swales 1990b, 23). Speech communities share similar norms of speech and cultural concepts. Despite the similarities of the concepts, Swales does make a distinction between a "sociolinguistic" grouping and a "sociorhetorical" grouping. He maintains that sociolinguistic variation is acquired, whereas sociorhetorical variation is learned.

Research has addressed the existence of conventions in the verbal practices of discourse communities and has focused on how these conventions are learned in social contexts. Researchers in applied linguistics have identified linguistic and rhetorical conventions within discourse communities. Three important volumes contribute to our knowledge about how scientific discourse is shaped in its social context. Myers (1985, 1990) focused on differences between early and late drafts in biologists' writing in a variety of genres – grant proposals, scientific articles, and popular science articles. Bazerman contributed to knowledge about the genre of a scientific research article, focusing on the processes in the construction of texts through observations of physicists' reading and writing processes and habits. Swales (1990b) provides a discourse analytic base for describing research articles linking L1 work on writing across the curriculum with L2 work in English for academic purposes.

Composition experts in the United States such as Bizzell (1982a; 1982b; 1992) and Berkenkotter, Huckin, and Ackerman (1988) have shown that students entering academic disciplines need to learn the genres and conventions that members of the disciplinary community employ. Berkenkotter et al. and others maintain that students learn language conventions and ways of arguments as well as "the conversations of the discipline" or issues and problems under discussion in the discipline (Bazerman 1985; 1988), "the prevailing paradigm" (Myers 1990), or the accepted knowledge and paradigms of the discipline. In other words, novices in discourse communities need to learn both the conventions of language and writing as well as the accepted world view of the disciplinary values and practices.

Researchers have begun to investigate how students and other novices become members of their chosen disciplinary communities. In first-language composition studies, Berkenkotter et al. (1988) report on the initiation of a graduate student into a Ph.D. rhetoric program at Carnegie Mellon University. Using participant-observer and case-study data collecting techniques, the study analyzed the student's written products as well as the processes through which he learned new subject matter and linguistic and rhetorical conventions. Their findings suggest that "achieving disciplinary literacy requires that the writer be able to integrate procedural with substantive/declarative knowledge, in this case, the student's knowledge of appropriate discourse conventions with his developing knowledge of a disciplinary community's issues and research methodology" (9). Other studies examining the acquisition of academic literacy in the first language include Herrington's two-course, senior engineering sequence (Herrington 1985), an undergraduate literature class (Herrington 1988), and a graduate seminar in second language education (Prior 1991).

Findings from the research suggest that learning to write in one's academic discourse community is complex, involving reading and writing processes specific to each class, professor, and student. Initiated into a disciplinary community through writing, reading, and discussion, students learn values and practices as well as writing skills. Swales' (1990b) case studies of international graduate students writing dissertations was among the first to study the initiation and socialization processes that graduate students go through to become literate professionals in their discourse communities. Other relevant research is that of Prior (1995), Belcher (1994), and Casanave (1995).

Prior (1995), in a series of case studies involving graduate students in six different disciplines, used a variety of methods (professor's comments, class observations, questionnaires, interviews, student assignments, and text-based interviews) to learn about the socialization of graduate students in their disciplines. His findings reveal that academic literacy is a complex process situated in the specific context. Some of the findings show that writing tasks are not static but instead are explicitly and implicitly negotiated throughout the semester by the professor and students. Professors interpret student writing as representations of the class as well as of the student, and student reactions to professors' comments on written work depend on what they know about the professor and how much time they think they need to spend in order to get a certain grade.

Belcher (1995) reports three case studies of international graduate student/professor mentor relationships at the stage of dissertation writing. She examined types of modeling and coaching provided by the mentors as the students fit into the academic community. Only one of these academic apprenticeships was successful in that the student and professor had a collaborative, consensual relationship rather than a hierarchical, one-way enculturation.

Casanave (1995) argues for abolishing the one-way enculturation model of a novice into a community where the novice writer learns values, practices, and language conventions of the disciplinary community only from the professor. Instead, based on her case studies of first-year graduate students in sociology, Casanave argues for considering disciplinary communities as "intellectual villages," which are local and interactive. Thus, discussions with peers, other professionals, and self-dialogue are important when students are learning to think and write in their disciplinary communities.

Research examining the socialization of novice writers into their disciplinary communities is currently popular among first-language (L1) and second-language (L2) composition specialists. Researchers in these areas emphasize the existence of discrete disciplinary communities, on one hand, and speak of writing specific to context and situation on the other.

The movement of the social construction of meaning in composition has helped contrastive rheoricians appreciate the roles of situation and task in cross-cultural contrasts. Not only have methods of study improved in that contrastive rhetoricians are more careful in controlling text types in comparisons so that expository essays are no longer being compared to academic journal articles, but the range of text types has been expanded, as Chapter 8 shows.

Summary

The teaching and research of composition at the college level, particularly in North America, has had an important role in transforming contrastive rhetoric. Four major approaches were discussed in this chapter: classical rhetoric, the expressionist approach, the cognitive approach, and the social constructivist approach. Classical rhetoric has given researchers and teachers tools for analyzing invention and text strategies of persuasion and argumentation cross-culturally, with the "new rhetoric" providing a focused examination of audience. The expressionist approach, focusing on the discovery of meaning in the writer herself – a Western concept – has helped highlight cross-cultural difficulties in second language writing. The cognitive approach focuses on understanding the cognitive processes writers go through while writing. It has encouraged many cross-cultural studies of writing, but the findings seem inconclusive with regard to the universality of any process or activity. Finally, the social constructivist approach focuses on the context and situation of writing. In addition, this approach emphasizes the different assumptions that writers from different groups and cultures bring with them.

5 Contrastive rhetoric and text linguistics

Text linguistics is a relatively new development that has greatly affected contrastive analysis. It helped revitalize contrastive rhetoric in the 1980s by providing it with new, valid, and reliable tools for the analysis of texts. This chapter is an introduction to the concepts and methods of text linguistics, and it reviews the most influential research in contrastive rhetoric that has had a text linguistic orientation.

Brief overview of the history of text linguistics; definitions

In the 1970s and 1980s, many linguists felt that traditional morphological and syntactic tools were not adequate to explain texts and that new discourse tools needed to be developed. The resulting new field has been given a variety of names: text linguistics, written discourse analysis, and discourse linguistics. These terms are used almost interchangeably in the literature. (See the discussion of definitions and connotations of the terms in Chapter 2.) However, recent publications treat text linguistics as written, not spoken, discourse analysis – as an analysis of texts that extends beyond the sentence level and considers the communicative constraints of the situation.

Discourse analysis was developed in many countries simultaneously. It appeared in France in the middle of the 1960s. Van Dijk (1985b) describes how, in the United States at the same time, Hymes's *Language in Culture and Society* (1964) marked the beginning of sociolinguistics, a departure from the transformational grammar of Chomsky, in that it emphasized the social bases of communication and thus was a precursor of discourse analysis. Simultaneously, in Czechoslovakia, the orientation in functional grammar gave further impetus for the rise of discourse analysis by continuing the development of the concepts of "theme" and "rheme" (or topic and comment) and "functional sentence perspective." Finally, about the same time, the systemic grammar of Halliday in Britain focused on relations between sentences and discourse or cohesion.

By the 1970s, discourse analysis was an established field of study, with numerous treatments in several countries, among them Enkvist's introduction to text linguistics in Finnish (1974); Dressler's introduction to text linguistics in Germany (1972); van Dijk's book on text grammars in the Netherlands (1972); and Halliday and Hasan's grammar of cohesion in English in Britain (1976).

The 1980s experienced an explosion of discourse studies, which continued to develop new theories and apply them in a variety of fields such as business, law, and medicine. Van Dijk's four-volume *Handbook of Discourse Analysis* (1985a) provides a comprehensive overview of the interdisciplinary trends. Major developments in discourse analysis are reviewed in a 1990 special issue of the journal, *Text,* and in the 1990 issue of the *Annual Review of Applied Linguistics.*

Major schools of thought in text linguistics

In the following discussions we will focus on the three most important text linguistic schools of thought, which help establish a context for the growth of discourse theories.

Prague school of linguistics

The Prague school of linguistics was initiated by Mathesius in the 1920s and was developed by a large number of Czech linguists such as Firbas and Daneš in the 1950s and 1960s. Their linguistic analysis was unique in that they were the first to show how the presentation of information in whole texts needed to be studied along with the formal structures of sentences, such as subject–predicate relations.

The Prague school's greatest contribution to text linguistics was the study of "theme" and "rheme." Theme and rheme concern the pattern of information flow in sentences and the relation of the pattern to text coherence. Theme is what the sentence is about; rheme is what is said about it. Other, almost synonymous terms given to the concepts of theme and rheme are "old" or "given" information vs. "new information" or "topic" vs. "comment." Old or given information refers to what the writer thinks the reader already knows. New information, on the contrary, refers to what the writer believes the reader does not know. In most sentences in Western Indo-European languages such as English, new information is placed at the end, in the predicate. In most texts, the comment or the new information of one sentence becomes the topic or the old information of the next sentence. This constitutes the information dynamics of texts. The Prague term for this concept is "functional sentence perspective." An old–new analysis of a sentence illustrates a typical placement of information: "*This book* (old) deals with contrastive rhetoric (new). *Contrastive rhetoric* (old) is a relatively new field (new)."

Studies of second language writing have applied Prague school concepts. Examples of text analytic studies based on the theories of the Prague school are studies of "coherence" using theme–rheme, topic–comment, or given–new distinctions, samples of which are discussed later in this chapter.

Systemic linguistics

Influenced by the Prague school of linguistics is "systemic linguistics," which emerged in the 1960s and has had an impact on educational studies throughout the world. Developed by linguists such as Halliday, the emphasis is on the content of discourse as well as on choices writers make when they use language. Halliday writes that language has three major functions: an ideational or content-bearing function; an interpersonal function, which signals the writer's attitude; and a textual function, which is "an enabling function, that of creating a text"; "it is this component that enables the speaker to organize what he is saying in such a way that it makes sense in the context and fulfils its function as a message" (Halliday 1973, 66).

Halliday's systemic linguistics has had a major influence on text analysis. The most popular application has been the theory of cohesion, perhaps because it is easy to quantify cohesive links between sentences using Halliday and Hasan's taxonomy (1976). Other specific contributions include the study of register and metadiscourse. (Sample studies were discussed in Chapter 3.) Significant theoretical and empirical contributions concerning the interrelationships among language, register, genre, and ideology are being explored by Martin (1993). His work points to directions for future research in the systemic linguistics school.

New school of discourse analysis

In the 1970s and 1980s, discourse analysis was embraced by many linguists, psychologists, and composition specialists around the world. Leaders of this movement were linguist Nils Enkvist in Finland; psycholinguist Teun van Dijk in the Netherlands; the linguist Robert de Beaugrande in the United States and in Austria; applied linguist and contrastive rhetorician John Hinds in the United States and in Japan; and composition expert Stephen Witte in the United States. The efforts of these text analysts have helped develop coherent text grammars and applications of text analysis to the teaching of writing. The new school of text linguistics is characterized by an interdisciplinary emphasis in which psychological and educational theories have equal status with linguistic theories. This is in contrast with the foci of the Prague and systemic schools of text analysis, the primary emphases of which have been linguistic.

Concepts and methods of text linguistics and their application to the study of writing

Cohesion

Cohesion is defined as the use of explicit linguistic devices to signal relations between sentences and parts of texts. Cohesive devices are words or phrases that act as signals to the reader in order to help the reader make connections with what has already been stated or soon will be stated. In their work on cohesion, Halliday and Hasan (1976) identified five general categories of cohesive devices that signal coherence in texts: referential, ellipsis, substitution, lexical, and conjunctive cohesion. Figure 1 gives an example of each of these categories.

Many first language researchers have studied the relationship between the cohesiveness of student writing and its overall quality and/or coherence. Among these studies, Witte and Faigley's pioneering research (1981) showed a relationship between cohesion and coherence in college students' writing. In contrast, Tierney and Mosenthal (1983) found no relationship between cohesion and coherence in American twelfth-grade students' essays. It seems that most researchers have noted that cohesive texts are not necessarily also coherent texts. Cohesion is determined by lexically and grammatically overt intersentential relationships, whereas coherence is based on semantic relationships. These two aspects of writing interact somewhat, and yet a text need not be coherent to be cohesive, as is seen in an example from the linguist Charles Fillmore (Witte and Faigley 1981, 201):

The quarterback threw the ball toward the tight end. Balls are used in many sports. Most balls are spheres, but a football is an ellipsoid. The tight end leaped to catch the ball.

The word "ball" provides the cohesion of these lines, but this cohesive passage will sound incoherent to the reader. One of the characteristics of coherence, on the other hand, is that it allows "a text to be understood in a real-world setting" (Witte and Faigley 1981, 199) and thus contributes to an understanding of its quality. Writing quality is defined, in part, as a fit of a text to its context, which includes the writer's purpose, the discourse medium, the knowledge of the audience, and so on.

Second-language writing studies have been characterized by innovative probing of the underlying premises of cohesion and coherence. Scarcella (1984b) examined patterns of cohesion in the ESL academic writing of

1. *Reference*   "John makes good meals. Last night *he* cooked spaghetti."
2. *Substitution*   "I want an ice cream cone. Do you want *one*?"
3. *Ellipsis*   "Which hat will you wear? This is the best."
4. *Lexical Cohesion*   "There's a boy climbing that tree."
   a. The *boy's* going to fall if he doesn't take care.
   b. The *child's* going to fall . . . .
   c. The *idiot's* going to fall . . . .
5. *Conjunction*   "For the whole day he climbed up the steep mountainside, almost without stopping. *And* in all this time he met no one."

Figure 1   Summary of major categories in Halliday and Hasan's Cohesion in English *(1976).*

different language groups studying at a U.S. college. One of the groups, Korean students, showed a greater difference in cohesion behavior when compared to native English speakers. Connor's (1984) study examined the relationship between cohesion and coherence in the writing of native English speakers vs. Japanese and Spanish ESL college-level subjects in the United States. She found that general cohesion density was not a discriminating factor between native speakers and ESL writers. The ESL writers were found, however, to lack the variety of lexical cohesive devices used by the native speakers. Johns (1984) found, based on close observation of Chinese ESL writers, that reference and adversative conjuncts were the most problematic cohesive devices for the Chinese student.

Coherence

As was noted, cohesion does not create coherence. Instead, to be coherent, texts need to make sense to the reader. Two competing theories for the definition of coherence have emerged: one that emphasizes the reader's interaction with the text, and another that focuses on the text itself. In recent years, definitions emphasizing the interaction between reader and text have prevailed.

Applications of coherence theories as in Connor and Johns (1990) suggest that such applications can improve writing instruction. One particularly promising attempt to describe discourse-based coherence, which is applicable directly to writing instruction, is "topical structure analysis." Drawing on theories of the Prague school of linguistics, Finnish text linguist Liisa Lautamatti (1978; 1987) developed topical structure analysis to describe coherence in texts, focusing on semantic relationships that exist between sentence topics and the overall discourse topic. Topical structure analysis examines how topics repeat, shift, and return to earlier topics in discourse. Coherence in texts can be charted using a system of three different kinds of progressions: parallel progression (topics of successive sentences are the same), sequential progression (topics of succes-

Parallel progression (Sample 1)
(1) <u>Chocolates</u> are a national craving. (2) Records show <u>they</u> are sold in huge quantities – 11.2 pounds per capita per year. (3) <u>Designer chocolates</u> often sell for nearly $30/lb. (4) It is obvious that <u>these candies</u> are America's number one choice.

  1. Chocolates
  2. they
  3. Designer chocolates
  4. these candies

Sequential progression (Sample 2)
(1) <u>Computer interviews</u> are used by market researchers to assess product demand. (2) Using <u>these</u>, many different <u>products</u> are analyzed. (3) For example, people may be asked about <u>detergents</u>.

  1. Computer interviews
  2.   products
  3.   detergents

Extended parallel progression (Sample 3)
(1) <u>Body language</u> varies from culture to culture. (2) To say yes, <u>Americans</u> nod their heads up and down. (3) <u>Japanese and Italians</u> use the same nod to say no. (4) <u>Body language</u> is an important skill for international managers.

  1. Body language
  2.   Americans
  3.   Japanese and Italians
  4. Body language

Figure 2   Sample passages showing three types of sentence progression (Table 2 in "The teaching of topical structure analysis as a revision strategy for ESL writers," by Connor and Farmer, in Second Language Writing: Research Insights for the Classroom, *edited by Barbara Kroll, © Cambridge University Press, 1990, p. 131. Reprinted by permission.)*

sive sentences are always different, as the comment of one sentence becomes the topic of the next), and extended parallel progression (the first and the last topics of a piece of text are the same but are interrupted with some sequential progression).

Figure 2 includes sample passages of three types of sentence progression. The topic of each sentence is underlined. Beneath each passage is a diagram showing the topical structure of the passage. Sentence topics with parallel progression are placed exactly below each other. Sequential topics are indented progressively, and extended parallel progression is aligned under the parallel topic to which it refers.

Topical structure analysis has been used to explain differences among high- and low-rated essays. Significant differences have been found between the low-rated and high-rated essays in the frequency of the three topical progressions (Witte 1983a, b). In an ESL context, Schneider and Connor (1991) used a sample of essays written for the TOEFL's Test of Written English (TWE) and found that topical structure analysis correlated well with readers' judgments of writing quality. Figure 3 displays a

1 There often exists in our society *a certain dichotomy* of art and science./ 2 *Supporters* of either disciplines sometimes are of the opinion that one is more valuable to society than the other./ 3 But is this *a fair judgement* to make?/ 4 Should *a judgement* be made at all?/

5 I believe that *art and science* sustain and support each other./ 6 *The developments and knowledge* we gain from science can be used to give us a better understanding of our art forms and even improve existing styles and techniques./ 7 On the other hand, *art* in its continuous search for new ways to express beauty, often provides the impetus and support for scientific research./

8 An example of *a discipline* where art and science interact is architecture./ 9 *The architectural discipline* makes use of forms, shapes, lines, and other aesthetic components of art./ 10 *It* also involves principles of physics, engineering, and understanding of chemistry in order to build a sound structure and design./ 11 Where will *society* be without the structures and buildings produced from the interplay of art and science?/

12 *Gymnastics* is also a good example of such an interplay./ 13 *Gymnasts* strive to perfect the beauty of human form and grace./ 14 However, this will not be possible without *some understanding of biology, physics, or physiology.*/

15 *The examples* are endless./ 16 Even *art forms* which many consider "pure" would not have advanced without science./ 17 *Painting benefits from chemistry,*/ 18 *theater* benefits from breakthroughs in acoustics,/ 19 and *the list* goes on./ 20 *Einstein* himself was a lover of many art forms./

21 *Science and art* are both integral and inseparable products of society./ 22 *They* come from the same harmonious body of universal knowledge./ 23 *Both* are of tremendous and equal value to humankind./

```
 1.  a certain dichotomy
 2.    supporters
 3.      a fair judgement
 4.      a judgement
 5.        art and science
 6.          the developments and knowledge
 7.            art
 8.              a discipline
 9.              the architectural discipline
10.              it
11.                society
12.                gymanstics
13.                gymanasts
14.                  some understanding
15.                  the examples
16.                  art forms
17.                    painting
18.                      theater
19.                    the list
20.                          Einstein
21.        science and art
22.        they
23.        both
```

Figure 3   Sample highly scored essay with its topical structure diagram (In "Analyzing topical structure in ESL essays," by Schneider and Connor, in Studies in Second Language Acquisition, 12, © *Cambridge University Press, 1991, p. 420. Reprinted by permission.)*

coherence diagram for a highly rated essay in the sample. The results of the study showed that more highly rated essays, like the one shown in the figure, have the following characteristics: a high proportion of sequential progression (see sentences 2–18) and an extended parallel progression (sentence 21), which helps pull the essay back to its main theme.

In addition to distinguishing between low- and high-rated essays, topical structure analysis has received attention as a teaching method to help students check for coherence in their own writing and to revise accordingly (Cerniglia, Medsker, and Connor 1990; Connor and Farmer 1990). As a revision strategy, topical structure analysis for checking coherence works best if it is applied after an early draft, when students are still prepared to make substantive changes. According to Connor and Farmer, student response has been positive and writing has improved, specifically with regard to clearer focus (owing to added extended parallel progression) and better development (owing to a reasonable ratio of parallel and sequential progressions). Through topical structure analysis, which forces students to focus on the meaning of individual sentences and their interrelations, students become careful and critical readers of their own texts. Connor and Farmer recommend the use of topical structure analysis as a revision strategy, which should be used in conjunction with teacher and peer comments.

Superstructures or global text structures

Several top-level discourse structure theories have been advanced in the past decade, such as van Dijk's "macrostructures" (1980), Meyer's "rhetorical predicates" of expository prose (1975), Hoey's "problem-solution" text patterns (1983, 1986), Mandler and Johnson's "story grammars" (1977), and Tirkkonen-Condit's superstructure of argument (1985).

Theories of superstructures have been developed for different types of texts such as exposition, argumentation, and narration, and have been applied to student writing for the purpose of evaluating and describing quality. For example, in order to evaluate students' narratives or teach students to write well-formed stories, linguists James Martin and Joan Rothery (1986) developed a story grammar analysis, adapted from Labov and Waletsky's terminology (1967). The schematic structure of the typical narrative written for school assignments includes four parts:

1. Orientation (the major characters are introduced and a setting is established)
2. Complication (a series of events unfolds, and a crisis develops)
3. Resolution (the crisis is resolved)
4. Coda (the final stage, in which the writer may express an attitude toward the story or give her perspective on its significance)

"My Most Frightening Experience"

Orientation
1. One evening I was not feeling well
2. and so my father put on the television for me.
3. My parents were sleeping
4. and on the television there was a horror film going on
5. and I was wrapped up in blankets
6. because I was scared.

Complication
7. Suddenly the light went out,
8. I got up to take a flashlight.
9. The television went on all the same because of the batteries
10. and still there was the horror film going on
11. and just as the thief was going to strangle her,
12. I stumbled on the floor
13. and I felt a strong hand on my neck
14. and on the television the thief was saying "It's the end . . . !"
15. I thought that the voice was that of the person who was gripping my neck
16. and I was still more frightened
17. and I thought there were thieves
18. because the television went off,
19. then I do not know how it happened that I fell asleep thinking that if the thieves would have seen me sleeping they would have ignored me.

Resolution
20. The following morning I woke up
21. and that hand was a doll with a weight on.
22. Then I woke my mother and told her everything.

Coda
23. And for me this has been the most frightening moment in my life.

Figure 4   Sample essay with its story structure analysis.

Based on their research in Australian schools, Martin and Rothery report that "the stories classified by teachers as the best or most successful pieces usually conform closely to a structure of this kind" (1986, 255).

Figure 4 shows a sample essay written by a 12-year-old high school student in the United States as part of the IEA Study of Written Composition. I analyzed the structure of the story using Martin and Rothery's system, shown in the left column.

Another superstructure analysis, for argumentative texts, was developed by the Finnish text linguist and translation theorist, Sonja Tirkkonen-Condit. Tirkkonen-Condit's (1985; 1986) system includes a four-unit structure consisting of situation, problem, solution, and evaluation. The system was applied by Connor (1987a) in a cross-cultural study, which compared argumentative essays written by 16-year-old students in the IEA sample. The study included essays written by American, Finnish, and German students. The results showed that highly rated essays followed the pattern of situation–problem–solution–evaluation, suggesting that Tirkkonen-Condit's superstructure is a viable analysis.

Research on the role of superstructures in writing is just beginning, and applications of well known discourse theories of global text structures have been relatively few. The contrast with the many studies of cohesion and coherence is striking. Based on my own experience, I suggest that cohesion and coherence studies have been numerous because of the relative convenience of applying Halliday and Hasan's cohesion taxonomy or Lautamatti's topical structure analysis. Both systems of analysis can be applied to texts of any type, independent of the purpose or task. Analyses of superstructures, on the other hand, tend to be specific to a text type such as narrative or argument. Also, applied linguists in the past have not been interested in analyzing prose other than exposition and have not needed to consider whether global structures differ from one text type to another. I expect, however, that the increased interest in genre-based research will soon stimulate further research on superstructures of different kinds of texts.

NORDTEXT and NORDWRITE text linguistic projects of student writing

Before reviewing individual contrastive studies, it is appropriate to discuss the contributions of a large research project for the study of contrastive writing. The NORDTEXT project and its subgroup, NORD-WRITE, focus on the explicit connections between text linguistics and the teaching of composition. The NORDTEXT project (the Nordic Research Group for Theoretical and Applied Text Linguistics) was initiated at a symposium on "Coherence and Composition" at the Research Institute of the Åbo Akademi Foundation in Turku, Finland, in 1984; the proceedings provide one of the earliest careful examinations of the connections between text linguistics and the teaching of composition (Enkvist 1985a). The proceedings of the 1985 Nordtext Symposium, held in Trondheim, Norway, were published in a special issue of *Text* (Enkvist 1985b).

More recently, a subgroup, the NORDWRITE project, has been formed. This group concentrates on the development of written EFL skills in the Nordic countries, including Finland, focusing on the discourse level in writing. The analyses to date have been organized according to a common core of variables (for example, lexical cohesion, theme dynamics, and superstructure markers). Evensen (1986) provides an overview of the project; papers by Linnarud and Lindeberg in the Evensen volume describe results of specific studies in the project. Other publications relating to this work appear in recent volumes on applied linguistics edited in the United States. Particularly worth noting are Evensen's (1990) research on superstructure markers, Enkvist's (1987; 1990) writings on discourse theory and theories of coherence, and Wikborg's (1990) empirical study on coherence breaks in Swedish EFL students' writing. These NORDTEXT and NORDWRITE projects have identified many important problems and have come up with solutions for describing student texts in terms of discourse-level properties such as cohesion, coherence, and superstructures.

Survey of contrastive rhetorical studies with a text linguistic emphasis

This section surveys contributions to and the impact of text linguistic theories and methods on contrastive rhetoric. The purpose of the survey is not to prove or disprove the contrastive rhetoric hypothesis that culture-specific patterns of writing exist and cause interference in L2 writing. Instead, the survey is intended to demonstrate the comprehensiveness of text linguistic approaches in the study of contrastive rhetoric as well as to expose areas in need of study.[1]

Studies in this survey are designated either as research on student writing or writing done for academic or other professional purposes, here called "accomplished" writing. Three additional distinctions allow for further classification: concept and text analysis, language (native language = L1; target language = L2), and genre. Brief discussions of the last three categories follow.

General concept categories such as paragraph development and discourse development are used in the present survey rather than the four models of text analysis proposed by Enkvist (1984), whose framework is sentence, predication, and cognition based and includes interactional text models. Enkvist's models deserve brief mention, however.

Sentence-based text models, according to Enkvist, regard texts as strings of sentences. They explain such phenomena as intersentential coreference (for example, cohesion as in Halliday and Hasan 1976). They

---

1 Some overlap occurs with studies in Chapter 3. The emphasis of this chapter is on a brief survey of types of studies, whereas the focus of Chapter 3 is on the cross-cultural results of the studies.

also show how sentences get their textual fit through theme–rheme or topic–comment focus. Predication-based models, on the other hand, see texts as peculiar arrangements depending on a specific strategy; and they maintain that the same input of sentences can be textualized into different text types such as narrative, argumentative, or descriptive. Cognitive text models help explain reasons why writers in given situations use certain text strategies, and emphasize the role of cognition in text processing. For example, coherence is a function of the text and of the equipment the reader brings to its interpretation. Finally, the fourth model in Enkvist's framework, "interactional text models," is concerned with the interactional behavior patterns of the people communicating through texts. They account for writers' intentions. Enkvist's framework is comprehensive, yet the inherent overlap among the four models makes the classification difficult to apply (Connor 1987b), and with the increased emphasis on process-centered text research in the past decade, few applied researchers would admit that they conduct sentence-based research.

Survey of contrastive text linguistic studies of student writing

Figure 5 lists concepts, analyses, references for the studies, language, and genre related to the surveyed studies. Three major categories emerged from the studies: paragraph development, discourse development, and metadiscourse. A review of studies follows in the order listed in the figure.

Two studies, those of Evensen (1987) and Ingberg (1987), contrasted the use of topic sentences in Norwegian high school students' ESL essays (Evensen) and college-level Finnish-Swedish students' (Ingberg) Swedish and English essays. Both studies compared the sample data to the Anglo-American norm of the deductive style in which a topic sentence begins a paragraph. Both studies found a tendency toward induction (topic sentence at the end) in the essays of the L2 students in the samples.

Bickner and Peyasantiwong (1988) examined fifty Thai and forty American student essays written in the L1 using the IEA study data text analyses developed for the study. They examined the paragraph developments in the essays using a system something like that of Kaplan (1966), who examined the placement of topic sentences in paragraphs. In addition, they analyzed the content of the essay with regard to the theme and attitudes toward the text (personal vs. impersonal; formal vs. informal). They found that both groups tend to begin their essays with topic sentences, but that there were differences in how students concluded the essays. There was a firmer conclusion in most of the American essays than in the Thai essays. In addition, it was found that the Thai essays were less personal and informal and included more definitions and terms.

Concept	Text analysis	Reference	Language L1	Language L2	Genre
Paragraph development	– Topic sentence	Evensen (1987)		EFL (L1 = Norwegian)	Expository essay
	– Topic sentence	Ingberg (1987)		EFL (L1 = Swedish)	Expository essay
	– Topic sentence	Bickner and Peyansantiwong (1988)	Thai		Argumentative essay
Discourse development	– "Story graph"	Sóter (1988)	English	EFL (L1 = Arabic, Vietnamese)	Expository essay
	– Discourse bloc; T-unit	Ostler (1987)	English	EFL (L1 = Arabic)	Expository essay
	– Orientation	Scarcella (1984a)	English	EFL (L1 = Japanese, Korean, Romance, Taiwanese)	Expository essay
	– Coherence	Connor and McCagg (1983)	English	EFL = (L1 = Japanese, Spanish)	Paraphrases of reading passages
	– Cohesion	Reid (1992)	English	EFL (L1 = Arabic, Chinese, Spanish)	Expository essay
	– Coherence, topical structure analysis; argumentative structure	Connor and Lauer (1988)	English (England, New Zealand, USA)		Argumentative essay
	– Cohesion; narrative structure; clause functions	Indrasuta (1988)	Thai; English		Narrative essay
Metadiscourse	– Metadiscoursal devices	Crismore et al. (1993)	English; Finnish		Argumentative essay

Figure 5 Summary of contrastive text linguistic studies of student writing.

Söter (1988) studied story structures in the essay writing of English-, Vietnamese-, and Arabic-speaking students in Australian schools. The story structure analysis was developed by Söter to determine the amount of "story about story," setting, scene, and plot. The students in Söter's study displayed differences in story structures due to cultural background. The Vietnamese stories placed greater emphasis on the relationship and dialogue between the characters than on the plot. The Arabic students' writing contained more information about the scene of the story than the writing of the other students.

Ostler compared English essays written by Saudi Arabian students entering a U.S. university with English paragraphs selected randomly from books. The results of T-unit analyses showed that there was a significant difference between the two language samples in the number of coordinate clauses. (The T-unit, or "minimal terminable unit," is defined by Hunt as "one main clause plus any subordinate clause or non-clausal structure that is attached to or embedded in it" (Hunt 1970, 4). The results of a discourse bloc analysis showed that more of the Arabic students' essays began with a superordinate statement, "generally a universal statement only globally related to the topic" (Ostler 1987, 182), than did the English paragraphs, that formulaic or proverbial statements occurred frequently in the Arabic students' papers, and that they had fewer subdivisions.

Scarcella (1984a) examined the function of initial sentences in native- and nonnative-English-speaking American university freshman essays. Interested in comparing how writers introduce a topic to their readers, she found that nonnative speakers tended to use longer but less effective "orientations" (introductions to the topic). Scarcella explained the difference as being due to the native subjects' greater familiarity with their readers, who were their teachers.

Connor and McCagg (1983) used Meyer's (1975) rhetorical content structure to examine the coherence of students' English paraphrases of a reading passage. Three groups of students, native English speakers and Japanese and Spanish-speaking ESL learners, participated. Intended to investiate the effect on the paraphrases of different rhetorical patterns potentially transferred from L1, the study found no culture-specific patterns of organization emerging from the task. Although it is frequently cited by opponents of Kaplan's research as a study that proves universal patterns in student writing, the research has been criticized justly by Péry-Woodley (1990), among others, for its research design and the lack of contrastive rhetorical hypotheses concerning Japanese and Spanish vs. English.

Indrasuta (1988) compared narrative essays written by Thai high school students with narrative essays written by U.S. high school students. Three methods of analysis were included: cohesion analysis (Halliday and Hasan 1976), an analysis of narrative structure (plot, conflict, setting, theme, character, scene, and figurative language), and an analysis of clause functions. The two groups differed in the use of cohesion (a higher use of reference by the U.S. students), in the use of the narrative components (a higher use of implicit themes among the U.S. students than among others), and in the functions of sentences (the Thai students used more mental state verbs whereas Americans used more action verbs).

In a major study, Reid (1992) examined the use of four cohesive devices – pronouns, coordinate conjunctions, subordinate conjunction openers, and prepositions – in expository essays written by native English-speaking, Spanish-, Chinese-, and Arabic-speaking students for the Test of Written English. Using the "Writer's Workbench," a computer text-analysis program, she found some significant differences among the groups in the frequency with which cohesiveness was employed. For example, native English speakers used more pronouns than the three other groups. Arabic writers used significantly more coordinate conjunctions than the other three language groups. Chinese writers relied more on subordinate conjunctions than the other students did. English speakers used more prepositions than the other groups.

Connor and Lauer (1988) studied argumentative essays of fifty English-speaking students each from England, New Zealand, and the United States. The research combined linguistic and rhetorical text analysis; syntactic variation using Biber's (1988) multidimensional system; argument structure using Tirkkonen-Condit's argument superstructure (1985); and effectiveness of argument using Toulmin's (1958) rhetorical model consisting of the analysis of claim, data, and warrant. Cross-cultural differences were found in the use of syntactic devices and the effectiveness of arguments. The U.S. students used less formal and less edited language than did the students from the two other countries. The U.S. students' arguments were less effective because they lacked evidence.

A relatively new area of investigation in contrastive student writing is the study of metadiscourse strategies. The term "metadiscourse" is used to refer to the linguistic material in texts that does not add anything to the propositional content but helps the reader organize, interpret, and evaluate the information. Metadiscourse thus serves the textual and interpersonal functions of language (Halliday 1973). Metadiscourse enables the writer to show the reader how parts of the text are related as well as to express his or her own evaluation of the content and his or her attitude.

Crismore et al. (1993) analyzed the metadiscourse strategies of college student writers composing in L1 in Finland and the United States. Fifty students from each country wrote a persuasive essay. Twenty essays from each country were analyzed for the use of metadiscourse. Following previous definitions of metadiscourse, primarily Vande Kopple's (1985; 1986), the research examined linguistic material in the essays that does not add to the propositional information but allows the writer either to organize what is being said or to express personal feelings and attitudes and interact with the reader. The study and its related research (Markkaren et al. 1993) is discussed in detail in Chapter 3.

Reviews of contrastive text linguistic studies of "accomplished" texts

Discourse development and metadiscourse are the two categories that delimit the empirical studies covered in this section. Hinds (1983a; 1987) examined the first in relation to the *ki-shoo-ten-ketsu* pattern of Japanese prose development, an organization characterized by an unexpected topic shift. The Japanese pattern in expository prose first develops an argument, which is then turned into a subtheme with no direct connection, before the conclusion is reached – a pattern of prose development that is alien to the Anglo-American reader. Moreover, Japanese texts rely on fewer transitions, thus making more cognitive demands on the reader. Hinds asked Japanese-speaking and English-speaking readers to evaluate the Japanese version of a newspaper article, which had been translated for the English-language version, for unity, focus, and coherence. Not surprisingly, the Japanese readers consistently rated the Japanese-language version higher than did the English-speaking readers.

Eggington (1987) examined writing patterns in Korean. A rhetorical structure preferred by Koreans is the four-unit style, *ki-sung-chon-kyui,* similar to the Japanese pattern described by Hinds. According to Eggington, this is a nonlinear development of text and hence is unfamiliar to Anglo-Americans and not preferred by Koreans who have earned American college degrees.

Clyne (1987) compared the linear organization of academic papers and articles written by English-speaking and German linguists and sociologists. He examined the hierarchical development of macropropositions, the development of arguments, the symmetry of text segments, and the uniformity of formal structuring. It was found that English-speaking writers favored a linear development, whereas the German speakers tended to digress. The German texts exhibited more textual and propositional symmetry and greater discontinuity of arguments. For example, a new argument would begin before a previous one had been developed. English papers used "advance organizers" (explicit statements about the organization) in order to clarify the organization of the paper, whereas German papers scattered the organizers if, indeed, they used them at all.

Connor (1988) compared the writing of a Japanese and an American marketing manager during a two-year business negotiation. After analyzing the correspondence, including faxes, reports, and electronic mail (forty-seven pieces altogether), she found culture-specific differences in the organization of argumentative policy reports and in the strength of argumentative claims, data, and warrants. Using Toulmin's model of argument, she found that the Japanese reports followed a nonlinear organization of argument and used many hedges and indirect requests. (The study is discussed in more detail in Chapter 8.)

A great deal of research on contrastive rhetoric in Finland has begun to focus on genre-specific texts. In particular, the language of Finnish academics writing in their specific disciplines has been compared with the writing of native-English-speaking academics. The most comprehensive research agendas are those pursued by Eija Ventola and Anna Mauranen. Much of this research was reviewed in Chapter 3; a brief listing of three representative studies will suffice here, with the emphasis on the text linguistic features involved in the analysis.

Ventola and Mauranen (1991) compared the writing of six Finnish scientists with the writing of native-English-speaking scientists. The text linguistic analyses dealt with examinations of cohesion, thematic development, and reference. The results showed that the Finnish writers used cohesive devices less frequently than the English writers did. The range of connectors was also limited, and the Finnish writers' thematic development differed from that of their English-speaking colleagues, as did their use of reference.

Mauranen (1992) analyzed the use of cohesion and the placement of main ideas in scientific paragraphs written by Finnish and native-English-speaking scientists. The results showed that Finnish writers employed fewer selective demonstrative references ("this") than native English speakers did, which reduced the feeling of solidarity with the reader in the Finnish texts. Another difference was the relatively late introduction of the central points written by the Finns in comparison to texts written by native speakers of English.

Mauranen (1993) examined a variety of other textual features when she compared Finnish and English academic texts written by economists. The results show that Finnish economists used relatively little metalanguage in organizing the text and orienting the reader. In contrast, native speakers used numerous metalinguistic features to orient the reader, telling the reader what was to follow in the text and how the reader needed to understand the functions of the sections of the text.

Summary

Text linguistic studies of contrastive rhetoric have come a long way from Kaplan's 1966 research on paragraph organization and the well-known accompanying diagrams. Text concepts, text analyses, and types of writing studied are the areas of greatest advance. Instead of examining paragraph-level organization of texts, contrastive rhetoric studies more and more are designed to compare discourse-level features of texts such as superstructures and theme–rheme relationships. Furthermore, thanks to advances in text linguistics toward a comprehensive text theory, which allows for a study of interacting levels of texts (such as sentences, words, and text structures), contrastive studies have been including a combination of analyses including several text levels (for example, Connor and Lauer [1988]; and Indrasuta [1988], in Figure 5; and Ventola and Mauranen [1991], in Figure 6).

Because contrastive rhetorical research is deeply embedded in the empirical traditions of applied linguistics, quantitative analyses are expected. This fondness for quantification probably accounts for the popularity of analyses such as cohesion and metadiscourse, both of which rely on counts of discrete linguistic items. Neither of these requires much adaptation before application. Other text theories that have been used in contrastive rhetoric research have gone through a variety of modifications. Some have undergone extensive work for the purpose of operationalization; topical structure analysis, based on theme and rheme relations in texts, was operationalized by Lautamatti (1978; 1987), who used an "accomplished" text to show how it works and how it can be used to compare simplified and nonsimplified texts in EFL instruction. Witte (1983a; 1983b) further refined topical structure analysis to evaluate L1 student essays. Several subsequent studies have refined topical structure analysis even further for use with L2 writing. In particular, categories of topic progression have been subjected to rigorous interrater reliability (Schneider and Connor 1991).

Much of the contrastive rhetoric research surveyed here, however, lacks explicitly described steps of analysis, and this makes the studies nonreplicable. It seems to me that not only are the applied linguists to be blamed for the lack of stated text theories, but that theorists should strive harder to make their theories more accessible for a larger number of appliers.

Needless to say, quantifiability of research does not guarantee sound contrastive text research. Too many researchers are satisfied with easy solutions and count cohesive devices mechanically, without adequate theory and expectations. In an article in the *Annual Review of Applied Linguistics* (1990b) I discuss this problem, which is particularly acute in the research of educational psychologists in the United States who are

| Concept | Text analysis | Reference | Language | | Genre |
			L1	L2	
Discourse development	– Coherence; *ki-sho-ten-ketsu* pattern	Hinds (1983a)	Japanese, English		Expository newspaper article
	– Reader/writer responsibility; *ki-sho-ten-ketsu* pattern	Hinds (1987)	Japanese		Expository newspaper article
	– Paragraph organization; induction vs. deduction	Hinds (1990)	Chinese, Japanese, Korean, Thai		Expository newspaper article
	– Coherence; *ki-sung-chon-kyui* pattern	Eggington (1987)	Korean		Academic articles
	– Coherence; linearity	Clyne (1987)	German, English		Academic articles
	– Argument structure	Connor (1988)	English	EFL (L1 = Japanese)	Business correspondence
	– Cohesion	Mauranen (1992)	English, Finnish	EFL (L1 = Finnish)	Medical journal articles
	– Cohesion; thematic development; reference	Ventola & Mauranen (1991)	English, Finnish	EFL (L1 = Finnish)	Scientific journal articles
Metadiscourse	– Metadiscoursal devices	Mauranen (1993)	English	EFL (L1 = Finnish)	Economic articles

Figure 6 Summary of contrastive text linguistic studies of "accomplished" (vs. student) tests.

interested in problems of reading and writing instruction of school children. My study of cohesive devices in ESL writing (1984) and Reid's (1992) study resemble slightly the research on cohesion in educational psychology.

In contrast to earlier studies of contrastive rhetoric, the research surveyed in this chapter includes a variety of languages and combinations. Two directions emerge: the study of numerous different L1s, and the increased number of comparisons among different L1s and L2s. Bilingual and bicultural researchers have joined the ranks of English-speaking contrastive rhetoricians. This has resulted in a less ethnocentric stance about the role of English, as in the work of Mauranen and Hinds, for example.

One of the biggest changes in contrastive rhetoric research is the diversity of genres that has been studied. Essay types now include narrative and argumentative in addition to exposition. A variety of text types has also been studied: academic journal articles, business correspondence, and so on. The new trend of diversification of genres reflects the need in ESL to teach English for specific purposes, especially at the college level in Europe, where students specialize from the very beginning of their studies. In North America also, there is an increased emphasis on ESL instruction for graduate students, who demand English instruction that is specific to their fields.

As Swales (1990b) shows, it is not enough to describe text types (e.g., narrative, descriptive, argumentative) or situations (writing in certain discourse communities); one also needs to consider the specific tasks and purposes of writing. For example, an engineer in the community of engineers may be expected to write memos, letters, reports, and proposals. It is worth noting that Swales speaks of the importance of contrastive rhetoric studies that consider the variable of genre. He is critical of some published contrastive rhetoric research that has compared student essays with the writing of literary authors.

To conclude, the 1980s introduced a new type of text analysis in contrastive rhetoric research. The 1990s is the decade when these text analyses became fully operationalized for the testing of specific contrastive rhetoric hypotheses.

6 Writing as an activity embedded in a culture

Kaplan's landmark article (1966) was concerned with the transfer of first-language cultural conventions to second language performance. It dealt with the rhetorical organization of ideas in writing, which was assumed, without much question, to be culturally determined. The emphasis of the work was on rhetorical styles; little attention in that early work was paid to reasons for culture-specific writing styles.

In a later work, Kaplan took up the issue of culture in the context of the difference between writing and speaking. As he observed, "written language is different from spoken language" (1987, 12). Spoken language is primarily an innate, biologically determined ability; writing, on the other hand, according to Kaplan, is a "post-biological" step and obviously is not universal to all people. It is, he claimed, the invention of literacy that allows the search for truth in terms of cultural universals and particulars.

Although Kaplan's traditional approach to rhetoric did not focus on reasons for cultural differences in writing, more recent scholarship has shed new light on the role of culture and its inculcation through schooling. The 1980s witnessed a proliferation of studies examining the processes whereby one becomes literate in one's native language and culture. Anthropologists, psychologists, and researchers in education are among those who have particularly investigated the processes of learning literacy and the effects of literacy on learners' thinking as well as social behavior.

This field is still just beginning, at least in its contemporary form. Still, important discoveries have been made about the embeddedness of discourse and writing in culture and about the roles that schooling and instruction play in inculcating this embeddedness. Most significantly, research points to the fact that written texts and the ways they are used vary according to cultural group. It also shows that people learn many of the conventions and uses of writing through schools or some kind of instruction.

This chapter, which begins with a tentative definition of the term, "culture," gives an overview of scholarship examining writing as an activity embedded in Ll culture. Relevant studies in three disciplines are discussed: psychology, anthropology, and applied linguistics.

100

Definition of "culture"

A widely accepted definition of culture considers it a set of rules and patterns shared by a given community. Cultural anthropologist and linguist Ward Goodenough writes:

As I see it, a society's culture consists of whatever it is one has to know or believe in order to operate in a manner acceptable to its members, and do so in any role that they accept for any one of themselves. Culture, being what people have to learn as distinct from their biological heritage, must consist of the end product of learning: knowledge, in a most general, if relative, sense of the term. By this definition, we should note that culture is not a material phenomenon; it does not consist of things, people, behavior, or emotions. It is rather an organization of these things. It is the forms of things that people have in mind, their models for perceiving, relating, and otherwise interpreting them. As such, the things people say and do, their social arrangements and events, are products or by-products of their culture as they apply it to the task of perceiving and dealing with their circumstances. (1964, 36)

This definition allows an individual to be considered a member of several different cultural communities. The definition is appropriate for the newer parameters of contrastive rhetoric in that one may view science writers, for example, as members of a cultural community of scientists, probably an international community, who also belong to an ethnic and probably a local community.

Psychological investigations of culture and literacy

Empirical studies examining the relation between culture and cognition fall into two categories. The first type of research describes cultural differences in social behavior. It assumes the existence of unchanged patterns of behavior, which it attempts to discover, and it locates particular patterns along these universal dimensions. The second type examines interrelations among culture, cognition, orality, and literacy.

Study of cultures according to dimensions of value orientations

The work of three researchers illustrates this approach. Hofstede's (1980) study of cultural differences deals with work-related value orientations. His approach is based on the assumption that human beings are imbued with "mental programs" that are developed during childhood and are culturally reinforced. These mental programs are expressed through a culture's dominant values. Through statistical analyses, Hofstede came up with ratings of forty countries on four major dimensions along which dominant patterns of culture can be ordered: power distance, uncertainty avoidance, individualism–collectivism, and masculinity–femininity. Power distance refers to a culture's value orientation about the importance of status differences and hierarchies. Uncertainty avoidance is related to the means that cultures select to adapt to changes and cope with uncertainties. Individualism–collectivism is related to people's relationships to the larger social groups of which they are a part. Masculinity–femininity pertains to the extent to which cultures prefer either achievement and assertiveness or nurturance and social support.

One should exercise caution in applying Hofstede's dimensions in writing research, because the survey subjects were business managers in the early 1970s. Many cultures were not included, such as those of most African, Arab, and Soviet bloc countries. Contrastive rhetoricians have been quite careful in adopting Hofstede's dimensions, even though references to his work are frequent. Nelson and Carson (1995), for example, cite Hofstede to support their expectation of the collectivist stance of Chinese students to collaborative peer response in contrast to Americans' individualistic goals in peer response groups.

Triandis (1981) proposed twenty-five dimensions of cultural variation under broad categories of "patterns of thought," "patterns of perception," "patterns of behavior," "values," and "social organization." Among Triandis's dimensions related to thought patterns and communication are "universalism" (preference for broad ideologies with an emphasis on the deductive mode of thought); "associative" (communication that can be indirect because everything is considered as being related to everything else); and "abstractive" (communication that is strictly relevant to a particular situation). Triandis mainly compared Mediterranean culture (Greece, Latin America) to North European and North American cultural patterns.

Glenn and Glenn (1981) proposed a model with the dimensions of "particularism–universalism" and "association–abstraction." Their model exemplifies some of the pitfalls since found in psychological models of the 1980s. According to Glenn and Glenn, universalism and abstraction are associated with literate cultures, whereas particularism and association, both representing lower levels of cognition, are characteristic of preliterate cultures. As they write:

The abstractive approach is capable of organizing much richer information (or the description of much broader environments) than the associative approach. Once an item is described as a stone, there is no more need to seek additional information concerning animation in the case of particular stones. On the other hand, the expression of individuality of experience is made more difficult; beliefs and dreams involving animate stones are no longer fully acceptable. (1981, 11)

Glenn and Glenn provide a most helpful discussion about differences between the West and the Eastern bloc of the 1960s and 1970s in the areas of politics and international negotiations. Scholars of international relations will find useful linguistic and anecdotal evidence about traits of Americans, Russians, and French, for example. However, for an understanding of cultural characteristics, Glenn and Glenn's, Triandis's, and Hofstede's theories are too formalistic and ethnically oriented. Contrastive rhetoricians are familiar with these types of psychological representations of cultures but find that they stereotype cultures.

Contrastive rhetoric, which originated as an applied linguistics inquiry, has never been very closely associated with psychological investigations of culture. It skipped over the psychological mode of investigation that was dominant in the 1980s, a method in which speakers in a given culture were labeled along a cognitive dimension, as in Glenn and Glenn. Instead, contrastive rhetoric's continuing viability in the 1980s was due to a renewed interest in disciplines such as text linguistics and anthropological studies of literacy.

Relation between orality and literacy

A study by psychologists Sylvia Scribner and Michael Cole, *The Psychology of Literacy* (1981), was designed to examine the cognitive consequences of literacy and compare the effects of different scripts. In their impressive study, which relied on multiple quantifiable psychological measures, the authors investigated the cognitive abilities of three different groups among the Vai people in northwestern Liberia in West Africa. They tested more than 1,000 subjects over a 4-year period to measure the cognitive capacities of literates and nonliterates as well as documented uses of literacy.

The Vai situation is unique in that, in addition to illiteracy, four different literacies are evident in the culture: Vai, Qur'anic, Arabic, and English. The Vai script, a syllabary of 200 characters with a common core of twenty to forty, has been used in this rural society for a century and a half, for writing notes, keeping logs and diaries, and writing bills. Arabic writing for the Qur'anic script is taught in the Qur'anic schools by learned Muslims. (About 90 percent of Vai are Muslims.) The majority of Vai people trained in Qur'anic schools learn Arabic at the level of repetition for the purpose of reciting, reading, and writing Islamic religious passages. Knowledge gained in the Qur'anic schools qualifies an individual for many important functions religious and trade-related in the community; it makes one a learned individual in the culture. The few students who go on to advanced study of the Arabic language – beyond the Qur'anic school – study Islamic religious, legal, and other texts. English script has the least impact in the rural society. It is taught in Western-type government and mission schools, located outside the Vai country. Students need to leave their homes to pursue education in these schools.

Although little English is used in the villages, some clan chiefs employ clerks to record court matters in English as well as to correspond with administrative functionaries.

Scribner and Cole's results were "in direct conflict with persistent claims that 'deep psychological differences' divide literate and nonliterate populations" (251). On no tasks – logic, abstraction, memory, communication – did they find all nonliterates at lower levels than all literates. They admit that literacy promotes skills among the Vai but claim that literacy is not a necessary and sufficient condition for any of the skills they assessed.

In an attempt to discover whether different literacies have different cognitive effects, Scribner and Cole assessed cognitive abilities such as categorizing, memory, and logical reasoning. Figure 1 shows the results. Each row in the figure represents one of the three scripts for which Scribner and Cole studied literate practices: English (school), Vai script, and Arabic. Each column represents a cognitive task or aspect of a cognitive task that was used to measure cognitive skills. The shaded intersections of script and task in the figure indicate that the designated cognitive skill has been enhanced by practice in the corresponding script.

The results show that English schooling contributes to performance on most tasks but that script literacy "shows no such similar spread to the general ability tasks that historically have demonstrated the influence of schooling" (p. 253). In other words, it is not so much the type of literacy but the existence of formal schooling that accounted for such spectacular differences. In other words, those who go to school are better at skills practiced at school.

Furthermore, the figure shows that Vai literates, Arabic literates, and English literates showed different patterns of skills. For example, Qur'anic and Arabic literates were better at incremental recall, whereas English (school) literates were better at free recall.

Scribner and Cole's research is significant for contrastive rhetoric research in two ways. First, it shows that although some literacy groups are less skillful at certain cognitive tasks (e.g., difficulty in beginning to call the sun "moon" and vice versa when asked to do this by a researcher), one should not draw an overall conclusion concerning these people's way of thinking or their "thought patterns."

Scribner and Cole's work is significant in another respect. Their research proves that the appearance of writing in itself does not substantially change the quality of culture. What Kaplan describes as a "post-biological evolutionary step" is in fact only potentially a revolutionary achievement. Goody and Watt (1968) also mention that it is not simply the emergence of writing but its proliferation and general availability that matter.

Broad category of effect		Type of literacy			
		English/ school	Vai script	Qur'anic	Arabic language
Categorizing	Form/number sort	▨	▨		▨
Memory	Incremental recall			▨	▨
	Free recall	▨			
Logical reasoning	Syllogisms	▨			
Encoding and decoding	Rebus reading	▨	▨		
	Rebus writing	▨	▨		▨
Semantic integration	Integrating words	▨	▨	▨	▨
	Integrating syllables		▨		
Verbal explanation	Communication game	▨	▨		
	Grammatical rules	▨	▨		
	Sorting geometric figuess	▨			
	Logical syllogisms	▨			
	Sun-moon name-switching (Because of ambiguities in this task, we include only those literacy effects appearing in more than one administration.)	▨			

Figure 1   Scribner and Cole's literacy categories and their effects. (From The Psychology of Literacy *by Sylvia Scribner and Michael Cole, © Harvard University Press, 1981, p. 253. Reprinted by permission.)*

Anthropological study of culture and literacy

A ground-breaking contrastive research on the relation of literacy practices to culture is American anthropological linguist Shirley Brice Heath's ethnographic study, *Ways with Words: Language, Life and Work in Communities and Classrooms* (1983). Heath studied three geographically close communities in South Carolina: the white working-class Roadville, the black working-class Trackton, and middle-class townspeople consisting of both white and black professionals. Her ethnography compared the literacy development of the two working-class groups with that of the urbanized middle-class whites and blacks.

The results showed differences in types and uses of literacy between the working-class and middle-class groups. The working-class children had a concept of print, but they did not have an experience of seeing their parents read and write extended pieces of prose. Although quantity of talk at home was not lacking, its quality was different from that of the townspeople's. Townspeople structured their socialization with children to include "extended narratives, imaginative flights of establishing new contexts, or manipulating features of an event or item" (Heath 1983, 352). These activities taught the children to acquire new concepts as well as learn the role of elaboration and turn taking in conversation, all important aspects of succeeding at school. As a result, the townspeople's children were much more prepared for literacy readiness when they entered school than the children of the two rural groups.

Heath's study is important to contrastive rhetoric for at least three reasons. First, it shows that speakers of the same language often experience sharper cross-cultural conflicts than speakers of different languages. Second, one of the most significant findings of Heath's ethnographic inquiry was the relationship between language socialization at home and subsequent success in literacy at school. The implication is that schooling in all cultures is experienced as a mild form of culture shock, with its strength depending on how different the person's literacy background is from the literacy expectations of the school. Third, Heath's work is significant in that it shows the power of ethnography as a research method in contrastive rhetoric.

Partly inspired by Heath's ethnographic research, a dissertation by a Chinese doctoral student at the University of New Hampshire analyzed teachers' comments on student writing in America and China (Li 1992). The author, Xiao-Ming Li, sought to build a dialogue between teachers of writing in China and America on what "good writing" is in order to show that "good writing" resides not only with student texts but with the teachers who read and evaluate student papers.

The study consisted of a case study of four writing teachers, two from China and two from the United States, and a survey of six other teachers in both countries. Li studied the four writing teachers through extensive interviews, personal observations, and their comments on six pieces of narrative writing – three from each country – recommended as samples of "good writing."

Differences were found in the rhetorical values between the American and Chinese teachers. For example, the Chinese teachers considered writing as a vehicle for disseminating the accepted morality of the society, whereas the American teachers "consider morality the last place for teachers to exert their authority" (Li 1992, 159). The American teachers valued the uniqueness of a writer's voice but did not care for the expression of too much emotion in writing, whereas the Chinese teachers allowed imitation and considered the expression of emotion a sign of good student writing. Other differences dealt with requirements for form (the Chinese favored them, the Americans did not), description versus explicit opinion (the Americans prefered "showing" not "telling," whereas the Chinese expected "moral tags" in good writing), and an oral versus a literate emphasis in writing (the Americans considered formal and overly ornate language phony and prefer "natural" language, whereas in Chinese the difference between the written and spoken languages is still large).

Although substantial "national" differences were found between the teachers of the two countries, there was similarity in the teachers' reactions to the student texts. For example, each teacher was moved by the student writer's anguish in an essay about a friend's suicide. However, Li has good reason to conclude that teachers, when they read student papers, bring to their judgments not only their personal history, but a whole set of culturally defined and prescribed criteria. Li writes:

But their identity is defined to some extent, if not to a large extent, by their nationality, for individuals can choose to resist or comply, but they operate in a particular social environment, and they are invariably subject to the influence and constraints of the cultures to which they belong. The four key teachers are fully aware of societal influence on them and talked about it eloquently in the discussions. Mr. Zhang pointed to the restraints posed on his teaching by entrance exams, and Mr. Wang analyzed how centuries of political oppression has shaped the writing and temperament of writers in China. Jack expounded on the outcome of the Vietnam War and the moral climate in America after the sixties, and Jane had to adjust her teaching strategy and expectations according to the student mores. Besides, they all teach literature produced by native writers, chosen not by the teachers but the literary community in each country. These "great works" are held as models of "good writing" for both the writing teachers and their students. (Li 1992, 156)

This study may initiate a promising new development in contrastive studies aimed at discovering what good writing in a culture is and how it is taught. Such ethnographic case studies, rather than formalistic studies such as those of Glenn and Glenn, Triandis, and Hofstede (discussed previously), enable researchers to go beyond the study of writing handbooks in order to learn how writing and the teaching of writing really take place.

Educational study of culture and literacy

Significant contributions to knowledge about writing instruction and culture have emerged from the International Study of Written Composition as part of the International Association for the Evaluation of Educational Achievement (IEA) (Gorman, Purves, and Degenhart 1988). The Study of Written Composition, begun in 1980, examined the teaching and learning of written composition in schools in fourteen countries: Chile, England, Finland, the Federal Republic of Germany, Hungary, Indonesia, Italy, the Netherlands, New Zealand, Nigeria, Sweden, Thailand, the United States, and Wales. The goals of the project, as explained by Takala (1988), were multifold: (1) to conceptualize the domain of school writing internationally; (2) to develop an internationally appropriate series of writing tasks; (3) to describe recent developments and the current state of instruction in participating countries, and, most relevant here, (4) to identify factors which explain differences as well as typical patterns in the performance of written composition with particular attention to cultural background, curriculum, and teaching practices.

From 1981 to 1986, thousands of 12-, 16-, and 18-year-old students in the participating countries wrote essays in their mother tongues on a variety of topics in styles ranging from reflection to persuasion. The dependent variable in the study was student performance in written composition. The independent variables were numerous. They were related to student characteristics, characteristics of home, community, school, curriculum, and teaching practices. Data on the independent variables were collected by means of questionnaires and case studies.

Careful planning among the national coordinators of the IEA study went into the test development and test performance phases. Test development involved the specification of test domains and essay topics. The development of the tasks and scoring procedures are explained in *The IEA Study of Written Composition I: The International Writing Tasks and Scoring Scales* (Gorman et al. 1988). Each student wrote on three tasks, each related to different areas of writing ability. The different essay tasks required paraphrase, descriptive, persuasive, or reflective essays.

Although data analyses are still underway, a number of important contributions of the study are already evident. First, the research has made it possible to compare domains of school writing such as narration cross-culturally (Kádár-Fülop 1988; Vähäpassi 1988a,b). Second, the study has made it possible to describe universal characteristics of school writing and student performance (Purves and Hawisher 1990; Purves and Purves 1986).

Kádár-Fülop, a national coordinator of the IEA study in Hungary, describes the model for comparing curricula of school writing cross-culturally that is used in the IEA study. She bases her model on a linguistic theory proposed in Werlich's *A Text Grammar of English* (1976), which shows how a text is a functional unit of linguistic elements. Werlich's text identifies text types – description, narration, exposition, argumentation, and instruction – each associated with a different function of writing. Each text type favors certain linguistic forms related to syntax, organization, and style. Each also appears in situation-specific text forms as either with a writer's personal point of view or with an objective point of view. Kádár-Fülop provides a summary of Werlich's five major text types as shown in Figure 2.

Using this classification of text types, Kádár-Fülop describes how text types and forms appear in a Hungarian school context. The text forms dominating writing education at the elementary level are narration and summaries, which start "with the help of the teacher usually from the third or fourth grade" (1988, 46). In grades 5–8, text forms in which composition skills are practiced and developed are the impressionistic description, the personal narrative, summary writing, text interpretation, and technical definition and description. In grades 9–12, the essay, text interpretation, the comment, definition, explication, and the summary are the tasks that occur with some likelihood.

Another system that was developed in the IEA study to assure that topics and tasks were appropriate cross-culturally was Vähäpassi's (1988a,b) "general model of writing domain" in school settings. Her model can be applied to the specification of writing tasks or assignments. It considers such important factors in writing situations as cognitive processing demands related to the topic and content, social and intersubjective demands of writing concerning the purpose and audience, and linguistic and rhetorical demands of writing concerning the mode of discourse. (Figure 3 shows Vähäpassi's 1988b model.) The first two fac-

(1) Descriptive text forms
    (1.1) Impressionistic description (personal)
    (1.2) Technical description (objective)
(2) Narrative text forms
    (2.1) The narrative (personal)
    (2.2) The report (objective)
    (2.3) The news story (objective but related to the writer's personal view)
(3) Expository text forms
    (3.1) The expository essay (personal)
    (3.2) The definition (objective)
    (3.3) The explication (objective)
    (3.4) The summary (objective)
    (3.5) Summarizing minutes (objective)
    (3.6) The text interpretation
(4) Argumentative text forms
    (4.1) The comment (personal)
    (4.2) Scientific argumentation
(5) Instructive text forms
    (5.1) Instructions (with reference to personal authority)
    (5.2) Directions, rules, regulations, statutes (with reference to impersonal authority)

Figure 2   Kádár-Fülop's summary of Werlich's text forms. (From "Culture, Writing, and Curriculum," by Kádár-Fülop, in Writing Across Languages and Cultures, *edited by Alan C. Purves,* © Sage Publishers, 1988, *p. 44. Reprinted by permission.)*

| Cognitive Processing | | | I Reproduce | II Organize/Reorganize | | III Invent/Generate | |
| Primary Content → | | | Linguistically Precoded/Predetermined Information | Known | | New or Alternative | |
Dominant Intention/Purpose ↓	Primary Audience ↓			Spatial/Temporal	Phenomena, Concepts or Mental States	Spatial/Temporal	Phenomena, Concepts or Mental States
1. To learn (meta-lingual, mathetic)	Self		Copying Taking dictation	Retell a story (heard or read)	Note Resume Summary Outline Paraphrasing	Comments on book margins Metaphors Analogies	
2. To convey emotions, feelings (emotive)	Self Others		Stream of Consciousness	Personal story	Portrayal Personal diary Personal letter	Reflective writing -- Personal essays	
3. To inform (referential)	Others		Quote Fill in a form	Narrative report News Instruction Telegram Announcement Circular	Directions Description Technical description Biography Science report/ experiment	Expository writing -- Definition -- Academic essay/article -- Book review -- Commentary	The traditional literary genre and modes can be placed
4. To convince persuade (conative)	Others		Citation form authority/expert	Letter of application Statement of personal views, opinions	Advertisement Letter or advice	Argumentative/ persuasive writing -- Editorial -- Critical essay/article	under one or more
5. To entertain, de-light, please (poetic)	Others		Quotation of poetry and prose	Given an ending-create a story Create an ending Retell a story	Word portrait or sketch Causerie	Entertainment writing -- Parody -- Rhymes	of these four purposes.
6. To keep in touch (phatic)	Others		Postcards	Postcards, letters			
			Documentative Discourse	Reportorial Discourse		Exploratory Discourse	

Figure 3   Vähäpassi's general model of writing discourse. (From "The Problem of Selection of Writing Tasks in Cross-Cultural Study," by Vähäpassi, in Writing Across Languages and Cultures, edited by Alan C. Purves, © Sage Publishers, 1988, p. 58. Reprinted by permission.)

tors (cognitive processing/demands and dominant intention/purpose) are the main dimensions. Modes of discourse are the complementary dimension.

Vähäpassi's model was used in the beginning stage of the IEA study to analyze topics in school-leaving examinations in the fourteen participating countries. The data showed that "writing in order to learn" as well as "to inform" were emphasized in all the school systems. Pragmatic, functional tasks whose purpose is to inform a given audience were neglected, as were writing tasks involving persuasion and argumentation. Finally, "writing in order to convey emotions and feelings" also appeared infrequently in school-leaving examinations.

In addition to establishing general parameters of school writing cross-culturally at the level of school leaving, Vähäpassi reports that the model was useful when the national coordinators of the IEA study met to decide on specific tasks and topics at all three age levels in the study (12, 16, and 18 years). These international deliberations led to a final number of fourteen writing tasks, which Vähäpassi classified into four major categories (Vähäpassi 1988, 67–68): organizing and reorganizing information in order to inform, organizing and reorganizing information in order to learn, organizing or inventing in order to convey emotions, and inventing or generating in order to convince.

Working from the entire empirical data set of the IEA study, Alan Purves has proposed that there are both an "international interpretative community" and "national communities." Evidence of the existence of an international interpretative community is the fact that all participants were able to agree not only on the same set of topics but also on the criteria for scoring the writing. On the other hand, differences were found in the style, content, and pragmatics of the essays across cultures. Purves and Hawisher write:

There are strong national differences in perception however, such as the relatively low emphasis on "organization" in Chile and on "style and tone" in the Netherlands. In New Zealand and Sweden, teachers appear to emphasize "process" more than in other countries, but in Sweden more of this emphasis concerns choice of topic than is the case in New Zealand. (1990, 190)

The findings have led Purves and Hawisher to infer that "good writing" is a "culturally defined phenomenon" and that "written tests, and the ways in which they are used and perceived, vary according to the cultural group to which an individual belongs" (1990, 183). The IEA study found systematic differences by culture along a number of continua, as follows: personal–impersonal, ornamented–plain, abstract–concrete, single–multiple, and propositional–appositional (Purves and Hawisher 1990, 188).

In addition to evaluating the quality and characteristics of student essays across languages and cultures, the IEA study revealed cross-cultural characteristics of "writing activity." Purves and Purves (1986) note that cultural variation characterizes specific styles of writing activity. They observe that in some cultures greater emphasis appears to be placed on criteria for editing, whereas in others there appears to be a greater emphasis on criteria for planning and drafting.

Purves and Purves (1986) suggest that we need to study further how and where individuals learn what constitutes "good" writing and "appropriate" writing in a given culture. Guidelines on rules for "good" or "appropriate" writing determine cultural models for finished texts as well as cultural models for good writing in specific contexts. The authors list three basic forms of required knowledge: "semantic knowledge" (knowledge of words and structures), "knowledge of text models" (discourse models of texts for different purposes), and "knowledge of social and cultural rules governing both when it is appropriate to write and when it is obligatory to write as well as knowledge of the appropriate procedures to use in the activity of writing" (Purves and Purves 1986, 179).

Purves and Purves admit that the IEA study examined writing solely in Ll and in Ll cultural contexts, a limitation that does not lend itself to generalizing for L2 contexts. However, they refer to the research that Söter (1988) conducted under the auspices of the IEA study, which showed that Ll models of narrative structure are translated to L2 writing. Story structures in the English writing of English-, Vietnamese-, and Arabic-speaking children in Australian schools were examined. The students in Söter's sample displayed variation in their story structures and in the content of their stories. The Vietnamese and Arabic students' stories had features that may be derived from elsewhere than English models. The Vietnamese stories appeared less goal oriented and less focused on the plot than the typical English story. Greater emphasis was placed on the relationships between characters; dialogue between them was frequent. The Arabic students' writing differed from the others in that it typically contained more information about the scene of the story.

The work conducted in the IEA project and the theoretical implications discussed by Alan Purves and his colleagues are significant in expanding contrastive rhetoric in three important directions. First, the sample writing in the IEA project was in the students' mother tongues, allowing for a more direct discussion of cross-cultural differences. Second, the sample sizes were large enough to allow statistical inferences and generalizations. Third, the project saw the importance of going beyond static linguistic and discourse analyses for learning about the cross-cultural conventions of writing.

Several reports describe the results of the IEA study in participating countries. Detailed reports are available for Sweden (Lifqvist 1990), New Zealand (Lamb 1987), Hungary (Kádár-Fülop 1990), Italy (Lucisano

1988), Germany (Lehmann and Hartmann 1987), Thailand (Devahastin and Methakunavudhi 1986), and England (Gubb, Gorman, and Price 1987). These reports describe sample populations, tasks conducted (types of essays, surveys, questionnaires), and results by age groups in each country.

Studies of culture and literacy conducted by applied linguists

Models of cross-cultural writing that emerged from the IEA study and the psychological and anthropological studies of literacy development suggest that writing is an activity that is acquired in and outside of school. Writing development is seen as part of the synthesis of culturally preferred patterns of rhetorical texts and the related cognitive cultural models. A strong relationship is seen between Ll language and communications skills and the development of literacy in both Ll and L2. This kind of model allows for positive transfer of shared linguistic and cultural features from the first language to writing in English as a second language.

According to such a cultural model of writing, it is not enough to examine texts and speculate about the reasons for rhetorically preferred conventions in cultures. For this reason, ESL researchers have turned to studying language acquisition and the literacy development of children in their native cultures when explaining Ll influences on L2 acquisition. For example, research on children's acquisition of culture-specific patterns of communication helps us to understand deeply rooted styles of communication.

Thus Clancy's research informs us about Japanese children's learning socially accepted communication patterns, which may affect writing patterns. Japanese communicative style places "speaker and hearer in the prototypical social relationship, namely, one that is based on 'amae' – to depend upon and presume upon another's benevolence" (1986, 219). The values reflected and reinforced by this mode of communication constitute an integral part of Japanese culture. In Clancy's study of five Japanese children and mothers, the children were taught early on the principles of "amae." Hence, Japanese children, according to Clancy, learn to become good listeners by being taught to rely on "verbal strategies that foster empathy and conformity" (1986, 219).

The concept of "amae" could be useful in explaining conflict situations that arise in cross-cultural communication between Japanese and American writers. For example, after analyzing 2 years of written communications between a Japanese and an American manager of marketing, Connor (1988) described the seeming incoherence and structural indirectness of the Japanese manager's style as contrasted to the direct approach of the American manager. However, a different and more precise explanation, based on the concept of "amae," would be that the initial report and request, long and rambling in American eyes, was the Japanese manager's attempt to establish personal rapport and trust with the American manager.

A beneficial research direction in ESL related to this general area is the one charted by Carson (1992), Folman and Sarig (1990), and Liebman (1992). Each of these studies has originated research that will provide valuable knowledge for the teaching of ESL literacy.

An article by Carson (1992) about the effects of an L1 educational system and orthography on the subsequent acquisition of L2 was discussed in Chapter 2 as an example of the directions contrastive rhetoric is taking in applied linguistics. Another paper by Carson and Nelson (1994) discusses the emphasis put on the collective common good in Chinese and Japanese upbringing and education. This creates problems for Japanese and Chinese ESL students in writing groups in ESL classes, the purpose of which is to improve the individual student's paper. Chinese and Japanese students strive to achieve harmony in peer groups and are hesitant to offer comments on their fellow students' papers for fear that they might hurt other students.

Folman and Sarig (1990) conducted a quantitative study that was planned to find out whether and to what extent rhetorical structures preferred by native Hebrew speakers differ from those preferred by native English speakers when constructing meaning in reading and writing in their native languages. One hundred and fifty-six students took part in the study. Folman and Sarig found differences in the rhetorical patterns used by the two groups of subjects. They then compared U.S. English with Israeli writing instructional norms using a taxonomy for cross-cultural comparison of writing instruction developed in the IEA study discussed above. They concluded that although there is considerable similarity between the two systems concerning norms for written expression, the rhetorical differences found in their constrastive studies:

> . . . do not seem to lie only within the realm of "different thought patterns," but more – [we] would like to suggest within the realm of the professed and implemented syllabuses of language arts and educational linguistics of each of the instructional systems, the formal agents of each of the cultures. (1990, 73)

Still another ESL study that has considered the Ll literacy backgrounds of the subjects is Liebman's (1992) survey study of ESL students' instructional backgrounds in Ll. Questionnaires were distributed to eighty-nine ESL students studying in an ESL program in the United States. Of these students, fifty-four were Arabic speakers and thirty-five Japanese speakers. The questions dealt with what kind of writing instruction the students had received in their Ll countries.

The survey results showed differences in the answers given by the two groups of students. Unlike what we would expect of the writing of Japanese students based on Carson's theoretical discussion, Liebman's subjects reported that writing instruction in Japan emphasizes the more expressive function of writing. Liebman adds that, in her own experience, "Japanese students adapt comfortably to writing journals" (1992, 157). The Arabic students in her study reported a positive experience with "transactional writing" related to argumentative writing, at which, according to Liebman, they excel. Liebman concludes by speaking of the importance of continued studies into Ll literacy backgrounds of ESL students:

> But this study suggests that, if ESL writing teachers want their students to succeed at a variety of academic writing tasks, they must become aware not only of these different forms but also of differences in instructional background. It is not enough to determine what will be expected of ESL students in the university and then give them models of what we want them to produce. We must also determine what these students' prior experiences are. Students from different backgrounds will require different approaches. When we seek to help ESL students use expressive writing more effectively, for example, we may find it necessary to use different techniques for Japanese and Arabic students in order to help these students achieve the goals reflected in the models we show them. Similarly, when we teach argument, we may need to approach it differently with Arabic and Japanese students. (1992, 157–158)

The three recent approaches looking at Ll literacy and its effect on L2 are pioneering in contrastive rhetoric in that they expand the scope of contrastive rhetoric beyond the point where the students are at the time of a particular study. It is noteworthy that the studies use different approaches in their explorations, which adds to the richness of the theory. However, we need to note that the findings of these studies are contradictory. Carson speaks about the difficulty experienced by Japanese students when they were asked to write in the expressive mode; Liebman found in her study that the Japanese students enjoyed writing in the expressive mode. It is fair to say that ESL teachers need to be very careful before they implement suggestions stemming from these small-scale, single studies. Future research needs to explore questions raised by Carson through replications of research like Liebman's.

Summary

An interdisciplinary interest in cultural literacy has produced important insights about relationships among orality, literacy, schooling and instruction, and cultural tendencies. Research employing a wide variety of approaches – experiments and surveys, educational tests, ethnographies, and case studies, conducted by psychologists, educational researchers, anthropologists, and applied linguists – reveals universal as well as "national" writing patterns. However, research has just begun. More explorations need to be made into the relationships between culture, writing and its instruction, and L2 instruction. Future studies need to investigate what good writing is in a given culture and how it is taught. Previous scholarship has determined features of good writing in written products and through analyses of writing handbooks, but if we consider culture to be a set of varied rules and patterns, representative of different groups within a community, readers' perceptions of written texts need to be investigated further.

7 Contrastive rhetoric and translation studies

Contrastive rhetoricians working on second language writing, not only in North America but in other countries, are often unfamiliar with the theories and research of scholars in translation studies. Translation theorists seem to be equally unaware of developments in contrastive rhetoric. This mutual ignorance is curious considering the many goals and research methods these two disciplines have in common. Both are applied rather than theoretical, in the sense that linguistics is used in each field for equally practical purposes: Contrastive rhetoric assists language teaching experts and translation theory assists translators. Both contrastive rhetoric and translation studies deal with first language and second language processing and benefit from the same literature on language acquisition. Both have experienced changes in methodology in the past decade as their individual theories were supplemented with relevant hypotheses and methods of literary study, education, and cognitive science. The explanation for the mutual ignorance may rest in social differences between educational systems: In countries with "small" national languages such as Finland, translation is a must; whereas in countries with "big" languages such as the United States, England, or France, composition is emphasized together with the need to teach ESL.

This chapter addresses three broad issues: first, current theories and practices of translation; second, the issue of "transfer" in contrastive rhetoric and translation theory; and finally, the potential of translation theory to contribute to the solution of some of the outstanding problems in contrastive rhetoric.

Development of theories of translation studies

Translation studies in Europe and the United States

Since the early 1970s, translation studies have become established as a legitimate field of study, much as applied linguistics did (see Gentzler [1993] for the development of translation studies as a separate discipline). Gideon Toury, a respected Israeli theorist of translation studies, traces the serious development of translation as a discipline of its own

117

to a paper by Holmes presented at the Third International Congress of Applied Linguistics in 1972 in Germany, "The name and nature of translation studies," later published in 1975. Holmes advocated translation as an empirical science divided into main categories of "pure" vs. "applied" translation studies. The former was further broken down into "theoretical" vs. "descriptive," with "descriptive" branching into three foci of research: function, process, and product oriented. Included in the applied branch are "translation training, translation aids, and translation criticism."

This evolution in translation studies in the past 20 years has resulted in active interrelations between the categories of Holmes's model. Toury (1991) discusses Holmes's model in terms of the need to interrelate the pure and applied branches. Andrew Chesterman, a translation scholar working in Finland (1993), also recognizes the multiple functions of translation theories, distinguishing the translation product, the processes involved in translating, and the functions of translation products for the target audiences.

Not only is the field of translation theory active, the training of translators is a major function of European language departments. Many European universities also have schools of translation studies, which offer specialized graduate training for students majoring in language studies and turn out teachers of foreign languages, while translators appear as well from language departments. A recent review of the teaching of English studies in Finland (Svartvik, Blake, and Toury 1994) recommended that translation and language studies at the graduate level be separated and stronger graduate level translation programs be developed. They write:

We wish to preserve the character of the schools as schools of translation studies and to maintain and enhance their academic credibility, especially in view of the prospect that Finland will soon join the European community, which would make translation even more important. . . . Schools of translation should become postgraduate institutions offering an MA degree with a well-balanced integration of the professional and academic aspects as well as a Ph.D. . . . Resources should be deployed in such a way that the country has at least one or two schools of translation studies of substance and international standing. (40)

Translation studies in Europe, spearheaded by German translation theorists, and translation studies in the United States have taken different directions. According to Pochhacker, German theorists have led the academic, "scientific" tradition of translation scholarship, whereas "Anglo-American scholars of translation have tended to adopt a much more praxis-oriented approach to the theory and teaching of their subject" (1989, 563). Pochhacker laments the lack of communication between the theoretically oriented European and the practically oriented Anglo-

American translation scholars. As an example of the British scholar's relatively negative view of the role of theory in translation, Pochhacker cites Newmark, one of the most popular authors in the Anglo-American translation studies, quoting from his book, *Approaches to Translation:*

There can be no valid single comprehensive theory of translation and no general agreement on the element of invariance, the ideal translation unit, the degree of translatability, and the concepts of equivalent-effect and congruence in translation. (1981, 113)

In sum, German translation scholars have been more interested in developing theories and models of translation than Anglo-American scholars. Both seem to agree, however, on the basic distinction between "literal" and "free" translation or the nearly synonymous terms "semantic" and "communicative" – Anglo-American – (Newmark 1981) and "overt" and "covert" translation – German – (House 1977). They agree that there is a need for free or communicative translation instead of literal translation, depending on the purpose of the translation. For example, translation theorists agree that methods of translation need to vary between informative and expressive texts because of different expected effects on the reader.

Expansion of methods of translation

The field of translation studies in the past decade has experienced changes similar to those that have occurred in contrastive rhetoric. An expansion of influences from related disciplines has contributed to new emphases in the methods of translation studies; a trend toward empirical work is strong, and an interdisciplinary emphasis has evolved. All are treated in the work of the Finnish translation scholar, Sonja Tirkkonen-Condit. Discussing the "frustration with existing translation theories" and the search for new tools for solving research problems in translation, she advocates an interdisciplinary approach to problems in translation studies:

It depends on the nature of the problem whether it is linguistics, psychology, pragmatics, literary studies or some other discipline or a combination of disciplines which turns out to be methodologically useful. In some instances, of course, the research problem will have to be redefined, if it appears to be unaccessible by conceivable methodologies. (1989, 4)

Using three different translations, Tirkkonen-Condit demonstrates the inadequacy of traditional translation theory, which stresses linguistically accurate, "semantic," translation. The first example deals with the Finnish translations of popular romantic fiction published by the American publisher, Harlequin. The research was reported by another Finnish translation researcher, Anne Kemppinen (1988). Kemppinen was interested in learning how the poorly paid Harlequin translators handled the task. The translators were given instructions about details such as omissions and linguistic structure; they were instructed to omit "boring descriptions" of characters as well as lengthy and "harping" dialogues. Linguistic simplication required short rather than long sentences and an emphasis on main clauses rather than subclauses. The publisher thus determined the "acceptability" norms of the translation.

After having read Harlequin books in the original and in Finnish translations, Kemppinen suspected a mismatch between the publisher's ideas about acceptability and those of the readers. The Finnish translations seemed dull. In order to investigate this suspected mismatch, Kemppinen resorted to research methods from outside of translation studies. She analyzed the educational backgrounds of typical readers and, through studying Finnish literary research about reader responses, discovered that Finnish readers were most interested in the main characters. The plot itself had a subsidiary role – after all, these books always have a happy ending.

The other two examples provided by Tirkkonen-Condit deal with the translation of summaries of research articles in education and a failed translation of a novel. In the first case, a researcher resorted to asking English-speaking readers' reactions to summaries in order to find out what was wrong with them. In the latter case, a researcher focused on the frequent dialogue in the book and saw that it carried dialectal and sociopolitical information, which is almost impossible to translate. In both cases, the researchers found the methodological tools in their research to be in domains beyond traditional translation theory.

Transfer in contrastive rhetoric and translation theory

Interlanguage transfer has been widely studied in second language acquisition. As discussed in Chapter 2, transfer is a problem-solving procedure utilizing L1 knowledge in order to solve a production or learning problem. In the procedure of "transfer," a language user activates both languages. Accordingly, it has been claimed that "transfer" applies similarly to both translation and contrastive studies. Toury notes the similarity between transfer and translation, observing that both involve the processing of two languages at the same time:

Translating is a mode of speech production in one language where another language is necessarily involved. The very presence of two distinct languages in any act of translating leaves no room for doubt that, at least in principle, transfer may accompany translating, too, as is the case with any other mode of speech production by bilingual speakers. (1986, 81)

Toury differs, however, from some theorists who maintain that the transfer procedure is the same in both translation studies and second language acquisition. He points out that the concept of transfer, as it is used in L2 studies, has characteristics that set it apart from the kind of transfer that takes place in translation. First, all knowledge of the source language is thought to be activated when a second language speaker produces target language utterances. In translation, on the other hand, only a translatable utterance is the object of transfer. The difference is between the language system as the object of transfer in second language acquisition and the utterance in translation.

Toury's point is especially well taken when one considers translation and writing in a second language, the domain of contrastive rhetoric. Whereas a translator has available a source text, a second language writer composing a piece of writing goes through a variety of writing processes. In translation, one has a source text as a starting point. In second language writing, one has available a complete knowledge of the first language and especially of writing in it in order to complete a second language text.

Issues in common: theories of "acceptability" and "adequacy" in translation

Theories of translation in both Europe and the United States used to be source-text oriented. Older models of translation presupposed that particular features in the source text (the text to be translated) or its role in the source culture determined the way in which the text needed to be translated. For example, Tirkkonen-Condit (1989) cites Nida's (1964) theory of dynamic equivalence, which, as a guideline for translation, assumes the response of the readers of the source text in the source culture. Also in the same category is the model of translation of the German translation scholar, Juliane House (1977), which defined functional equivalence in terms of sociolinguistic dimensions in the source text. For both Nida and House, the evaluation of translations involves the determination of equivalence between the translation and the source text.

Toury (1980, 1991, 1993) has presented an alternative to these older, source-text-oriented models of translation, which seems to have become accepted by leading translation experts, at least in Europe. Toury's criticisms of the source-text-oriented models of translations is that they prescribe aspects of translation in advance, on the basis of the source text and its environment alone, and do not provide a framework for describing existing translations against the background of the target language and culture.

Toury's model allows one to look at existing translations from two perspectives: as approximations of their source texts and as genuine members of the target literary systems, as texts among other texts in the target culture. As a result of these two perspectives, translations are said to possess varying degrees of two qualities, "adequacy" and "acceptability," the two theoretical poles of the continuum in which all translations can be found. For a translation to be acceptable, it is not enough merely to be adequate. For example, a piece of literature – say, a haiku – may take a totally different form translated from the original into English. Toury writes:

Thus, what may be said to operate in translation is not any *fact* about the reception of its end-product (which is not yet there, in the first place); only certain *assumptions* with respect to it, namely, assumptions as to the prospects of a text whose structure and linguistic make-up follow a certain pattern which is *acceptable* to the target end. Being members of the target culture, or tentatively assuming the role of ones, translators are more or less aware of the factors which govern the acceptability of texts and textual-linguistic features in that culture, or certain sector thereof. To the extent that they choose to subject themselves to these factors and resort to the appropriate translation strategies, the act itself is executed under the initial norm of acceptability; whether the end-product will indeed be admitted into the target system or not. (1993, 16)

The concepts of adequacy and acceptability have much to offer for contrastive rhetoric research. The concept of acceptability by the target audience is an important issue. In early phases of ESL, ESL teachers or their colleagues were their students' only audience. There was an accepted English norm that dealt with school writing. However, with the increasing emphasis on professional writing in the workplace and on writing for academic purposes, contrastive rhetoricians may know little about the expectations of their students' audiences. Students need to learn to write for different genres in discourse communities with varying norms.

An example from Ventola and Mauranen's (1991) study illustrates the important role of the theory of acceptability in contrastive research. In this study, the researchers examined academic journal articles written in English by Finnish- or Swedish-speaking physicists. Two other versions of the articles were also studied: revisions made by native-English-speaking professional reviser/translators and revisions made by the two researchers. The analyses showed that the Finnish physicists had difficulties with article use, lexical choices, and the construction of phrases and sentences in addition to the main problem of not connecting ideas in a "logical" manner. Particularly troubling was the lack of systematic theme-rheme development; instead, "themes and rhemes seem to have been constructed on a stream-of-consciousness principle" (1991, 484). The language revisers' versions included mainly grammatical and lexical corrections such as articles, spelling, the number of nouns, tense in verbs, and prepositions. The text researchers made changes "with the aim of making the text easier to read" (1991, 486). They added connectors as well as phrases to help the reader sort out information. All three versions of the results section of one article are shown in Figure 1 (pp. 124–125).

The Finnish researchers argued that the professional revisers' changes (see version 2) did not necessarily improve the Finnish scientists' academic writing. Instead, Finnish writers should receive better training and more practice in effective use of textual transitions and organization of ideas, as shown in version 3. When asked to evaluate the three versions, the original writer agreed that the text developed by the researchers (version 3) was the best.

Using Toury's definition of adequacy and acceptability, one could say that version 3 is the most adequate. But is it acceptable? For a text to be acceptable, it should be acceptable in the target culture, which in this case is represented by applied physicists. Therefore, if one wanted to test the acceptability of the passage, one would need to ask physicists to read it. Text linguists' or text revisers' points of view reveal the level of adequacy but not of acceptability.

Summary

Translation studies and contrastive rhetoric both are new fields. Contrastive rhetoric began in 1966 with Kaplan's article. It has been claimed that modern translation studies began in 1972 with Holmes's paper, "The Name and Nature of Translation Studies." Originally embedded in linguistic theory, both contrastive rhetoric and translation studies have expanded their goals and research methods. While doing so, each discipline has been interdisciplinary, drawing on linguistics, psychology, pragmatics, and literary studies, among other disciplines. But there are inescapable dissimilarities, as, for example, in the concept of "transfer." In second language writing all second language knowledge is thought to be activated, whereas in translation only a translatable utterance or passage is the object of transfer.

Several concepts developed for the study of translation have much to offer for contrastive rhetorical research. The focus of translation studies on the acceptability of a text for the target audience is an important issue for constrastive rhetoric as well.

Version 1

Results

(1) *Welder's age and welding experience distributed normally, but the luminances viewed through filter plates distributed log-normally (fig. 1).* (2) *The latter was expected, because the glare sensation is known to be a logarithmic function of the source luminance.*

(3) *Table 1 presents the age, welding experience, luminance and filter shade characteristics of the subjects.* (4) *When examining the shade numbers of the filter plates as a function of the welder's age a slight change towards lighter filters was observed.* (5) *The number of young welders was 36, whose average age was 20.7 years and welding experience an average 1.1 years.* (6) *Young welders and aluminum welders viewed at much lower luminances than the whole group of subjects.* (7) *Luminances increased both with the age of subjects and the welding experience (fig. 1 and 2).* (8) *The luminance difference was very significant between both young welders and whole group, and aluminum welders and whole group at 0.1 risk level.* (9) *The mean luminances were 540 cd/m² for young welders, 401 cd/m² for aluminum welders, 1586 cd/m² for women, and 1448 cd/m² for men.* (10) *The mean luminance for whole group of subjects was 1462 cd/m².* (11) *There was no significant differences between the mean luminances of whole group, men, and women.*

(12) *The questionnaire study showed that 69% of welders used fiber-board type welding helmet and the rest of the subjects used fiberglass type.* (13) *21% of welders were fully contented with their welding helmets.* (14) *8 welders had mounted a piece of leather on the lower edge of the welding helmet to protect their neck from radiation.* (15) *Welders complained of inadequate protection of the neck and heaviness of the fiberglass helmet.* (16) *The drawbacks of the fiber-board helmet were lack of space on the inside and a feature of bending the edges.* (17) *The edges bended outward when the helmet got wet.* (18) *The advantages of the fiber-board helmet was without exception its lightness.* (19) *The helmet with liquid crystal filter, which transmits visible light and darkens within 3–10 ms after the arc ignition, were highly approved by the subjects.*

482–83

Version 2

Results

(1) *Welder's age and welding experience distributed normally, but the luminances viewed through filter plates distributed log-normally (Fig. 1).* (2) *The latter was expected, because glare sensation is known to be logarithmic function of the source luminance.*

(3) *Table 1 presents the age, welding experience, luminance and filter shade characteristics of the subjects.* (4) *On examining the shade numbers of the filter plates as a function of the welder's age a slight change towards lighter filters can be observed.* (5) *The number of young welders was 36, their average age was 20.7 and average welding experience 1.1 years.* (6) *Young and aluminum welders worked at much lower luminances than the group of subjects taken as a whole.* (7) *Luminances increased both with the age of subjects and the welding experience (Fig. 1 and 2).* (8) *The luminance difference was very significant between both young welders and the whole group, and aluminum welders and whole group at the 0.1 risk level.* (9) *The mean luminances were 540 cd/m² for young welders, 401 cd/m² for aluminum welders, 1586 cd/m² for women, and 1448 cd/m² for men.* (19) *The mean luminance for entire group of subjects was 1462 cd/m².* (11) *There was no significant differences between the mean luminances of whole group, men, and women.*

(12) *The questionnaire study showed that 69% of welders used fiber-board type welding helmet and the rest of the subjects used the fiberglass type.* (13) *21% of welders were fully contented with their welding helmets.* (14) *Eight welders had mounted a piece of leather on the lower edge of the welding helmet to protect their necks from radiation.* (15) *The welders complained of inadequate neck protection and weight of the fiberglass helmet.* (16) *The drawbacks of the fiber-board helmet were a lack of space on the inside and the tendency for its edges to bend.* (17) *The edges bent outward when the helmet got wet.* (18) *The advantage of the fiberboard helmet for all the workers who used it was its lightness.* (19) *The helmet with a liquid crystal filter, which transmits visible light and darkens within 3–10 ms after the arc ignition, were highly regarded by the subjects.*

484–85

Results

(1) *In the present study the welder's age and welding experience were found to be normally distributed.* (2) *Furthermore, as Figure 1 shows, the luminances which were viewed through filter plates were distributed log-normally.* (3) *This could be expected, because it is known that glare sensation is a logarithmic function of the source luminance.*

(4) *Table 1 presents four variables: age, welding experience, luminance and the filter shade used.* (5) *The values of these variables are first presented for all subjects and then separately for men, women, young welders and aluminum welders.*

(6) *The values of men and women on all four variables did not differ significantly from those of the group as a whole, or from each other.* (7) *In contrast, the values of young welders (N = 36), whose average age was 20.7 and average welding experience 1.1 years, differed from the whole group in two respects.* (8) *Firstly, the younger welders tended to use darker filter plates than the entire group.* (9) *Secondly, as shown by Figures 1 and 2, they worked at lower luminances.* (10) *Their mean luminance value was 540 cd/m² as opposed to 1462 cd/m² of all the subjects.* (11) *The difference was highly significant at the 0.1 risk level.* (12) *The values of the last group, the aluminum welders, were similar to the mean values of the whole group, except with respect to luminance.* (13) *Their mean luminance value of 401 cd/m² was similar to that of young workers, being thus lower than that of the group as a whole.* (14) *The difference from the total group mean was again highly significant at the 0.1 risk level.*

(15) *One of the aims of the questionnaire was to find out what type of a helmet the welders used and whether they found the helmet satisfactory.* (16) *Two major types were found; 69% of the subjects used a fiber-board type welding helmet and 31% a fiberglass type.* (17) *As to workers' assessment of their helmets, it was found that only 21% were fully content with the type they were using.* (18) *The disadvantages associated with the most common type, the fiber-board helmet, were that it lacked space inside and that its edges tended to bend outward when the helmet got wet.* (19) *The advantage of this type was considered to be its lightness.* (20) *In contrast, the fiberglass type was found to be heavy.* (21) *Furthermore, the workers complained that it did not protect their necks adequately.* (22) *Therefore eight of the welders had mounted a piece of leather on the lower edge of the welding helmet to give their necks better protection from radiation.* (23) *In addition, the welders wee generally highly satisfied with those helmets which had a liquid crystal filter.* (24) *The filter transmits visible light and darkens within 3–10 ms after the arc ignition.*

485–86

Figure 1   Three different versions of a results section of a scientific paper: Version 1 is in the original text written by a Finn; Version 2 is a revised version by a native English speaker; and Version 3 is a version revised by Ventola and Mauranen. (From "Non-native Writing and Native Revising of Scientific Articles," by Ventola and Mauranen, in Functional and Systemic Linguistics, *edited by E. Ventola, © Mouton de Gruyter, a division of Walter de Gruyter & Co., 1991, pp. 482–486. Reprinted by permission.)*

8 Genre-specific studies in contrastive rhetoric

Contrastive rhetoric studies of the 1960s, 1970s, and early 1980s focused on expository essay writing by ESL students. In the 1980s, however, student essays written for other aims, such as narration and argument, were analyzed cross-culturally. More recently, contrastive rhetoric has expanded to examine other modes and domains in addition to student writing. For example, important cross-cultural research examines writing in academic and workplace situations for specific tasks, such as the writing of research reports and abstracts, articles, grant proposals, and business letters. This chapter examines the relevant concept of genre. Then the findings of contrastive rhetoric studies are reviewed in three domains: student writing at the primary, secondary, and college level; academic writing; and professional writing, a category that includes political writing. Finally, how students learn to write in an academic environment is discussed.

The concept of genre

In the 1990s, the concept of "genre" has become a significant issue in applied linguistics. Dissatisfied with linguistic and rhetorical definitions such as Biber's (1988) linguistic analysis or Kinneavy's (1971) rhetorical study, experts in genre analysis have defined genre as a linguistic realization of some social activity. Perhaps Swales's (1990b) genre analysis, developed for the examination and teaching of academic discourse, has become best known. Swales's analysis is based on the examination of constituent parts or "moves" in written academic writing, especially the organization of the content of research papers. Another approach to genre is that of Berkenkotter and Huckin (1993). This approach, emphasizing the social and communicative aspects of writing, is also significant for contrastive studies.

In *Genre Analysis: English in Academic and Research Settings* (1990b), 58), Swales provides a definition of genre which focuses on the communicative purpose of discourse:

A genre comprises a class of communicative events, the members of which share some set of communicative purposes. These purposes are recognized by the expert members of the parent discourse community, and thereby constitute the rationale for the genre. This rationale shapes the schematic structure of discourse and influences and constrains choice of content and style. Communicative purpose is both a privileged criterion and one that operates to keep the scope of a genre as here conceived narrowly focused on comparable rhetorical action. In addition to purpose, exemplars of a genre exhibit various patterns of similarity in terms of structure, style, content and intended audience. If all high probability expectations are realized, the exemplar will be viewed as prototypical by the parent discourse community. The genre names inherited and produced by discourse communities and imported by others constitute valuable ethnographic communication, but typically need further validation.

Important in Swales's definition is the centrality of a discourse community whose members agree upon the acceptable features of specific genres. According to Swales, research articles, presentations, grant proposals, and books all represent different genres because their sets of communicative purposes, hence their schematic structures, are different. A genre in Swales's definition differs from a linguistic "register" in that genre sets structural conditions on the different parts of a text, such as its beginning, body, and ending, whereas registers set the overall correlation of linguistic features with appropriate contextual and situational features, usually on a continuum of stylistic formality-informality. Thus the language of scientific reporting often (but not always) represents a different register from that of a newspaper columnist, but the two genres employ quite different schematic structures imposed by expert members of their discourse communities.

Bhatia's (1993) work on genre adds to the discussion an important consideration, that of subgenres within genres, which differ because of their different communicative purposes and the different strategies writers use to accomplish these purposes. Thus the research article, considered as a genre, has several subgenres such as a survey article, a review article, and a state-of-the-art article. Letters of application and sales letters similarly belong to the same genre, promotional writing. The communicative purpose of both subgenres is to persuade prospective employers or buyers about the value of the application or sale.

Swales's and Bhatia's approaches to genre contribute to categorical discriminations among discourse forms. Briggs and Bauman (1992) point out that such definitions of genre are influenced by the categorical orientation toward genres laid down by Aristotle in *Poetics*. Aristotle asserted that distinctions such as "epic" and "tragedy" are based on the way epics and tragedies are organized, presented, and received, and he suggested that rules and conventions impose structural and content-based constraints on the writing of these genres.

Definitions have also been proposed that consider genres as dynamic, social texts. These definitions help describe how writers utilize genre knowledge as they engage in writing reports, research proposals, and articles in their academic and professional situations. The approach that sees genres as dynamic, social texts emerges from diverse fields such as literary theory. Bakhtin, the early twentieth-century Russian literary theorist, has helped to shape this definition of genre. Briggs and Bauman discuss Bahktin's influence on the definition of genre, which is highly relevant for modern anthropology and linguistics. According to Briggs and Bauman (1992), Bakhtin locates the linguistic dimensions of genres in social groups. Hence, genres are not static, stylistically homogeneous texts. Although texts, according to Bakhtin, have ordered, unified forms (for example, stories have a structure), they are also "intertextual"; that is, texts are ongoing processes of discourse production and reception that are always tied to other texts or utterances in a culture.

Berkenkotter and Huckin (1993), sharing this dynamic view of genre, develop a model that is applicable for the teaching of composition. However, although their work is directed toward teachers and researchers in first language writing, their model of genre is highly relevant for ESL and contrastive rhetoric. Dissatisfied with the "traditional rhetorical approach" to genre, one that makes generalizations about "what some writers refer to as a genre's 'form, substance, and context'" (1993, 476), Berkenkotter and Huckin argue that the knowledge of genre is a "form of situated cognition embedded in disciplinary activities" (1993, 477). According to the authors, "writers acquire and strategically deploy genre knowledge as they participate in their field's or profession's knowledge-producing activities" (1993, 477).

Five principles constitute their theoretical framework: (1) Genres are dynamic rhetorical forms developed as responses to recurrent situations, which change over time in response to users' needs; (2) knowledge of genres is derived from participation in the communicative activities of daily and professional life; (3) this knowledge embraces form and content, including a sense of appropriate topics to write about; (4) through participation in organizational and disciplinary genres, humans constitute social structures and reproduce these as they draw on genre rules while engaging in professional activities, and (5) genre conventions signal the norms and ideologies of a discourse community.

Berkenkotter and Huckin's approach, therefore, locates genre in disciplinary and professional cultures where humans as "social actors" learn, monitor, and reproduce the content and form of language they deem appropriate. Their approach is unique in at least two ways. First, it locates genre knowledge in institutional discourse that involves oral conversations because much academic and professional discourse takes place, in addition to writing and written comments, through hallway chats with colleagues, student-teacher conferences, and peer responses (see principle 2). Second, as stated by principle 3, genre knowledge includes knowledge of content. Often, traditional genre definitions are too general to be able to deal with content. For example, many textbooks describe a format for a typical business letter but give little guidance about content.

An approach to genre that considers genre knowledge as a dynamic, social activity provides a useful framework for describing the process involved in a student's learning of disciplinary genre knowledge. It suggests, among other things, that rather than merely comparing textual features of a student's research paper with a prototype of a research paper of the discipline, we should examine the processes whereby a student acquires genre knowledge. Such a dynamic approach is represented by contrastive research on the acculturation process into academic discourse communities of international graduate students at American universities.

All these approaches are differently useful. However, it should be noted that they depend on working or emergent definitions. "Genre" is not yet a term that can be used to classify all the varieties of writing found in cross-cultural settings. Hence, in this chapter, the term "domain" will sometimes be used to refer to larger contexts in which writing takes place, contexts which, like professional or school writing, may include more than one discourse community.

School writing

School writing, if considered in Swalesean terms as a set of communicative events whose structures are determined by members of a discourse community, has traditionally been concerned about expository (or informative) essay writing. In the United States, the school essay is often called the five-paragraph essay, in which writers first tell the readers what they are going to write about, then develop it in three paragraphs with a main point in each, and finally tell the readers what they have written. Kaplan's first work (1966) dealt with school essays as written by students from various countries, thus as social texts emerging within distinctive cultures as conceived by the Berkenkotter and Huckin model. As examples in Chapter 3 show, Kaplan found that the organization of an expository essay varies in different languages. (See the Chinese eight-legged essay, for example.) It is fair to say that although the organization of the expository essay in different cultures has been investigated in numerous studies, some other aspects of exposition need further examination. For example, we know little about the aspect of choice – about preferences for topics of writing in different cultures. Takala (1983), in a model of writing (Figure 1), suggests four such aspects worth examining: angle, approach, atti-

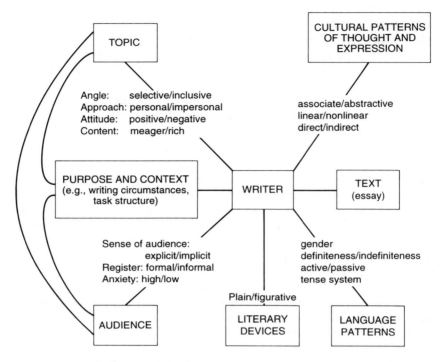

Figure 1   Takala's model of writing (From On the Domain of Writing, *by Takala Vähäpassi, © Institute for Educational Research, 1983, p. 58. Reprinted by permission.)*

tude, and content. Angle, according to Takala, is either selective or inclusive, approach is personal or impersonal, attitude is negative or positive, and content is meager or rich.

Other types of essays besides expository have also been studied cross-culturally following recent theories of rhetoric that suggest that different skills and strategies are required of students when they write for different purposes or aims. Clearly, students need to learn to use different modes or forms of expression when writing for different purposes.

Contrastive Essay Studies

Contrastive studies of student writing beginning in the 1980s expanded the repertoire of genres studied. For example, essays written for narrative, reflective, and persuasive purposes were compared cross-culturally. Some essay studies, given as examples of the range of school writing in this section, may have been discussed in other contexts in this book. Söter

(1988) examined narratives written by native English-, Arabic-, and Vietnamese-speaking schoolchildren in Australia. She found differences in the structures of their stories that depended on the cultural backgrounds. Though all three groups wrote stories that included setting, character, and action, the order of these elements varied. All three groups placed different emphasis on action. For example, the Vietnamese students were more concerned about context than the Arabic- and native-English-speaking students, whereas the Arabic-speaking students showed a preference for more detailed description. All three groups included a characteristic story opening such as "once upon a time. . . ."

Bickner and Peyasantiwong (1988) examined reflective essays written by Thai and American students. Students were asked to reflect and state their own viewpoints on topics such as whether watching television makes it more difficult to think independently, what the world would look like if the role of women in society really changed, whether preoccupation with possessions prevents people from living freely and nobly, and why many young people find it difficult to talk to and understand middle-aged people. The results showed that the Thai students seemed to consider potential counterarguments more than did the American students. For example, given the topic about teenagers, the Thai students discussed characteristics of teenagers and adults and looked for a common ground, whereas the American students dealt with the topic from the teenagers' point of view. There were differences in language use as well. The Thai students used less colloquial language than did the Americans. The Thai essays were also less personal in style.

Connor and Lauer (1988), using data from the IEA study, analyzed argumentative essays written by high school students in three English-speaking countries. They found no significant difference in the use of the superstructure of arguments (setting–problem–solution–evaluation) among the groups. There was a significant difference, however, on other persuasive variables tested. In the Toulmin analysis of reasoning (claim–data–warrant), the U.S. compositions as one group were significantly lower than the English and New Zealand compositions. Furthermore, the U.S. compositions were significantly lower on the use of persuasive appeals (rationality, credibility, and affectiveness).

Contrastive research dealing with specific genres has also investigated college-level ESL students' writing. A persuasive essay task was used by Crismore, Markkanen, and Steffensen (1993) in a study in which Finnish and American college-level students participated. The two groups of students wrote on different topics, deemed controversial and culturally appropriate. The writing prompt in the United States was "the banning of smoking in public places," and the topic in Finland was "the industrial economic responsibility for environmental damage." The researchers found differences in the use of metadiscoursal strategies: the Finns used more hedging behavior whereas the Americans stated their opinions with less hesitation.

In addition to studying student essays, some researchers have focused on reading-to-write assignments in school settings. Folman and Connor (1992) conducted a study that identified strategies for writing research papers of high school seniors in the United States and Israel. Although the results showed some differences between the two groups (e.g., the U.S. students used more superficial sources as references), the overall finding was that writing a research paper is a difficult task for all high school students. Students' processes, strategies, and final products clearly reflect expectations and standards set by their teachers and national curricula.

In summary, contrastive studies of student writing in school and college contexts have dealt with a variety of genres ranging from exposition to narration and persuasion, as well as reading from sources for writing purposes. The trend toward diversification of text types is positive; studies reflect the demands of school and college writing more accurately than the previous focus on exposition. It needs to be pointed out, however, that only a few isolated studies in contrastive rhetoric have examined each genre, nor have many studies been replicated. In order to learn more about the characteristics of essay genres and students' performance in them cross-culturally, more studies need to be conducted.

Academic writing

Two genres, research articles and grant proposals, are discussed here.

Research articles

Genre analysis helps identify the features of research articles. Swales (1981) investigated forty-eight article introductions, sixteen of which were taken from the "hard" sciences, sixteen from the social sciences, and sixteen from the life and health sciences. He found that the majority of articles followed a four-move pattern as follows: (1) introducing the field, (2) reporting previous research, (3) preparing for present research, and (4) introducing present research.

Swales's "moves" [or slight adaptations of them such as Swales 1990b; or Weissberg and Buker (1990)] seem to be present both in "hard" science as in well as social science articles. Figure 2 presents my analysis of the four moves in the introductions of two articles: a research report article, "Ethanol Patch Test – A Simple and Sensitive Method for Identifying ALDH Phenotype," in *Alcoholism: Clinical and Experimental Research;* and a research review article, "Ethnography in ESL: Defining the Essentials," in the *TESOL Quarterly.*

I.   Many Orientals exhibit a flushing response after ingesting a small amount of ethanol. This is characterized by flushing of the face and other parts of the body, tachycardia, headache, dizziness, nausea, etc.

II. The flushing phenomenon has received considerable attention in an attempt to explain the lower incidence of alcoholism among Orientals. Recently it was found that the response is caused by a high blood acetaldehyde concentration due to the lack of low K_m-aldehyde dehydrogenase (ALDH I). In Japan, lack of this isozyme was seen in 41% of the normal population but it was found in only 2% of alcoholics. Hence it is speculated that ALDJ isozymes might play a protective role against alcoholism. To confirm this hypothesis, further epidemiological studies in diverse racial populations concerning the isozyme patterns and drinking behaviors are needed.

III. At present, however, special techniques and large samples of hair roots are required to detect the presence of the ALDH I isozyme, and large-scale mass examinations have not been performed.

IV. Accordingly, a problem requiring further study is how to identify simply and appropriately each individual's ALDH phenotype. Although some studies using a flushing questionnaire were conducted, the relation between the self-reported flushing response and ALDH phenotype has not been demonstrated. Recently Wilkin et al. reported that individuals who flush after oral alcohol intake are more likely to have cutaneous erythema after topical ethanol application. We investigated the relation between this cutaneous reaction (ethanol patch test) and the ALDH phenotype, and part of that work was published previously. The purpose of the present paper is to confirm the reliability and utility of the ethanol patch test. Using a larger number of Japanese subjects we performed the acute ethanol patch test as well as a flushing questionnaire survey, and compared the results with the ALDH phenotype.

I.   Classroom research in ESL, second language acquisition, and bilingual education has drawn on a variety of research methodologies over the past decade (for reviews, see Allwright 1983; Chaudron 1986; 1987; Gaies 1983; Long 1980; Mitchell 1985). Recently, ethnographic methods have become fashionable in both educational and ESL research. Ethnography has been greeted with enthusiasm because of its promise for investigating issues difficult to address through experimental research, such as sociocultural processes in language learning, how institutional and societal pressures are played out in moment-to-moment classroom interaction, and how to gain a more holistic perspective on teacher-student interactions to aid teacher training and improve practice.

II. Yet an understanding of what constitutes high-quality, scientific ethnographic work has not kept pace with ethnography's increasing popularity in ESL. For some, *ethnography* has become a synonym for qualitative research, so that any qualitative approach may be called ethnographic in whole or part, as long as it involves observation in nonlaboratory settings. Some qualitative or "naturalistic" studies are structured by coding schemes based on predetermined categories. Others involve impressionistic accounts and very short periods of observation (e.g., Lightfoot 1983). The superficial nature of many studies, which caricature rather than characterize teaching-learning settings, has led Rist (1980) to call them "blitzkrieg ethnography": The researcher "dive-bombs" into a setting, makes a few fixed-category or entirely impressionistic observations, then takes off again to write up the results.

III. If impressionistic accounts are not ethnography—and they are not—what *is* ethnography? What constitutes a methodological framework for ethnographic study? Why should we study second language learning and teaching ethnographically?

IV. The purpose of this article is to address these questions through an overview of some essential characteristics of ethnography. It is not my intent to critique existing studies or to conduct a comprehensive review of the ethnographic literature. Instead, ethnography as a research perspective and method is outlined, and ways in which ethnography can serve second language learning and teaching are suggested.

Figure 2 Sample "Moves" analyses in article introductions. (From "Ethanol patch test: a simple and sensitive method for identifying ALDH Phenotype," by Taro Muramatsu et al., in Alcoholism: Clinical and Experimental Research, 13, 2, *© Williams and Wilkins, 1989 p. 229; and* TESOL Quarterly, 22, 4, *© Teachers of English to Speakers of Other Languages, Inc., 1988, pp. 575–576. Reprinted by permission.)*

In 1990, to emphasize the theory that the article introduction is meant to explain research motivation and justify publication, Swales revised his earlier four-move model and developed his three-move, "Create a Research Space" (CARS) model, as follows: (1) establish a territory, (2) establish a niche, and (3) occupy the niche. Contrastive studies have employed one or the other of Swales's models to examine whether the prototypical introduction exists universally. Lopez (1982) analyzed a corpus of twenty-one articles from Latin-American journals in a range of fields published in Spanish and found that establishing a niche occurred only in twelve articles. Najjar (1990) examined forty-eight article introductions in Arabic in agricultural sciences. Of them, twenty-seven fit the CARS model and of these only thirteen included establishing a niche. Finally, Taylor and Chen (1991) analyzed science papers by Chinese and Anglo-American researchers and found that the Chinese scholars, writing both in English and in Chinese, omitted or truncated the step of reviewing previous research in the move of establishing territory. Taylor and Chen offer interesting speculations such as that there may be a lack of bibliographic resources in China or that Chinese scholars are reluctant to discuss the work of colleagues for fear of rendering that work subject to exposure in subsequent descriptions of the gaps between established and new territory. (Taylor and Chen's study is discussed in more detail in Chapter 3.)

Grant proposals

Grant proposals are an important genre in many academic disciplines. Grant proposals are particularly important in experiment-based disciplines such as biology (Myers 1985; 1990) and engineering (Johns 1993). Applied linguist Greg Myers has described grant writing as "the most basic form of scientific writing: the researchers must get money in the first place if they are to publish articles and popularizations, participate in controversies, and be of interest to journalists" (1990, 41). According to Myers, every sentence in a proposal is meant to persuade, and, "In classical rhetorical terms, the forms of appeals in the proposal are ethical and pathetic as well as logical; one shows that one is able to do work, and that the work is potentially interesting to one's audience of other researchers, as well as showing that one is right" (42).

Myers reports on the processes of proposal writing by two U.S. biologists. In one case, several proposals were submitted to several agencies over the course of 18 months; in the other, drafts of one proposal were analyzed over the course of 10 months. Myers' analysis reveals that the rhetoric of proposals varies from one discipline to another and depends on the researcher's relation to the discipline. For example, a well-known researcher's arguments are different in tone from a newcomer's arguments. Meyers makes an interesting point about the learning process related to scientific writing and proposals in particular: "Scientists learn the rhetoric of their discipline in their training as graduate and postdoctoral students, but they relearn it every time they get the referees' reports on an article or the pink sheets on a proposal" (61).

The significance of Myers's work is that he legitimizes the study of proposals as a genre. Also, his notion about the idiosyncratic nature of proposals from one discipline to another is noteworthy; it is in contrast to the position of other linguists, who argue that there are universal patterns in genres that are teachable across disciplines – for example, the teachability of the moves in research articles (Swales 1990b).

Johns (1993) discusses the proposal writing strategies of two bilingual engineers in the United States. She focuses on the issue of audience in proposals and concludes that successful grant writers need to be well aware of their real readers' (i.e., grant reviewers and panel members') agendas; these writers have to talk like experienced engineering researchers. According to Johns's informants, grammatical correctness, however, is not required by the reviewers. Almost every sentence in the engineers' successful grant proposals had an error such as the third-person singular present tense -*s* and the plural -*s* morpheme. It needs to be noted that Johns did not examine proposals written by the informants; her data included only interviews with the researchers, which did not seem to be discourse based.

The genre of grant writing is an important area of research for contrastive rhetoricians interested in the academic writing of advanced-level writers. Establishing prototypical structures of grant proposals as well as their variations depending on situations and contexts seems to be a worthwhile area of inquiry. The interrelations between genre knowledge and language proficiency are particularly worthy investigations in the realm of contrastive rhetoric.

Professional writing

With the globalization of business and other professional communications, writing in such metaprofessional genres as letters, résumés, and job applications for readers with a different language and cultural background than one's own is a reality for more and more people. It has been found that in these contexts, too, second language writers transfer patterns and styles from the first language to the second. Predictably, differing reader expectations cause misunderstandings. For example, requests in letters can be made too directly when directness is more esteemed in the first language than in the second. Résumés also differ in style cross-culturally and even intraculturally, as in the difference between the functional résumé and the traditional résumé in the United States.

A significant contribution to the theoretical framework of professional writing comes from the research of Swedish linguist Britt-Louise Gunnarsson. The leader of numerous projects on the language of professional writing, Gunnarsson describes her comprehensive model of professional communication in a report titled "Research on language for specific purposes in the past and in the future" (1993). Gunnarsson's model emphasizes the intertwinement of oral and written discourse and distinguishes three layers in the construction of professional discourse: cognitive, social and societal. The cognitive layer deals with the knowledge base of the field related to language, discourse, attitudes, and norms. The social and societal layers focus on the role of group identity and the roles of professionals within society.

Knowledge about genre-specific professional writing has been advanced significantly by Bhatia (1993). Bhatia's discussion of the theories of genre analysis and their applications in various settings is thorough. Examples are provided from the domains of academic research writing, legal discourse, and, most relevant here, businesses settings. Emphasizing the fact that the communicative purpose of a genre is the most important factor in genre identification, Bhatia takes examples from "two seemingly different and yet closely related areas of linguistic activity, namely, *product* and *self-advertising* through sales promotion letters and job applications, respectively" (46).

Bhatia argues that although job applications and promotion letters are typically considered two different types of texts, with little in common, when one looks at the communicative purpose of the two kinds of documents, one finds that they have the same communicative purpose – namely, they promote a particular product or service. Both are persuasive, use the same medium, and exploit the same form. The only difference may be that sales letters are usually unsolicited, whereas application letters respond to an announcement.

According to Bhatia's analysis, both types of letters employ the same general moves: establishing credentials, offering incentives, enclosing documents, using pressure tactics, soliciting response, and ending politely. Bhatia provides sample letters and careful discussions of the language use in the moves. In addition, a discussion of cross-cultural variation in letters of job application is offered based on some 200 applications for jobs and scholarships from India, Pakistan, Sri Lanka, and Bangladesh. Bhatia discusses how the function of the job application differs in South Asia from the Western model. The main function of a Western job application letter is to highlight and make relevant the qualifications and experience of the applicant to the specifications of the job, that is, to provide a self-appraisal. In Bhatia's sample from South Asia, however, many applicants used the cover letter just to enclose the *curriculum vitae,* without taking the opportunity to offer self-appraisal in order to persuade the reader about their strong application. Instead, many applicants, particularly those applying for scholarships, used strategies such as "self-glorification," "adversary glorification," target glorification," and "self-degradation." These latter strategies are interpreted as too "emotional" by the Western reader, who uses and expects self-appraisal in a "logical" manner.

Bhatia provides a useful model for analyzing promotional letters, and his work needs to be replicated in other cultures.

Professional writing takes place in businesses, newspaper offices, governmental agencies, and other workplaces. It is different from academic writing, involving different purposes and audiences. The concept of professional writing as a legitimate and distinct area of writing and research was reinforced by the publication of a significant anthology by Odell and Goswami (1985). The book is an excellent introduction to the theory and practice of professional writing and offers valuable information about how to conduct research on it, discussing what researchers have found about professional writing habits and practices in many contexts including business and engineering, suggesting how to set up classes in professional writing, and outlining how educational institutions and businesses can work together through consulting and research practices.

The next section discusses briefly the findings of cross-cultural research related to business communication, specifically letters, and three other genres of professional writing, editorials, résumés, and political writing.

Business writing

Business writing was recently defined by Yli-Jokipii (1991, 62) as covering at least the following areas: corporate communication, organizational communication, managerial communication, administrative or governmental communication, and technical communication. Earlier, Zak and Dudley-Evans (1986, 59) described written communication in business as consisting of letters, documents, memos, and telexes.

As Yli-Jokipii and Zak and Dudley-Evans show, there is relatively little linguistically oriented research on business communication cross-culturally. Furthermore, the sparse literature on cross-cultural business communication has been disappointing. After conducting a literature search on cross-cultural business writing, I concluded that much of the literature was in the form of opinions and anecdotes rather than findings based on empirical evidence (Connor 1988, 59). A great deal of the research has relied on examples from business writing textbooks. Experts in business writing echo the sentiments of applied linguists about the quality and scope of international research. In a review, Moran and Moran (1985) complain that:

. . a surprisingly small amount of serious research has been done on business correspondence. Most of the work published during the last 25 years has been redundant and derivative. Instead of designing innovative research projects, writers in the field have tended either to rely on a kind of folk wisdom handed down from generation to generation of writers or to depend on rather limited personal experience. This has led to a great deal of repetition in published articles. (313)

In another review article, business writing experts Limaye and Victor (1991) criticize the current U.S.-based research for its theoretical weakness and false assumptions about comparability.

Four published studies on international business writing are worth describing here: Jenkins and Hinds (1987), Connor (1988), Maier (1992), and Yli-Jokipii (1994). Jenkins and Hinds (1987) compared the genre of business letter writing in Japanese, English, and French. They found that the American English business letter is reader oriented, the French business letter is writer oriented, and the Japanese is "non-person-oriented, reflecting an overall tendency to frame communication in terms of the relationship between people rather than in terms of the people" (1987, 330).

According to Jenkins and Hinds, American business letter writers attempt to convince the reader that what the writer wants is in the reader's best interest. The writer's responsibility is to analyze the rhetorical situation from the reader's perspective and adjust the format, choice of language, and content accordingly. American English business letters are formal, yet friendly. However, their formality does not include an extensive use of the passive voice, nor does their friendliness extend itself to an extensive use of the pronoun, "I."

The French business letter, in contrast, is writer oriented. According to Jenkins and Hinds, "the primary virtues of the French business letter are prudence, conciseness, and precision" (1987, 333). Rarely is there an attempt to personalize or to establish a friendly tone. Requests are made in the writer's, not the reader's, terms. As a reason for the conciseness and impersonal flavor, Hinds and Jenkins mention the expectation that business letters could serve as legal recourses in case of disputes.

Japanese business letter writing, on the other hand, is neither writer nor reader oriented. It is oriented toward the space or relationship between the writer and the reader. The format, content, and style help establish or maintain this relationship. Stock phrases and formulas are typical throughout the letter with the exception of the body. Adherence to formulaic language, often selected from books, helps maintain the appropriateness of the relationship. Formal language is typical.

The structure of the Japanese business letter also differs from that of the American and French, in that seasonal greetings are expressed in addition to salutation and personal greetings. Typically, the seasonal

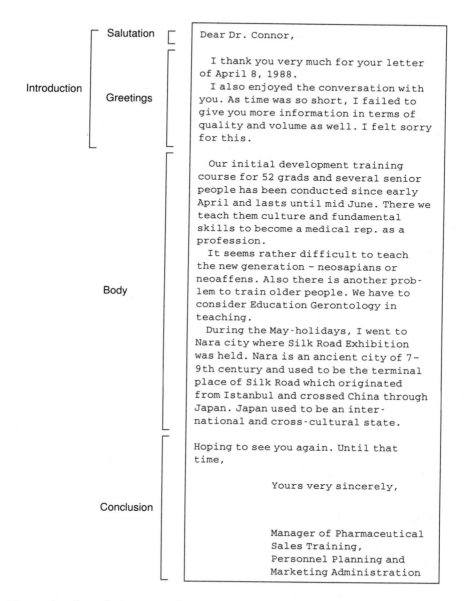

Figure 3   Sample Japanese letter (in Connor, 1988)

greeting appears in the introduction, preceded by the salutation, followed by personal greetings. Body and conclusion follow the introduction.

Figure 3 is a letter written by a Japanese business manager after a personal meeting I had with him. He had been an informant in a research study on Japanese–American business negotiations. The letter is a polite thank-you letter in response to my short letter thanking him for the interview. The tone of the letter is informative, continuing some of the discussion we had had. The letter includes an introduction with salutation ("Dear Dr. Connor") and greetings, body, and conclusion, as is the norm. The seasonal greeting, however, appears at the end of the body rather than in the introduction ("During the May-holidays, I . . ."). The Japanese manager's extensive experience with American English correspondence may have affected the out-of-the norm placement of the seasonal greeting, yet its mere existence is significant, confirming the results of Jenkins and Hinds's study.

The tone and formality of the exchange also echo Jenkins and Hinds's findings. The Japanese manager greets me politely: "I also enjoyed the conversation with you. As time was short, I failed to give you more information in terms of quality and volume as well. I felt sorry for this." His conclusion is also polite and formal: "Hoping to see you again. Until that time, Yours very sincerely."

With contrastive rhetoric research extending beyond exposition to other genres, persuasion and argumentation in both Japanese and English of native Japanese speakers has attracted attention. Connor (1988) examined the written correspondence between a Japanese and an American manager for marketing training of a large U.S. pharmaceutical company during a 2-year period. In the study, forty-seven documents of written correspondence (letters, faxes, and electronic mail messages) were analyzed for directness and concern for interpersonal harmony. The findings showed that the American manager did not hesitate to suggest changes and even improvements by openly criticizing the Japanese manager. The Japanese manager, on the other hand, used subtle ways of saying "no."

In addition to examining general patterns of communication throughout the interchange, the study analyzed in detail an important report written by the Japanese manager. The report was studied for its argumentative strategies. It employed a Japanese style of argument, as outlined by Hazen (1987). Hazen claims that Japanese argument differs from Western argument mainly because a Japanese claim is often stated indirectly, and the evidence and data for an argument are seldom expressed explicitly. In addition, the Japanese are said to make greater use of qualifiers and rebuttals. Using the terminology of Toulmin et al., qualifiers of an argument refer to the "strength or weakness, conditions, and/or limitations with which a claim is advanced" (1979, 79). These qualifiers often take the form of modal qualifiers, such as "necessarily," "certainly," "very likely," "plausibly," "maybe," and "so far as the evidence goes." Rebuttals, according to Toulmin and his associates, often occur in the conclusion and refer to "the extraordinary circumstances that might undermine the force of supporting arguments" (1979, 75).

"It is by all means impossible to achieve the 390-hour curricula of the training course by only three full-time training staffers with one part-time assistant."

"We cannot but be receptive to some inconveniences until our [subsidiary] has its own training facilities, sometime in the future."

"One thing to be improved in the future might be to develop more practical videotapes related to drug product detailings to supplement rather than general ones currently available."

"One thing to be considered in the future is to have if the situation allows, two visiting days per one trainee; one at the middle of the training period and the other toward the end."

Figure 4   Sample arguments in a Japanese manager's report (From "A Contrastive Study of Persuasive Business Correspondence," by Connor, in Global Implications for Business Communications, *edited by Sam Bruno, © University of Houston–Clear Lake, 1988, p. 68. Reprinted by permission.)*

An illustration of an argument that led to a misunderstanding was found in the report, which explained a marketing training session for new salespeople in Japan. In the report, written by the Japanese manager, the claim was not stated directly. Instead of arguing directly for extra funding, the manager only *suggested* extra funding and facilities. As Figure 4 shows, tentative expressions were used to ask for more inside lecturers, better personalized videotape programs, better training facilities, and easier access to sites to be visited. Several hedges and modifiers were employed: "by all means impossible," "some inconveniences," "sometime in the future," "might be," and "if the situation allows."

The reaction to the report by the American manager and his superior was negative. The Americans did not seem to take the Japanese manager's requests seriously. Instead, they refused to go along with his recommended improvements. In their response, they made statements such as "[we are] increasingly concerned about the escalating costs of training," "the proposed out-of-pocket modifications cannot be financed by the company," and "the balance of our resources and our needs is and will continue to be an important function for all of us." Specific recommendations made by the American manager were expressed in the imperative mode: "shorten the length of training," "reduce the involvement of outside lecturers." Perhaps the most critical point about the response was that it included no positive feedback.

Maier (1992) examined politeness strategies in letters written by eight native speakers and ten nonnative speakers in response to a fictional situation in which they had unavoidably missed a job interview and were requesting another interview. The native speakers used more negative politeness strategies such as apologies, were more indirect, and deferred to the reader more often than the nonnative speakers did. The nonnative speakers used positive politeness strategies and were more informal and direct in their language. The author suggests that "business writing in English by non-native speakers, even that which is grammatically flaw-less, may be perceived negatively by the reader because of the inappropri-ate use of politeness strategies" (1992, 189).

The most comprehensive linguistic study of real-life business letters, whose function is the request, is the dissertation of Hilkka Yli-Jokipii at the University of Turku in Finland (1994). The data consisted of 525 letters collected over several years from a number of English, American, and Finnish companies. All letters involved "interactive" communica-tion; they included requests in an ongoing business relationship involving real writers and readers. In the study, a "letter" was defined simply as a document that identified the addressee in the salutation, the writer in the signature, and the time of writing in the date. The real-life material represented ten broad lines of business, from large multinational com-panies to small family businesses. In addition, letters from British and American textbooks were analyzed.

The study analyzed requests and their linguistic realizations in the letters using a systematic framework in which forms were studied to-gether with their functions. A multilevel analysis including syntax, se-mantics, and pragmatics examined the politeness of the requests. Power relationships – subsidiary and headquarters, boss and employee – and levels of acquaintance, from casual to intimate, were noted.

The results showed that American requests were more explicit than British ones, yet the American letters attempted a reader perspective whereas the British letters favored a writer perspective. Differences were also found in the business letters in textbooks. Yli-Jokipii found that American textbook letters included bolder requesting tactics than were found in the real sample. The British textbook letters included safe, rou-tinized, formulaic ways of requesting.

From a cross-linguistic point of view, Yli-Jokipii's findings about Fin-nish- vs. English-language letters are noteworthy. The Finnish letters differed greatly from those of the other two cultural groups. They used implicit requests and employed evasive devices, such as refraining from indicating who should perform the requested action, using the name of the company instead of the name of the reader, and generally avoided the implication of human agents. The Finnish letters included deferential, respectful politeness, which did not impose on the reader and allowed the reader the opportunity to say no. In addition, the Finnish letters showed a reluctance to use "I" and an aversion to challenge the reader.

The study is significant in a number of ways. First, it includes a unique database, being the only good-sized databank of real-life business letters. Second, it provides an innovative system of analysis of requests, replica-ble in other languages. Finally, it adds another genre to research concerning differences between Finnish and English language use. A great deal of previous sociolinguistic research has described Finns as shy, or as "silent" (Lehtonen and Sajavaara 1985). Yli-Jokipii's findings suggest that Finns, at least when writing business letters, are not "silent" in the negative connotation of the term, but instead are nonintrusive and deferential.

Editorials

In most newspapers, the purpose of editorials is to influence the opinions of readers on some controversial issue. Nonnative speakers of English seldom need to write newspaper editorials in English, which may explain the relatively small set of published work on cross-cultural differences in editorials. The research that has been done in this area is important, however, because editorials, perhaps more than any other type of writing, reflect national styles regarding modes of persuasion.

Two studies are relevant: Dantas-Whitney and Grabe (1989) and Tirkkonen-Condit and Liefländer-Koistinen (1989). Dantas-Whitney and Grabe (1989) compared editorial texts in Brazilian, Portugese, and English. Twenty editorials were compared for fifteen linguistic variables. A significant difference was found on one dimension, presentation of information, which included six text features: use of nominalizations, prepositions, third-person singular, pronouns, and locative adverbs. The English texts used a more formal, detached style than the Portuguese editorials; they used more nominalizations and prepositions, whereas the Portuguese texts used more personal aspects of texts such as third-person singular and pronouns. The research was exploratory and used Biber's (1988) system, developed for English language studies, which may jeopardize the norms of comparability. The features and dimensions are based on analyses of large sets of English texts. Thus the six variables representing "presentation of information" in terms of formality and informality describe the phenomenon in English-language texts. As Lux and Grabe point out, there is a "need to perform multivariate analyses on large sets of Portuguese texts to determine whether or not a model of factor dimensions for Portuguese texts would look similar to the textual dimensions for English" (1991, 166).

Another study about cross-cultural differences in editorials is Tirkkonen-Condit and Liefländer-Koistinen's study of Finnish, English, and German editorials (1989), in which the authors compared the strength and placement of the main claim or argument of an editorial. They found that Finnish editorials were different from the others in that the Finnish editorials did not always argue a point a view, but rather informed. The desire to build consensus rather than divide was the stated policy of the newspaper. The German editorials placed the argument statement at the beginning of the editorial more often than the English newspaper did, whereas the Finnish editorials had no argument statement.

Research on editorials cross-culturally is significant even if ESL students do not become editorial writers for, in most cases, they are readers of editorials. Good editorials are considered some of the best examples of persuasive writing in all countries; they set standards for written persuasion. At the present time, little is known cross-culturally about the genre.

Résumés

Standards for résumés seem to vary from culture to culture, but no published research exists on the topic. At Indiana University in Indianapolis, a project on international business communication (the Indianapolis-Antwerp-Turku Project) is collecting student-written résumés and job application letters for fictional business jobs in Indianapolis (United States), Antwerp (Belgium), and Turku (Finland). For the past few years, students in business writing classes have collaborated in writing, reviewing, and critiquing résumés and applications letters. Connor, Davis, and De Rycker, in press, compare the functional components of letters of job applications written by U.S. and Belgian business students in the sample.

Differences in résumé writing may be worth investigating across several cultures. To illustrate and perhaps support this assertion, I would like to share a cross-cultural résumé writing exercise developed in a class at the summer TESOL institute in Bratislava, Czechoslovakia, in 1992. For a project on cross-cultural differences in résumé writing, Ildikó Melis, a Hungarian ESL instructor, and Steen Spove, a U.S. EFL instructor, collaborated and prepared two hypothetical résumés for a Hungarian undergraduate student, Istvan Horvath. Figure 5 (on pages 146 and 147) shows the two résumés, one in a Hungarian style, the other in a U.S. style. The differences between the two versions are immense. The résumé developed for an American setting is short and plays up Horvath's accomplishments. The résumé written for the Hungarian context takes a narrative form and includes details that Americans would find superfluous, such as a description of the sweet smell of mom's very special Sunday cookies.

These résumés raise many issues for ESL teachers: the cultural motives of résumé writing, the dimensions of the genre, and the importance of the context. Thus, the Hungarian version of the résumé in Figure 5, even when composed in English, follows the norm expected of Hungarian résumés. This raises an issue important for the future of contrastive studies as well as for the immediate attention of ESL teachers: whose English should be taught – Hungarian English, British English, or American English? The question is complex. I would argue that the audience is the deciding factor, a point of view supported by the theory of "acceptability" deriving from translation studies, discussed in Chapter 7. In summary, cross-cultural research of résumé writing and job applications in a variety of settings (professional and academic) presents a wide-open field for cross-cultural researchers.

Political discourse

Bolivar's (1992) study is a useful introduction to the cross-cultural study of political writing. She defines political discourse "as that related to political activity of a human group, and in consequence, linked with the actions of a government and the power relations that arise between the parties or groups, or between those representing the official power and the other social groups with less power in the same society" (161). Bolivar analyzed hundreds of political texts in a Spanish newspaper in Venezuela over 1 month, 6 months before the end of a political campaign in 1988. These texts were written by candidates to persuade people to vote for them. A multilevel analysis dealt with semantic content, structure, and appeals of arguments. More text in larger sizes with pictures and "artful combination of sequences of acts" were found to be favored by the leading candidates.

It would be interesting to replicate Bolivar's study in another culture in order to compare persuasive strategies. It might be found that even the form of the genre is not comparable. Candidates in other cultures may not be expected to advertise themselves in local newspapers.

Learning academic writing in sociocognitive perspective as a dynamic activity

In this area, research typically employs a case-study approach, with single or relatively few subjects. Data collected include interviews with students or professionals whose learning process is being studied, written products, observations of classrooms or workplaces, and interviews with colleagues and/or supervisors of the subjects. A model of this type of research is a case study conducted by Berkenkotter, Huckin, and Ackerman (1988), who examined the acculturation process of a doctoral student in rhetoric and composition at Carnegie Mellon University in the United States. Their study describes in detail how, in a year's time, the graduate student learned to write to the satisfaction of his professors, abandoning his more personal style and conforming to the demands of the discourse community in composition and rhetoric.

Cross-cultural case studies by Swales (1990b), Connor and Kramer (1995), Belcher (1994), Prior (1995), and Casanave (1995) investigate

```
                        Curriculum Vitae
     István Horváth   Kis utca 6.
                      1042-H Budapest

     Education:
        Eötvös Lorand University, Budapest, 1990-present (English
        major)
        King Laszlo Secondary Grammar School, Debrecen, 1985-1989

     Experiences:
        Hungarian Military Forces, 1989-1990
        IBM computer course, summer 1989
        Advanced Certificate of English, 1988
        Reading knowledge of Russian and French

     Accomplishments:
        Honorable mention of history paper at National Student
        Contest

     References:
        Ildikó Melis, ELTE English Dept. Budapest 1146
          As u. 6.II.9. Phone: 112-34456
        Gareth Dewar, ELTE English Dept. Budapest 1146
          As u. 6.II.9. Phone: 112-34456
```

(a)

*Figure 5   Sample U.S. and Hungarian résumés prepared by Ildikó Melis,
Hungary, and Steen Spove, United States, at TESOL Summer Institute,
Bratislava, Czechoslovakia, 1992.*

Curriculum Vitae

My name is István Horváth. My father is an engineer, my mother a shop-assistant. I have a 17-year-old sister. I was born in Hajduszenas, a small village in North-east Hungary. My village is very small and there is not much in it to be famous for. Yet I have pleasant memories of my childhood years, especially of those afternoons when the summer air was filled with the sweet smell of my mum's very special Sunday cookies.

After my nursery school I went to primary school called Dobo István. I was not an outstanding student, but I liked math, partly because I had a teacher who was more than a teacher: he was also a fantastic human being.

When I was in 8th grade my parents divorced and I and my sister moved to Debrecen with our mum who thought we could get a better education in a big city.

In Debrecen I attended the famous King László Secondary Grammar School. However, I wasn't very happy at first because I missed my friends from the village and often felt like a total stranger in town. It was in this school that I started to learn English and gradually became fond of languages. I also studied Russian and French, but I soon realized that I must specialize if I want to achieve.

Since I was best at history and English, I applied for admission in history and English at Eötvös Loránd University in Budapest. In 1989 I missed the required admission score by two points and of course was immediately conscripted in the army. Before I thought that military service was a necessary and inevitable phase in a boy's life. As my mum would say, the army is where the boy grows into a man. Now I know that it's not true. Unless "growing into a man" means meaningless exercise, drills, humiliation and losing your self-esteem. The only positive effect of that lost year of my life was that I began to work twice as hard as ever before to get admitted by the university, which would shorten my days of ordeal.

Since 1990 I have been the student of Eötvös Loránd University. My history studies are not quite what I had expected so I may drop history next year and become a single-major student in English. I would like to spend as much time to improve my English as possible. That's why I would like to get this scholarship because I believe that I would benefit a lot from direct contact with the target language and culture.

Yours sincerely,

(b)

how international graduate students in a variety of fields at U.S. universities learn to write term papers, reports, and dissertations in their graduate disciplines. (This research was introduced in Chapter 4 in the discussion of writing as a social construction of meaning, and the studies by Belcher, Prior, and Casanave were described there.)

Swales (1990b) conducted three insightful case studies of graduate student writers at a U.S. university – an Egyptian biologist, a Chinese economist, and an Iranian engineer. These case studies reinforce the relevance of discourse communities and reveal the diversity of writing strategies needed to become proficient writers. Despite the diversity, Swales emphasizes the proactive nature of these writers as the key to their success.

Connor and Kramer (1995) studied the task representations of three international graduate students (Belgian, Korean, and Brazilian) and two American graduate students when they read a business case study and wrote policy reports based on it. Through text analyses and interviews with the students and the professor of the business writing class, the authors found that the tasks of reading a long business case study and writing original policy recommendations were daunting for two of the international students. Only one of them, the one with lengthy business experience as well as high language scores, had the confidence to draw the "original" conclusions about the case study that were expected by the professor. The other two students were not successful in making the right choices in how they dealt with the task itself and how they went about it. For example, the international students did not know how to study in groups, nor did they seek advice from the professor. They lacked strategies to construct meaning socially.

In a survey study, Parkhurst (1990) analyzed the writing processes of native and nonnative research scientists and professors writing in English. Both native and nonnative writers agreed that extensive reading, discussing, and writing on scientific topics were needed to learn to write well, but there were differences between the native and nonnative speakers' surveyed processes. In learning to write scientific prose, the nonnative speakers were less likely to seek help from others. Instead, they reported finding "step-by-step" scientific writing assignments useful. Furthermore, they found sentence-level grammar issues to be very important. This latter finding agrees with Connor and Kramer's results but runs counter to Johns's (1993) study about grant proposal writing by two bilinguals. These differences in results may reflect the length of experience in the discipline. Connor and Kramer's subjects were novices, whereas Johns's informants were long-time researchers. Parkhurst, unfortunately, does not report the level of expertise of his subjects.

Research shows that learning academic literacy is a complex, dynamic process, which involves knowledge of discourse conventions as well as topic appropriateness. Expected interactions with professors, supervisors, and colleagues have been found to be important but to differ cross-culturally. Studies have been conducted to examine international students' acculturation into academic discourse communities at U.S. colleges. Few studies have looked at processes of learning genre knowledge by second language academics or professionals in other countries. A fruitful, although labor intensive, area of inquiry awaits.

Summary

Cross-cultural studies of writing have expanded the type of writing analysis from the first analysis of expository student writing to a variety of school writing genres as well as to academic and professional genres. Student writing has been studied for a variety of school purposes, ranging from in-class narrative and argumentative essays to research papers. Attempts have been made to describe prototypes of academic and professional genres such as research papers, résumés, editorials, and business letters. Cross-cultural research has begun to test the universality of these prototypes.

The attention given to genre by both rhetoricians and linguists in the past decade is useful for contrastive rhetoric research. It enables a more focused analysis by offering comprehensive systems of categorizing texts based on their communicative purpose. No longer are apples compared with oranges in contrastive rhetoric; student writing is not juxtaposed with "accomplished" writing. The consideration of genre has also extended contrastive studies to types of writing that had not been studied before, such as business writing, research articles, and résumés. The emphasis is on the communicative writing needs of all ESL learners, not only freshman level English writers but writers in specialized writing classes (e.g., business English), graduate programs, and in the workplace.

Despite the enhanced research activity on genre-specific writing cross-culturally, only a few isolated studies have examined each genre. More studies need to be conducted.

PART III:
IMPLICATIONS OF CONTRASTIVE RHETORIC

9 Methods of research in contrastive rhetoric

Studies of contrastive rhetoric, like a great deal of ESL research, have been interdisciplinary, reflecting the background and research training of the particular researcher. Linguistics, education, discourse analysis, sociolinguistics, and psycholinguistics have affected research approaches. Linguistics has provided tools for the structural analysis of texts, education and psychology have encouraged quantitative experimental methods, and sociolinguistic and anthropological investigations have favored qualitative research methods such as case studies and ethnographies. Early contrastive rhetoric was deeply embedded in an analysis influenced by structural linguistics. More recent contrastive research has been heavily influenced by quantitative and qualitative approaches derived from education, anthropology, and the other disciplines mentioned above.

Guidance from studies of composition pedagogy

Case studies, ethnographies, interviews, and text analyses are often labeled "qualitative" studies, whereas experiments and large-scale surveys are considered quantitative research. Books about research design and methods that explain the distinctions, such as Johnson's *Approaches to Research in Second Language Learning* (1992), are available for the second language teacher and researcher. For the researcher in contrastive rhetoric, treatments of research design by composition specialists may be more relevant. Three recent books devoted to the evolving design of composition research are Lauer and Asher's *Composition Research: Empirical Designs* (1988), Kirsch and Sullivan's *Methods and Methodology in Composition Research* (1992), and Hayes et al.'s *Reading Empirical Research Studies: The Rhetoric of Research* (1992). According to these sources, there is a healthy debate about methodology in composition studies, composition experts agree about the importance of multiple approaches in their research, hence historical, linguistic, philosophical, and rhetorical approaches are all prevalent.

Lauer and Asher's taxonomy of methods of composition designs is a straightforward classification based on educational research. Among empirical, data-bound approaches, Lauer and Asher distinguish between descriptive and experimental designs. There are five different types of descriptive studies in their system:

1. *Case studies* examine closely a small number of individuals and are guided by theory. Data collection methods include observations, interviews, protocols, tests, examination of records, and collection of writing samples.
2. *Ethnographies* engage researchers in a study of writing in a context. Researchers withhold initial judgements and allow data to determine research directions. Data collection includes a rich variety of material such as field notes, interviews, and writing samples.
3. *Surveys* seek information about larger groups, usually by means of sampling techniques.
4. *Quantitative research* is research that "goes beyond case studies and ethnographies to isolate systematically the most important variables developed by these studies, to define them further, and to *quantify* them at least roughly, if not with some accuracy, and to interrelate them" (1988, 82).
5. *Prediction and classification studies* seek to determine the strength of a relationship between several variables and criteria. Quantitative data are collected for predictor variables, and correlations and regression analyses are used.

Lauer and Asher describe two experimental designs, true and quasi-experiments. The features of a true experiment include randomization, treatments, hypotheses, criterion variables and analyses to determine statistical significance and effect size. In contrast, "the quasi-experiment is a research design that uses intact groups, treatment and control to make cause-and-effect statements" (1988, 200). Pretests and posttests are used to determine the equality of the groups.

A system of categories that stems more directly from composition studies than from educational research is a framework developed by Bereiter and Scardamalia (1983). Their system includes six levels of inquiry:

1. Reflective inquiry, which identifies problems and phenomena through observation, introspection, and literature review
2. Empirical variable testing, in which researchers test relationships by using surveys, correlation analysis, and factorial analysis of variance
3. Text analysis, in which researchers use error analysis, story grammar analysis, and thematic analysis to study rules the writer could be following

4. Process description, which tries to account for patterns or systems involved in composing by means of thinking aloud protocols
5. Theory imbedded experimentation
6. Computer simulation and simulation by intervention

Bereiter and Scardamalia's framework is useful because it provides a sequenced progression of research from inquiry to experimentation. Bereiter and Scardamalia favor the experimental approach. They suggest, among other benefits, that case studies will lead to more controlled experimental studies.

Methods of contrastive rhetorical research

The earliest studies of contrastive research were empirical. Based on student data, they were conducted by linguists interested in error and contrastive analyses of languages. In the past few years, contrastive rhetoric research has diversified its methods. Research is conducted by researchers in education such as Purves and Liebman, students of linguistic approaches interested in discourse analysis such as Ventola, Mauranen, Markkanen, and Grabe, and researchers employing anthropological approaches such as Carson.

Using a combined Lauer-Asher and Bereiter-Scardamalia set of categories, this chapter surveys contrastive rhetorical studies. Figure 1 summarizes the methods of research in contrastive rhetoric according to the combined system and includes sample studies.

Reflective inquiry

Reflective inquiries abound in contrastive rhetoric. They can be divided into three categories, depending on the purpose. First, some reflections, such as those of Leki (1991), provide surveys of the field. Second, Kaplan's reflections explain the origins and developments of the field from his unique perspective. Third, in the late 1980s and early 1990s there has been a flurry of activity in contrastive rhetoric, with numerous calls for a paradigm shift in the field by researchers such as Purves (1988), Carson (1992), and Connor (in press).

Kaplan has discussed developments in contrastive rhetoric in a number of publications, ranging from his book-length treatment of early contrastive rhetoric, *The Anatomy of Rhetoric: Prolegomena to a Functional Theory of Rhetoric* (1972), to reflections on the state of the art of contrastive rhetoric in the 1980s. In "Cultural Thought Patterns Revisited" (1987), he reinstates his hypothesis about cultural differences in writing patterns. He also discusses the importance of the study of written texts as

I. *Reflective inquiry* "identifies problems and phenomena through observation, introspection, and literature review" (Bereiter and Scardamalia 1983).

Sample CR studies: Kaplan (1972; 1988); Purves (1988); Leki (1991); Connor (in press)

II. *Quantitative descriptive research* "goes beyond case studies and ethnographies to isolate systematically the most important variables developed by these studies, to define them further, and to *quantify* them at least roughly, if not with some accuracy, and to interrelate them" (Lauer and Asher 1988, 82).

Sample CR studies: text analyses by Kaplan (1966); Ostler (1987); Hinds (1987; 1990); Eggington (1987); Connor (1990a); Crismore et al. (1993)

III. *Prediction and classification studies* "determine the *strength* of a relationship between several variables and a single criterion." (Lauer and Asher 1988, 109).

Sample CR studies: Reid (1992); Connor (1990a)

IV. *Sampling surveys* "Sampling survey research describes a large group, a *population*, of people, compositions, English courses, teachers, or classrooms, in terms of a *sample*, a smaller part of that group" (Lauer and Asher 1988, 54).

Sample CR studies: Liebman (1992)

V. *Case studies and ethnographies* "The case study is a type of qualitative descriptive research that closely examines a small number of subjects, and is guided by some theory of writing" (Lauer and Asher 1988, 33). "Ethnographic research, another kind of qualitative descriptive research, examines entire environments, looking at subjects in context" (Lauer and Asher 1988, 39).

Sample studies (but with no explicit CR hypothesis): Nelson and Murphy (1992); Johns (1991); Connor and Kramer (1995); Connor (1989)

VI. *Experiments (quasi and true)*

Hinds (1984); Eggington (1987); Connor and McCagg (1983)

Figure 1   Summary of methods of research in contrastive rhetoric

a separate inquiry from research on oral language, the focus of traditional linguistic analysis. In addition, Kaplan calls for contrastive rhetorical studies that distinguish among text types – for example, exposition and narration.

In "Contrastive Rhetoric and Second Language Learning: Notes Toward a Theory of Contrastive Rhetoric" (1988), Kaplan makes a number of specific claims about contrastive rhetoric. Notably, he asserts that (1) the primary impetus for contrastive rhetoric is finding solutions to immediate pedagogical problems, which explains why contrastive studies deal with the English writing of non-English students; (2) developments in text analysis have had an impact on the evolution of contrastive rhetoric as a research paradigm and as a useful tool for teachers; (3) because writing should be taught (it is not acquired), contrastive rhetoric strives to determine which of the several functions exists in a particular language as compared to English; and (4) contrastive rhetoric is not a methodology for teaching, even though some of its findings can be applied to the teaching process.

Because many of Kaplan's detractors have judged his work of the 1960s from the perspective of later decades, Kaplan has been put in a defensive position. He apologizes for the simplicity of his 1966 "doodles" article, as he calls it, pointing out that too much was expected of contrastive rhetoric, that it was never meant to be a teaching method, and that it reflected the analytic tools available for linguists at the time. Kaplan's reflections in the 1980s embed contrastive rhetoric deeply in text linguistics. This attracts criticism from many who emphasize the writing process and the sociocultural context of writing. Despite his admission in 1988 of the importance of audience in writing intended for different functions or genres, Kaplan does not seem willing to accept a paradigm of contrastive rhetoric that would extend itself beyond the analysis of written products.

Several researchers have called for the expansion of contrastive rhetoric to include not only the analysis of written products but also an examination of those educational, cognitive, and social dimensions of composition that enter into cross-cultural writing. The most prolific and influential has been Alan Purves, whose IEA study has helped change the new contrastive rhetoric paradigm. In addition to reports of empirical findings from the large-scale study, Purves has published numerous reflective essays on writing across cultures. In the introduction to his edited book on contrastive rhetoric (1988), Purves charts new directions for the discipline as follows: (1) extending the study from textual effects to sociocultural influence in written styles; (2) encouraging a "hybrid" approach to the study of cross-cultural writing that includes linguistics, psychology, and anthropology; and (3) encouraging linguistic approaches in the study of contrastive rhetoric. In several other publications, Purves has expanded on the concept that cultural communities and discourse communities shape the conventions of writing in those communities. Purves and Purves (1986) also focus on cultural communities, as do Purves and Hawisher (1990).

Quantitative descriptive research

Most studies of contrastive rhetoric can be classified as quantitative, descriptive research. Contrastive rhetoric began as the quantifiable analysis of texts. Error analysis was used by Kaplan and his followers, who compared organizational patterns of native and nonnative texts. As discussed in Chapter 3, the first contrastive text analysis dealt with the subordination and coordination of sentences as well as the organization of "discourse blocs." The hypothesis was that second language writers' patterns deviated from the English pattern because of the interference from L1.

In the 1980s a different approach to text analysis took hold. There was an emphasis on more sophisticated discourse analysis methods, which dealt with multiple levels of texts as well as allowed for examining processes of production and comprehension. In addition, researchers began analyzing L1 texts of second language writers. This led to a better appreciation of L1 backgrounds and a search for universals in addition to differences. Hinds (1987; 1990) introduced an approach that relies on a few chosen pieces of "accomplished" writing in a given culture. This approach, which analyzes texts that are presumably typical of a language and culture, is reminiscent of Chomskyan linguistics, which relies on language samples generated by a native speaker.

Kaplan's early studies included large sets of data – there were more than 600 essays in his 1966 study. The reliance on large numbers has continued in many studies of his followers (e.g., Ostler and Grabe), recently aided by the computerized text analyses of Biber (1988). The computerized text analysis developed by linguist Douglas Biber is based on the sociolinguistic principle of co-occurring features. The multifeature/multidimensional approach developed by Biber (1984; 1985; 1986; 1987; 1988) was designed to study variation of textual features among texts. This approach uses computer programs for frequency counts of linguistic features and multivariate statistical techniques to analyze co-occurrence patterns among linguistic features in texts.

Based on Biber's dissertation research, and explained in detail in a book (Biber 1988), the approach assumes that there is no single parameter of linguistic variation that distinguishes among different types of texts. Instead, Biber's approach seeks to describe systematically the linguistic characteristics of different types of texts in English and to explain variation in text types using a key notion of his framework, "textual dimension." According to Biber, "dimensions are bundles of linguistic features that co-occur in texts because they work together to mark some common underlying function" (1988, 55). Scientific texts, for example, differ in the dimension of formality versus informality when compared to conversations. Accordingly, frequency counts within dimensions show that when a text has many passives, it also has many nominalizations, as in a scientific text. Contrastingly, when a text has few passives, as in a conversational text, it also has few nominalizations. Thus, dimensions encompass features that consistently occur together and that consistently complement one another.

The identification of dimensions in Biber's research is unique in that frequency counts of particular features in texts were first used to identify the groups of features that co-occur in texts, and only afterward were these groupings interpreted in functional terms as dimensions. All previous research had started with speculative, functional terms, thus bypassing the empirical first step, which is a bottom–up distinguishing of dimensional chunks.

To examine variation in speech and writing in English texts, Biber (1988) analyzed sixty-seven different linguistic features in 481 texts. These analyses identified the following initial list of functional dimensions: informal/formal, restricted/elaborated, contextualized/decontextualized, involved/detached, integrated/fragmented, abstract/concrete, and colloquial/literary. After the initial functional interpretation of the dimensions, Biber used factor analysis to identify a grouping of linguistic features that co-occur with a high frequency along each dimension.

Several previous studies by Biber using a multifeature/multidimensional approach to identify textual dimensions in speech and writing in English texts have identified three primary dimensions of linguistic variation among texts in English. To reflect their underlying functions, Biber labeled these dimensions as dimension 1: interactive vs. edited text, dimension 2: abstract vs. situated content, and dimension 3: reported vs. immediate style.

Biber's analysis has been used in contrastive rhetoric research by Grabe and Biber (1987), Dantas-Whitney and Grabe (1989), and Connor (1995). Dantas-Whitney and Grabe's study of editorials was discussed in Chapter 8. Connor applied the Biber model to persuasive essays written by high school students in England, New Zealand, and the United States. Two of Biber's dimensions – interactive vs. edited features and abstract vs. situated context – were examined.

The results showed that the American essays used more interactive style and had a large number of features such as "that" clauses, first- and second-person pronouns, contractions, and subordinate clauses. The British and New Zealand essays, on the other hand, had lower mean scores along this dimension, associated with greater lexical variety (shown by a higher type/token ratio), indicating a carefully produced, noninteractive style. The difference between the American essays on one hand and the British and New Zealand essays on the other was statistically significant.

There was a significant difference in the holistic ratings among students from the three countries. The Scheffé post hoc test showed that American students were significantly lower than the other two groups combined, whereas there was no significant difference between the English and New Zealand students. The raters tended to rate compositions more highly if they were less involved and more carefully edited and if they were more abstract and formal.

Interestingly, the differences found here are very similar to those found by Biber (1987) in a comparison of nine British and American written genres: American genres consistently use more colloquial and interactive features than British genres do, and American genres consistently use a more nominalized style than British genres. It was suggested in that study that both of these differences reflect a greater awareness of and concern about the forms of "good" writing in British English.

The strengths of Biber's multidimensional analysis are discussed by Grabe (1987), who points out that Biber's analysis is a needed beginning for any contrastive research in that it allows for a more accurate description of text types. Furthermore, the computerized nature of the analysis allows for the handling of large data sets.

Text analyses have always been at the core of contrastive rhetorical research, whether of large or small data sets. Such analyses have helped identify patterns favored by writers in a certain culture. In addition, advances made in text analytic procedures in the past couple of decades have enabled researchers conducting surveys, correlations, or experimental studies to use textual variables as measures of dependent and independent variables (Connor and Lauer 1988). Of course, such analyses have been criticized. As with criticisms associated with other descriptive research, it is asserted, for example, that research formulates hypotheses but does not help establish relationships, let alone establish causal relationships.

Prediction and classification studies

Reid's (1992) computerized text analysis of four cohesion devices in English text essays by native and nonnative writers (Arabic, Chinese, and Spanish) provides an example of empirical variable testing. The study analyzed coordinate conjunctions, subordinate conjunction openers, (i.e., first words in sentences), prepositions, and pronouns in 768 essays written for four different prompts. Complex relationships were found among the variables. (The major findings are discussed in Chapter 5.)

A benefit of this type of research is the identification of measurable variables of writing. A weakness is that variables can be mechanical without an adequate theoretical base. Also, relations between variables and underlying theory can be misinterpreted.

Surveys

Liebman's study (1992) is representative of surveys. (The major cross-cultural findings of the study are discussed in Chapter 6; here the focus is on the methodology.) She surveyed Japanese and Arabic ESL students in order to find out how writing is taught in these different cultures. Reacting to the traditional contrastive rhetoric paradigm, which favors linguistic text analysis of student writing, Liebman was interested in examining writing backgrounds and their effects on L2 writing. A questionnaire was distributed to eighty-nine students, thirty-five Japanese and fifty-four Arabic speakers enrolled in ESL writing classes at a U.S. university. The questionnaire consisted of twenty questions of three types: open-ended questions, Likert-scale questions (e.g., "Did you study writing in school? Circle one: every year, most years, some years, never"), and ranking questions, which asked students to identify and rank techniques used to teach writing at home or criteria used to evaluate writing.

Liebman admits to limitations in the study. For example, the responses are what students report and may not reflect what teachers actually do in writing classes. However, Liebman's point about the need for contrastive rhetoric to look beyond texts to students' educational backgrounds is well taken. Her study invites replication with students from other cultures.

Case studies and ethnographies

A prolific area of investigation involves case studies of peer responses in cross-cultural peer response groups. Studies by Nelson and Murphy (1992), Allaei and Connor (1990), and Connor and Asenavage (1994) have analyzed student interactions in peer response groups in ESL writing classrooms. Although the focus has been on the interactions themselves, contrastive hypotheses have been brought to bear to explain the results. For example, Nelson and Murphy (1992) found to their surprise that a Chinese woman student monopolized discussion in a writing group. The opposite was expected; Chinese students are expected to be quiet collaborators. Carson (1992) has taken up this issue in a paper on cross-cultural groups; her point is that collaboration in a Western sense is an alien concept for Asian students. Chinese and Japanese students collaborate for the common good; Western students collaborate for the good of the individual. Connor and Asenavage (1994) found that the independent variables of L1 language and culture as well as L2 proficiency interact in a complex manner in peer response groups when they analyzed the impact of peer comments on subsequent revisions.

A great deal of research focuses on the academic writing of nonnative English speakers. Several case studies in the United States have investigated problems of ESL students writing in different academic disciplines, as discussed in Chapter 8. (See also Johns 1991.)

True and quasi experiments

Contrastive rhetoric experiments are rare. Three are well known and are discussed in previous chapters: Hinds (1984), Eggington (1987), and Connor and McCagg (1983). All three are quasi-experiments, which tested contrastive hypotheses using reading passages to test the ease of comprehension of L1 and L2 texts. To my knowledge, no true experiments, involving randomization of subjects into control and experimental groups, exist.

Summary and implications

The review shows that contrastive rhetoric studies have employed major types of research methods used in the study of composition with the exception of true experiments and ethnographies. Contrastive rhetoricians, an interdisciplinary group of researchers, are comfortable doing surveys, text analyses, prediction studies, and reflective inquiries. Because they have not embraced experimentation, the field has been criticized for not producing firm results suitable for teaching practice. Contrastive rhetoric studies have also been criticized for using too small samples, a criticism directed at most qualitative research, and their validity, quality, and generalizing potential has also been questioned.

I believe in synergetic energy produced by a combination of research methods (cf. Connor 1989). Quantitative and qualitative contrastive research are both needed. To quote Salomon, "To achieve a fuller or more satisfactory understanding of a phenomenon, one would want to entertain a number of different views" (1991, 16). To understand war, for example, Salomon suggests that one would need to participate in one, interview people who had been in a war, study the phenomenon of violence, and so on. To understand contrastive writing, one needs to study L1 and L2 writing, observe and interview L1 and L2 writers, and study influences on L1 writing developments. If one agrees with Salomon's premise that both research paradigms, qualitative and quantitative, are needed to understand a phenomenon fully, then contrastive rhetoric needs both case study and experimentation. In the usual hierarchy of research methods, on the other hand, one moves from case studies to experiments in which hypotheses generated in case studies can be tested.

Contrastive rhetoric research has been criticized for design flaws. Design problems include small sample size, a mix of genres, and generalizing from L2 data to L1 behavior. Perhaps even more damaging have been charges of ethnocentrism and lack of adequate levels of comparability in the studies. Each issue warrants a discussion here.

Ethnocentrism

Ethnocentrism results from assuming that the world view of one's own culture is central to all reality. It results in denigration (negative stereotyping) of others' languages and cultures. The opposite of ethnocentrism is ethnorelativism, which has empathy for different behaviors and cultures.

Many early contrastive rhetoric studies were criticized for ethnocentrism because they considered Anglo-American writing logical and straightforward, implicitly holding it up as the standard. It has been pointed out, of course, that English writing appears linear to native English speakers, but not necessarily to speakers of other languages whose coherence patterns often differ from that of English (see Hinds [1987; 1990], for example).

More recently, native speakers of languages other than English have asserted the equivalent if different value of their language and culture. For example, Finnish text linguists have pointed out that although it is true that Finnish writers in English use fewer transitions than native English speakers, making the reader work harder to get the meaning, Finns are not unfriendly toward their readers, but respect the readers' intelligence and do not care to spell out things too explicitly. Although the Finnish point of view is refreshing, comments like these could be interpreted as ethnocentric and as denigrating native English speakers.

How can one avoid stereotyping languages and cultures in contrastive rhetoric studies? Clearly, it is advisable to collaborate with a native speaker of a language other than your own when doing contrastive studies. International collaborators can help each other to be sensitive to cultural perceptions at each stage of the research. A contrastive study in which native speakers of the two languages collaborated is the study on persuasive student writing in Finland and the United States by Crismore, Markkanen, and Steffensen (1993). Successful large-scale cross-cultural studies also include native speakers as collaborators and co-authors; the obvious example is the IEA Study on Written Composition (Purves 1988) and the cross-cultural study on speech acts in spoken language in Europe (Blum-Kulka, House, and Kasper 1989).

Establishing tertium comparationis

It is necessary to establish a joint basis for comparisons. Comparable phenomena are both similar and different. Any adequate description of their differences either presupposes an implicit understanding of the underlying similarities of the phenomena or it explicitly elucidates them. Too often in comparative rhetoric, however, such a common ground is assumed to be implicitly understood. When readers of the research belong exclusively to one linguistic and cultural community, however, such a commonality simply may not be known. Markkanen (1990) has pointed out that cross-cultural research on politeness, for example, has often failed to elicit such a common ground. Obviously, the fact that Finns do not use the Finnish equivalent of "please" in their requests does not exclude their possession of a ground of politeness strategies common with other cultures. So an adequate appreciation of Finnish politeness must depend on what Krzeszowsky (1990, 15–21) calls a *tertium comparationis,* a "common platform of reference." (See also Markkanen et al. 1993 for a discussion of methodogical problems in their contrastive study.)

A problem arises when analytic systems, developed within one culture and necessarily reflecting that culture's world view, are used to explore the speech acts of another culture. This is most clearly seen when Western science is used to "understand" the world views of non-Western people. In this case there may be no *tertium comparationis,* yet the structural categories of Western linguistics were assumed to reflect a common plat-form of reference in early contrastive analyses. Early comparative rheto-ricians attributed a universal applicability to Western analysis, and this may be true also of later developments in speech act theory, structural theories of register, genre, topics, and communicative needs. For exam-ple, Biber's multilevel analysis of texts (1988) was developed for English; its use in its original form with other languages – especially non-Indo-European languages – should be questioned. In contrast, Crismore et al. (1993), studying hedging behavior in student writing in English and Fin-nish, developed an equivalent system for Finnish based on an intermedia-tion or interpolation between the two cultural realizations of hedging. Suitable comparisons in contrastive rhetoric need to be established at a number of levels depending on the purpose of the study.

Structural form was the *tertium comparationis* of early contrastive analyses. Later, speech acts, registers, genres, topics, and communicative needs were added as bases for suitable comparisons.

Controlling for authorship

Related to the issue of establishing a joint basis for comparisons is con-trolling for authorship. Contrastive rhetorical studies have examined writers at many levels of proficiency: learners in educational systems (for example, Kaplan 1966; Mohan and Lo 1985), experienced academics in their fields of study (for example, Clyne 1987; Eggington 1987; Ventola and Mauranen 1991), and business professionals (Connor 1988). Al-though the diversity of data sources is useful in helping to build a com-prehensive theory of contrastive rhetoric, we need to be careful not to simply aggregate the results from the various studies to form a model of writing style in a culture. Furthermore, it seems obvious that one should not mix apples and oranges in a single study and compare, for example, student writing in one culture with professional writing in another.

Controlling for genre and content

A great deal of contrastive rhetorical research has focused on genre-specific writing, as discussed in Chapter 8. Comparisons have been made between writers with a variety of native languages in a number of academic and professional genres. As has been pointed out by many scholars, however, care needs to be exercised in the use of concepts such as "academic writing." Taylor and Chen point out that "where academic writing is the subject-matter to be investigated it is necessary to be specific not only about the discipline" but also about "schools of thought within disciplines" (1991, 321). Among scholars of academic writing, there is an increased understanding about the diversity in academic writing owing to subdisciplinary departmental and individual variation (Myers 1990; Swales 1990a,b).

Interrater reliability

Researchers need to provide objectivity in their analyses through interrater reliability. Procedures for conducting interrater reliability are available in books of research design (for example, Johnson 1992; Lauer and Asher 1988). An example of contrastive research with rigorously achieved interrater reliability is Connor and Lauer's (1988) study of argumentative student writing in three cultures, discussed in Chapter 4.

10 Conclusion: Implications and research directions

This book has defined an emerging contrastive rhetoric discipline that draws on several relevant interdisciplinary fields: text linguistics, composition and rhetoric, translation studies, and cultural studies of literacy. In English teaching situations, the extended definition of contrastive rhetoric takes us away from looking only at the effects of transfer from L1 to L2 products. It leads us to the analysis of processes of writing as well as to studying the development of literacy skills in L1 together with the effects of this development on L2 literacy. Thus, in addition to reviewing contrastive rhetoric research on cross-cultural writing styles and organizational patterns (Chapters 3 and 5), developments in the teaching of writing with emphasis on processes were discussed in Chapter 4. Chapter 6 discussed ways in which the acquisition and learning of literacy varies across cultures. The emphasis of Chapter 8 was on cross-cultural variation in writing for specific genres such as research articles, business letters, résumés, and newspaper editorials.

Although teaching implications were woven throughout the chapters, this final chapter pulls together the major implications for teaching from three sets of findings: text linguistics, process-based composition instruction, and genre-specific research in EFL settings. Most would not consider contrastive rhetoric to be a method of teaching. It is an inquiry that provides a knowledge base to help ESL/EFL teachers and students. Though Kaplan (1966) maintained that the ESL teacher needs to be aware of differences between paragraph organization in different languages so that she can make these differences apparent to students, in later work he reasserted that contrastive rhetoric was not meant as a teaching pedagogy but as a knowledge and awareness about differences in writing patterns across cultures. As Grabe and Kaplan write: "Contrastive rhetoric is not a methodology for teaching though some of its findings can be (and indeed have been) applied to teaching" (1989, 269).

Implications for the testing of L2 writing will be explored, and, finally, researchable topics for future research are suggested.

Implications from contrastive text studies

Text linguistic contrastive rhetoric research shows that different cultures have different expectations of writing and that these different expectations are internalized as different patterns of discourse. Writers of second languages transfer their L1 writing strategies to the new situation of the second language. Hence, before they learn the expectations of their second language audience, ESL writers may use textual and rhetorical strategies that are considered odd at the very least.

Contrastive rhetoricians maintain that different reader expectations are the primary reason for cross-cultural differences in writing styles and that students should be made aware of these differences by their teachers. A strong advocate for the employment of contrastive rhetoric insights in the ESL classroom is Leki (1991; 1992). According to her, it is important for ESL teachers in North America to make their ESL students aware of the following: English-speaking readers are convinced by facts, statistics, and illustrations in arguments; they move from generalizations to specific examples and expect explicit links between main topics and subtopics; and they value originality.

Leki maintains that insights from contrastive rhetoric both for teachers and students are valuable for psychological as well as practical reasons. Teachers learn that the "particular options ESL students choose in their writing are not random but may come as a result of rhetorical constraints not shared by English speakers" (Leki 1992, 102). On the other hand, students appreciate knowing that their ESL writing problems may be due to their writing experience in their first languages. They learn that certain problems do not reflect any personal inadequacies but are instead part of learning about another discourse community. Armed with this insight, students will better be able to acquire new strategies and to exercise choices in their second language writing.

Exercises for the improvement of writing based on contrastive rhetoric findings include work on thesis statements as suggested by Grabe and Kaplan, which include identifying topic sentences in texts, sorting supporting information from its generalization, brainstorming a thesis, and conferencing (1989, 277). Other teaching suggestions from contrastive rhetoric include the use of topical structure analysis as a revision tool that students can use to improve the coherence of their own writing, as discussed in detail in Chapter 5.

Implications from contrastive process-based writing

Changes in the nature of contrastive rhetoric and subsequent implications for teaching reflect changes in the teaching of writing in general. As discussed in Chapter 4, the teaching of writing in North America has undergone a paradigm shift. The emphasis is no longer on the product. Instead, writing is taught as a process, in which each stage – prewriting, composing, and editing – is important. In addition, writing is not considered a solitary act; it involves teachers, peers, and other readers. The responses of other readers are a vital part of writing considered as a social construction of meaning. The second language teacher who is familiar with the teaching of writing as a process does not teach her students to write through model compositions. Instead, she focuses on helping students make revisions in students' drafts from the beginning to the final editing.

Thus the broader definition of contrastive rhetoric advocated in this book has further implications for teachers of nonnative speakers of English in North American contexts where writing is taught as a process and as a social construction of meaning. For example, teachers need to be aware of cultural differences in their students' attitude toward collaboration in writing classes. As discussed in Chapters 2 and 6, students from different language and cultural backgrounds have different expectations about group work. In addition, group discussions and negotiations reflect sociolinguistically based variation in the directness of comment and topic initiation, among other things. Allaei and Connor discuss concerns resulting from different attitudes toward peer feedback among their international students as follows:

Some students (mostly East Asian) state that they are uncomfortable making negative statements about their peers' writing; they would rather focus on the things that they like. . . . Second, some students (mostly Middle Eastern) express reluctance about being asked to share their writing, particularly if it is expressive, personal writing, with other students. They feel that such writing is not appropriate for an academic context. Finally, some students feel constrained by weak language skills from making contributions to the peer response process. (1990, 24)

Allaei and Connor make several suggestions for the teacher. First, for collaborative peer response groups to be successful, it is essential that students understand why they are being asked to participate in these activities. To prepare them for peer response activities, they recommend nonthreatening interaction such as brainstorming and discussing various scenarios such as refusing requests, pointing out mistakes that a peer has made, or placing blame at the scene of an accident, with the purpose of highlighting cross-cultural differences and their implications for cross-cultural interactions.

Carson and Nelson (1994) warn against conflicting assumptions about student behaviors in groups. In their research project, the Chinese students saw their roles as nurturers whereas the Spanish-speaking students conceived their role to be a critical one. Similar findings about conflicting expectations in writing classrooms are evident in linguistically heterogeneous "mainstream" writing classes in North America (Hull et al. 1991). Increased numbers of nonnative speakers in American high schools and colleges have encouraged publications such as Severino, Guerra, and Butler's useful book about contrastive rhetoric findings for mainstream teachers (in press).

Implications from contrastive genre-specific research in EFL Settings

Insights from contrastive rhetoric help guide the EFL teacher around the world by providing information about the expectations of native-English-speaking readers. "EFL" means English taught as a school subject in order to give students a competence in a foreign language, in this case, English; the students are not necessarily expected to use the foreign language with native speakers. In EFL situations, teachers need a knowledge of the rhetorical contrast between English and the other language, the students' native language. Students typically have the same first language, such as Swedish in schools in Sweden. There are exceptions, of course. In some countries students possess native competence in one and a learned competence in the other of the country's national languages (e.g., Finnish and Swedish in Finland). Some societies are multilingual although one language may be used in schools and government, as in Singapore. In still other countries, large numbers of immigrants from a variety of backgrounds diversify some school populations, as in San Francisco and Los Angeles.

As discussed in previous chapters, a great deal of research on textual and rhetorical contrasts is being conducted in countries with EFL teaching emphasis. For example, the NORDTEXT project in Scandinavia has provided valuable insights for school teachers in the Scandinavian countries. Exciting research on English-native language contrasts is being conducted on genre-specific writing in Germany, Czech Republic, Finland, and several South American countries, and research results are finding their way into EFL classes and tutorials.

Ventola and Mauranen (1991) write about the value of awareness about contrasting coherence patterns for Finnish students and teachers of English. The awareness of differences in reader expectations about how texts are organized, how explicitly transitions should be stated, how directly requests are made, and so on, is crucial for a nonnative writer. Lack of awareness of such cross-cultural differences in text characteristics and reader expectations is believed to be the main cause preventing nonnative writers' successes in the international community. Ventola and Mauranen are critical of the approaches taken at Finnish universities, for example, where "language centers," meant to help Finnish writers revise their English writing, are manned by native speakers of English called "translator/editors." Typically, these translator/editors are not trained in text linguistics or contrastive rhetoric and are not tuned to revising at the text level. Instead, they often recommend revisions at the surface level only. (See Chapter 7 for a sample revision by a translator/editor, which relied on surface-level revisions.)

Contrastive rhetoric in EFL situations can empower the nonnative English-speaking teacher in a valuable way, making the teacher more confident because she knows explicitly how writing in different languages works. Advances in contrastive rhetoric research have revealed explicit textual and rhetorical differences about characteristics of written texts for specific purposes, how writers produce texts, and how readers interpret texts. Naturally, the teacher or the national curriculum of the country needs to determine the expectations of which English-speaking discourse community to follow.

Testing ESL/EFL writing in a cross-cultural setting

The general principles of contrastive rhetoric comprise relevant knowledge in the testing of second language writing. Because the testing of writing ability and achievement is typically done using a direct writing sample such as an essay, findings about cross-cultural differences in preferences for topics, discourse organization, and style are relevant for test makers and scorers, teachers, and students. Few studies have examined cross-cultural aspects of direct writing assessment, perhaps because direct assessment of writing as an area of study has existed only since the early 1980s. Insights from the IEA study as well as from second language experts involved with writing assessment follow.

Concerning the cross-cultural assessment of first language writing (that is, the comparison of first-language writing achievement), the International Association for the Evaluation of Educational Achievement (IEA) Study of Written Communication provides the most valuable information about universal and national topic types, writing styles, and rating criteria. (See Chapter 6 for a detailed discussion of the project.) The IEA study began with the premise that one could make conclusions about the effects of various factors on writing performance by examining the products of students as judged by trained raters. The study was carefully designed: It used multiple writing tasks rather than relying on a single sample, and the rating rubrics were agreed upon by the selected raters from the fourteen participating countries. In reflecting on the 10-year study, Alan Purves comments that despite the careful planning, the study did not succeed in guaranteeing uniform interpretation of topics across cultures: "Indonesian students, for example, tended to interpret all tasks as an invitation to a personal narrative; they would write stories about arguments rather than write arguments or embed their letters and notes in narratives. Students in various settings construed the task in ways that were meaningful to them" (1992, 115). The point is that trying to establish levels of writing achievement across cultures is close to impossible. However, the IEA study is a valiant effort; anyone interested in cross-cultural writing assessment needs to become familiar with the procedures and results of the project.

Concerning the assessment of second language writing, Carlson and Bridgeman (1986) discuss characteristics of good essay tests in large-scale assessments of international students' writing with special reference to the Test of Written English (TWE). The TWE is administered by the Educational Testing Service's TOEFL division to thousands of international students a year around the world. The writing stimulus or the prompt (i.e., the verbal statement that elicits the writing) needs to be carefully developed and pretested. The content implied by the topic should not favor or disadvantage students from any cultural groups. Neither should topics be emotionally too taxing, such as asking students to write about tests. Nor should topics assume of the test writers a strictly American, middle-class point of view. In addition to topic selection and prompt preparation, Carlson and Bridgeman's work offers insightful information related to many other aspects of a good international writing test such as the validity and reliability of rating criteria.

Culture-specific problems in second language testing are obvious, as Ballard and Clanchy (1991) point out, basing their conclusion on their experiences with East and Southeast Asian ESL populations at universities in Australia. In addition to different organizational patterns of texts, students from Asia bring to their second language writing different attitudes toward knowledge and its function in society. Asian students do not seem to approach a topic as directly as expected by the Western teacher. Second, the Asian students' use of sources is different in that they do not like to question published knowledge. For an Asian student, "an established text is to be studied with respect, not interrogated, not hastily skimmed or mined for the odd nugget of useful data, certainly not to be subjected to the criticism of a neophyte" (31). These are the skills that Western students are encouraged to master. A third problem, according to Ballard and Clanchy, is the criterion of "reasoned argument," expected by the Western rater. Again, as discussed in previous chapters, standards of what constitutes a reasonable argument vary from culture to culture. Ballard and Clanchy explain how Asian students prefer not to take a point of view, and argue for a clear-cut conclusion.

There is, instead, frequently a willingness to tolerate ambiguity, even contradictions, to allow them to sit easily in tension within the same piece of writing. The Japanese student who, when writing an essay involving comparison and contrast, directs his efforts towards justifying the bases of the differing interpretations in his source materials but makes no attempt to test or evaluate them, is working in a fundamentally different tradition from the Western academic who expects all roads lead to evaluation. The Japanese student is striving to achieve harmony, where his lecturer wants critical judgment. (p. 33)

The culture-specific potential problems discussed by Ballard and Clanchy are direct implications from contrastive rhetoric research whose primary emphasis has been on the teaching of writing. It is important, therefore, that contrastive rhetoric be taken seriously by second-language testing experts. With the increased emphasis on the direct assessment of writing of international students, an essay test is often rated by Western raters, or as in the case of the Test of Written English, solely by U.S. raters. Research needs to be conducted to study the issues of cultural sensitivity of prompts, rating rubrics, and rater behaviors in large-scale testing of international students' writing in English.

Research directions

The review of contrastive rhetoric conducted in this book reveals an interdisciplinary field of study that benefits from the theories and methods of such related fields as applied linguistics, text linguistics, composition pedagogy, education, anthropology, and translation studies. As Chapter 3 shows, since 1966 a great deal of research has been conducted in an applied linguistic framework using essays written by native-English-speaking and ESL students. However, using the framework of the "new contrastive rhetoric," which includes the study of processes of writing as well as the study of writing in academic and professional situations, less is known about cross-cultural differences. The following recommendations reflect the need to develop a better understanding of these new areas.

1. Text linguistic contrastive studies should gather evidence about differences in writing for a variety of text types and writing situations. The research by Ventola and Mauranen (1991) is a good example of cross-cultural genre-specific research on the academic writing of economists and physicists. Other academic and professional genres need to be studied involving a number of different first languages. The Indianapolis-Antwerp-Turku project on the writing of résumés and job applications is such an attempt. Folman and Connor's international project on the writing of research papers at the high school and college levels is another example of a large-scale cross-cultural analysis. Both the Indianapolis-Antwerp-Turku project and the international research paper project involve native speakers of several languages as collaborators. This helps to avoid ethnocentric perceptions and establishes a joint basis for comparisons or *tertium comparationis*. In addition, each project promises to

build an international databank available for other international researchers.

2. Research studies need to examine how writing is learned in different languages and cultures. Both ethnic cultures and cultures of different academic and professional discourse communities need to be included. Ethnographic research similar to the work of Li (see Chapter 6) should be encouraged in order to learn about national styles and preferences from teachers and students. Surveys similar to Liebman's (1992) also would be useful in building knowledge about culturally embedded practices of writing that ESL and EFL students employ.

An important area of investigation is the acquisition of genre-specific literacy in second language settings. Learning to write academic and professional discourse is a long process. A case-study approach points to the difficulty that native-English-speaking students experience in learning to write for specific purposes (Berkenkotter, Huckin, and Ackerman 1988). Few case studies have begun to examine how nonnative speakers learn to write in English in their chosen academic discourse communities (Swales 1990a,b; Connor and Kramer 1995; Belcher 1994; Casanave 1995).

3. With the globalization of discourse patterns (Fairclough 1989), contrastive rhetoricians should learn more about the levels of adequacy and acceptability of second language writing. Ringbom's (1993) project on what constitutes near-nativeness in EFL writing in Finland includes analyses of texts as well as rater judgments of writing quality. Preliminary results indicate that "the difference between near-native speakers and advanced learners is definitely not clear-cut" (301). Furthermore, the level of near-nativeness can vary from genre to genre. Ringbom's collaboration with the project, "International Corpus of Learner English" (Granger 1993) should lead to fruitful results. Naturally, any contrastive writing research will benefit from the insights of the researchers of international Englishes (Kachru 1984).

4. Both the "old" and the "new" contrastive rhetorics reflect the gender blindness of sociolinguistic and text linguistic research as well as the gender-biased empirical parameters of applied linguistics (which usually assumes no gender-based differences in L2 acquisition). As cultural anthropologists and others have long since demonstrated, female acculturation and therefore female language use differs from male acculturation and language use in every society studied (Cameron 1985), yet this significant finding is rarely reflected in applied linguistics. Useful research could be made along such lines as gender-based resistance in the learning of L2 rhetorical patterns. For example, do Japanese women learn English rhetorical linearity as easily as Japanese men do?

5. Research on effective classroom interactions in ESL and EFL settings is necessary for the effective implementation of "social construction

of meaning" among teachers and students in ESL and EFL writing classes. Interviews and "think-aloud" protocols with students as well as ethnographic and case study descriptions, similar to the research by Nelson and Murphy (1992), need to be conducted. This kind of classroom-based research is important not only for the findings but for the process of encouraging "dialogue across differences between teachers and students concerning different assumptions about texts, writers, and audiences."

The above research suggestions represent just a few of the most obvious directions that contrastive rhetoric research could take. These directions are diverse, reflecting the multidimensional theories and methods the emerging discipline of contrastive rhetoric has espoused. They also concur with current trends in ESL and EFL, where learners come from an ever-widening circle of settings and situations.

References

Al-Jubouri, A. J. R. "The Role of Repetition in Arabic Argumentative Discourse." In *English for Specific Purposes in the Arab World,* edited by J. Swales and H. Mustafa, 99–117. Birmingham, UK: The Language Studies Unit, University of Aston, 1984.

Allaei, S. K., and U. M. Connor. "Exploring the Dynamics of Cross-Cultural Collaboration in Writing Classrooms." *The Writing Instructor* 10, no. 1 (1990): 19–28.

Altehenger-Smith, S. "Language Choice in Multilingual Societies: A Singapore Case Study." In *Analyzing Intercultural Communication,* edited by K. Knapp, W. Enninger, and A. Knapp-Potthoff, 75–94. Amsterdam: Mouton de Gruyter, 1987.

Aristotle. "Rhetoric." In *The Complete Works of Aristotle.* rev. Oxford ed., edited by J. Barnes, vol. 2, 2152–2269. Princeton, NJ: Princeton University Press, 1984.

Bailey, N., C. Madden, and S. D. Krashen. "Is There a 'Natural Sequence' in Adult Second Language Learning?" *Language Learning* 24 (1974): 235–243.

Bain, A. *English Composition and Rhetoric: A Manual.* London: Longmans, Green and Co., 1866.

Ballard, B., and J. Clanchy. "Assessment by Misconception: Cultural Influences and Intellectual Traditions." In *Assessing Second Language Writing in Academic Contexts,* edited by L. Hamp-Lyons, 19–36. Norwood, NJ: Ablex, 1991.

Bar-Lev, Z. "Discourse Theory and Contrastive Rhetoric." *Discourse Processes* 9 (1986): 235–246.

Bazerman, C. Physicists Reading Physics: Schema-Laden Purposes and Purpose-Laden Schema. *Written Communication* 2 (1985): 3–24.

———. *Shaping Written Knowledge. The Genre and Activity of the Experimental Article in Science.* Madison, WI: The University of Wisconsin Press, 1988.

Belcher, D. "The Apprenticeship Approach to Advanced Academic Literacy: Graduate Students and Their Mentors." *English for Specific Purposes* 13, no. 1 (1994): 23–34.

Bereiter, C., and M. Scardamalia. "Levels of Inquiry in Writing Research." In *Research on Writing: Principles and Methods,* edited by P. Mosenthal, L. Tamor, and S. Walmsley, 3–25. New York: Longman, 1983.

Berkenkotter, C., and T. N. Huckin. "Rethinking Genre from a Sociocognitive Perspective." *Written Communication* 10, no. 4 (1993): 475–509.

Berkenkotter, C., T. N. Huckin, and J. Ackerman. "Conventions, Conversations, and the Writer: Case Study of a Student in a Rhetoric Ph.D. Program." *Research in the Teaching of English* 22, no. 1 (1988): 9–44.

Berlin, J. A. *Writing Instruction in Nineteenth-Century American Colleges.* Carbondale, IL: Southern Illinois University Press, 1984.

———. *Rhetoric and Reality: Writing Instruction in American Colleges, 1900–1985.* Carbondale, IL: Southern Illinois University Press, 1987.

———. "Rhetoric and Ideology in the Writing Class." *College English* 50, no. 5 (1988): 477–494.

Bhatia, V. K. *Analyzing Genre: Language Use in Professional Settings.* New York: Longman, 1993.

Biber, D. "A Model of Textual Relations Within the Written and Spoken Modes." Unpublished Ph.D. dissertation, Department of Linguistics, University of Southern California, 1984.

———. "Investigating Macroscopic Textual Variation Through Multi-Feature/Multi-Dimensional Analyses." *Linguistics* 23 (1985): 337–360.

———. "Spoken and Written Textual Dimensions in English: Resolving the Contradictory Findings." *Language* 62 (1986): 384–414.

———. "A Textual Comparison of British and American Writing." *American Speech* 62 (1987): 99–119.

———. *Variation Across Speech and Writing.* New York: Cambridge University Press, 1988.

Bickner, R., and P. Peyasantiwong. "Cultural Variation in Reflective Writing." In *Writing Across Languages and Cultures: Issues in Contrastive Rhetoric,* edited by A. C. Purves, 160–176. Newbury Park, CA: Sage, 1988.

Bizzell, P. "College Composition: Initiation into the Academic Discourse Community." *Curriculum Inquiry* 12, no. 2 (1982a): 191–207.

———. "Cognition, Convention, and Certainty: What We Need to Know About Writing." *PRE/TEXT* 3, no. 3 (1982b): 213–241.

———. *Academic Discourse and Critical Consciousness.* Pittsburgh, PA: University of Pittsburgh Press, 1992.

Bloom, A. *The Linguistic Shaping of Thought: A Study of the Impact of Language on Thinking in China and the West.* Hillsdale, NJ: Erlbaum, 1981.

Bloom, L. Z., and M. Bloom. "The Teaching and Learning of Argumentative Writing." *College English* 29 (1967): 128–135.

Bloomfield, L. *Language.* New York: Holt and Co., 1933.

Blum-Kulka, S., J. House, and G. Kasper, eds. *Cross-Cultural Pragmatics: Requests and Apologies.* Norwood, NJ: Ablex, 1989.

Bolivar, A. "The Analysis of Political Discourse, with Particular Reference to Venezuelan Dialogue." *English for Specific Purposes* 11, no. 2 (1992): 159–176.

Briggs, C. L., and R. Bauman. "Genre, Intertextuality, and Social Power." *Journal of Linguistic Anthropology* 2, no. 2 (1992): 131–172.

Britton, J., T. Burgess, N. Martin, A. Mclead, and H. Rosen. *The Development of Writing Abilities,* 11–18. London: Macmillan, 1975.

Brown, G., and G. Yule. *Discourse Analysis.* London: Cambridge University Press, 1983.

Bruffee, K. A. "Collaborative Learning: Some Practical Models." *College English* 34 (1973): 634–43.

Cai, G. "Beyond Bad Writing: Teaching English Composition to Chinese ESL Students." Paper presented at the College Composition and Communication Conference, San Diego, CA, March 1993.

———. "Texts in Contexts: Understanding Chinese Students' English Compositions." In *Evaluating Writing* (2d ed.), edited by C. R. Cooper and L. Odell. Urbana, IL: National Council of Teachers of English, in press.

Cameron, D. *Feminism and Linguistic Theory.* London: Macmillan, 1985.

Campbell, G. *The Philosophy of Rhetoric,* edited by L. Bitzer. Carbondale, IL: Southern Illinois University Press, 1963. (Originally published in 1776.)

Carlson, S., and B. Bridgeman. "Testing ESL Student Writers." In *Writing Assessment. Issues and Strategies,* edited by K. L. Greenberg, H. S. Wiener, and R. A. Donovan, 126–152. New York: Longman, 1986.

Carlson, S., B. Bridgeman, R. Camp, and I. J. Waanders. "Relationship of Admission Test Scores to Writing Performance of Native and Non-Native Speakers of English." In *TOEFL Research Report No. 19,* Princeton, N.J.: Educational Testing Service, 1985.

Carson, J. G. "Becoming Biliterate: First Language Influences." *Journal of Second Language Writing* 1, no. 1 (1992): 37–60.

Carson, J. G., and G. L. Nelson. "Writing Groups: Cross-Cultural Issues." *Journal of Second Language Writing* 3, no. 1 (1994):17–30.

Casanave, C. P. "Local Interactions: Constructing Contexts for Composing in a Graduate Sociology Program." In *Academic Writing in a Second Language: Essays on Research and Pedagogy,* edited by D. Belcher and G. Braine, 83–110. Norwood, NJ: Ablex, 1995.

Cerniglia, C., K. Medsker, and U. Connor. "Improving Coherence Using Computer-Assisted Instruction." In *Coherence in Writing: Research and Pedagogical Perspectives,* edited by U. Connor and A. M. Johns, 227–241. Arlington, VA: TESOL, 1990.

Chesterman, A. "From Is to Ought: Laws, Norms and Strategies in Translation Studies." *Target* 5, no. 1 (1993): 1–20.

Choi, Y. H. "Text Structure of Korean Speakers' Argumentative Essays in English." *World Englishes* 7, no. 2 (1988): 129–142.

Christensen, F. "A Generative Rhetoric of the Paragraph." *College Composition and Communication* 14 (1963): 155–161.

———. *Notes Toward a New Rhetoric.* London and New York: Harper & Row, 1967.

Clancy, P. M. "The Acquisition of Communicative Style in Japanese." In *Language Socialization Across Cultures,* edited by B. B. Schieffelin and E. Ochs, 213–250. New York: Cambridge University Press, 1986.

Clark, H. H., and E. V. Clark. *Psychology and Language: An Introduction to Psycholinguistics.* New York: Harcourt Brace Jovanovich, 1977.

Clyne, M. G. "Linguistics and Written Discourse in Particular Languages: Contrastive Studies: English and German." In *Annual Review of Applied Linguistics III,* edited by R. B. Kaplan, 38–49. Rowley, MA: Newbury House, 1983.

———. "Cultural Differences in the Organization of Academic Texts: English and German." *Journal of Pragmatics* 11, no. 2 (1987): 211–247.

Čmejrková, S. "Academic Writing in Czech and English." Paper presented at the Conference on Academic Writing – Research and Applications, University of Helsinki, Finland, May 21–23, 1994a.

———. "Non-Native (Academic) Writing." In *Writing vs. Speaking: Language, Text, Discourse, Communication,* edited by S. Čmejroková, F. Daneš, and E. Havlová, 303–310. Tübingen, Germany: Gunter Narr Verlag, 1994b.

Connor, U. "A Study of Cohesion and Coherence in ESL Students' Writing." *Papers in Linguistics: International Journal of Human Communication* 17, no. 3 (1984): 301–316.

———. "Argumentative Patterns in Student Essays: Cross-Cultural Differences." In *Writing Across Languages: Analysis of L2 Text,* edited by U. Connor and R. B. Kaplan, 57–71. Reading, MA: Addison-Wesley, 1987a.

———. "Research Frontiers in Writing Analysis." *TESOL Quarterly* 21, no. 4 (1987b): 677–696.

———. "A Contrastive Study of Persuasive Business Correspondence: American and Japanese." In *Global Implications for Business Communications: Theory, Technology, and Practice. 1988 Proceedings 53rd National and 15th International Convention of the Association for Business Communication,* edited by S. J. Bruno, 57–72. Houston, TX: School of Business and Public Administration, University of Houston – Clear Lake, 1988.

———. "Linguistic/Rhetorical Measures for International Persuasive Student Writing." *Research in the Teaching of English* 24, no. 1 (1990a): 67–87.

———. "Discourse Analysis and Writing/Reading Instruction." *Annual Review of Applied Linguistics* 11 (1990b): 164–180.

———. "Linguistic/Rhetorical Measures for Evaluating ESL Writing." In *Assessing Second Language in Academic Contexts,* edited by L. Hamp Lyons, 215–226. Norwood, NJ: Ablex, 1991.

———. "Contrastive Rhetoric: Implications for Teachers of Writing in Multicultural Classrooms." In *Writing in Multicultural Settings.* edited by C. Severino, J. Guerra, and J. Butler. New York: Modern Language Association, in press.

———. "Examining Syntactic Variation Across Three English-Speaking Nationalities Through a Multi-Feature/Multi-Dimensional Approach." In *Composing Social Identity in Written Language,* edited by D. L. Rubin, 75–88. Hillsdale, N.J.: Lawrence Erlbaum, 1995.

Connor, U., and K. Asenavage. "Peer Response Groups in ESL Writing Classes: How Much Impact on Revision?" *Journal of Second Language Writing* 3, no. 3, (1994): 257–275.

Connor, U., and D. Biber. "Comparing Textual Features in High School Student Writing: A Cross-Cultural study." Department of English, Indiana University in Indianapolis. Unpublished manuscript, 1988.

Connor, U., and M. Farmer. "The Teaching of Topical Structure Analysis as a Revision Strategy for ESL Writers. In *Second Language Writing. Research Insights for the Classroom,* edited by B. Kroll, 126–139. New York: Cambridge University Press, 1990.

Connor, U., and A. M. Johns, eds. *Coherence in Writing: Research and Pedagogical Perspectives.* Arlington, VA: TESOL. 1990.

Connor, U., and R. B. Kaplan, eds. *Writing Across Languages: Analysis of L2 Text.* Reading, MA: Addison-Wesley, 1987.

Connor, U., and M. Kramer. "Writing from Sources: Case Studies of Graduate Students in Business Management." In *Academic Writing in a Second Language: Essays on Research and Pedagogy,* edited by D. Belcher and G. Braine, 155–182. Norwood, NJ: Ablex, 1995.

Connor, U., and J. Lauer. "Understanding Persuasive Essay Writing: Linguistic/Rhetorical Approach." *Text 5,* no. 4 (1985): 309–326.

———. "Cross-Cultural Variation in Persuasive Student Writing." In *Writing Across Languages and Cultures,* edited by A. C. Purves, 138–159. Newbury Park, CA: Sage, 1988.

Connor, U., and P. McCagg. "Cross-Cultural Differences and Perceived Quality in Written Paraphrases of English Expository Prose." *Applied Linguistics 4,* no. 3 (1983): 259–268.

Connor, U., and S. Takala. "Predictors of Persuasive Essay Quality." In *Assessment of Student Writing in an International Context,* edited by E. Degenhart. (Research Report Series B. Theory into Practice No. 9), 187–206. Jyväskylä, Finland: Institute for Educational Research, 1987.

Connor, U., K. Davis, and T. De Rycker. "Correctness and Clarity in Applying for Overseas Jobs: A Cross-Cultural Analysis of U.S. and Flemish Applications," *Text,* in press.

Connors, R. J., L. S. Ede, and A. A. Lunsford. "The Revival of Rhetoric in America." In *Essays on Classical Rhetoric and Modern Discourse,* edited by R. J. Connors, L. S. Ede, and A. A. Lunsford, 1–15. Carbondale: Southern Illinois University Press, 1984.

Corbett, E. P. J. *Classical Rhetoric for the Modern Student.* New York: Oxford University Press, 1965.

Corder, S. P. "The Significance of Learners' Errors." *International Review of Applied Linguistics 5* (1967): 161–170.

Crismore, A., and R. Farnsworth. "Metadiscourse in Popular and Professional Science Discourse." In *The Writing Scholar,* edited by W. Nash, 118–136. Newbury Park, CA: Sage, 1990.

Crismore, A., R. Markkanen, and M. S. Steffensen. "Metadiscourse in Persuasive Writing: A Study of Texts Written by American and Finnish University Students." *Written Communication 10,* no. 1 (1993): 39–71.

Croft, K., ed. *Readings on English as a Second Language* 2d ed. Cambridge, MA: Winthrop, 1972.

Dantas-Whitney, M., and W. Grabe. "A Comparison of Portuguese and English Newspaper Editorials." Paper presented at the 23rd Annual TESOL Convention, San Antonio, Texas, March 1989.

De Beaugrande, R. "Textlinguistics and New Applications." *Annual Review of Applied Linguistics 11* (1990): 17–41.

De Beaugrande, R., and W. Dressler. *Introduction to Text Linguistics.* London: Longman, 1981.

Devahastin, W., and Methakunavudhi. *Achievement in Written Composition in Thailand (Grade II).* Hamburg: University of Hamburg, 1986.

Dressler, W. *Einfuhrung in Die Textlinguistik [Introduction to Text Linguistics].* Tuebingen, Germany: Niemeyer, 1972.

Dulay, H., and M. Burt. "Natural Sequences in Child Second Language Acquisition." *Language Learning 24* (1974): 37–53.

Dulay, H., M. Burt, and S. Krashen. *Language Two*. New York: Oxford University Press, 1982.

Edmondson, W. *Spoken Discourse: A Model for Analysis*. London and New York: Longman, 1981.

Educational Testing Service. *TOEFL Test of Written English Guide*. Princeton, NJ: Educational Testing Service, 1989.

Eggington, W. G. "Written Academic Discourse in Korean: Implications for Effective Communication." In *Writing Across Languages: Analysis of L2 Text*, edited by U. Connor and R. B. Kaplan, 153–168. Reading, MA: Addison-Wesley, 1987.

Elbow, P. "A Method for Teaching Writing." *College English* 30 (1968): 115–25.

———. *Writing with Power*. New York: Oxford University Press, 1981.

Emig, J. *The Composing Processes of Twelfth Graders*. Research Report No. 13. Urbana, IL: National Council of Teachers of English, 1971.

Enkvist, N. E. *Tekstilingvistiikan Peruskäsitteitä [Basic Principles of Text Linguistics]*. Helsinki: Gaudeamus, 1974.

———. "Some Aspects of Applications of Text Linguistics." In *Text Linguistics, Cognitive Learning, and Language Teaching*, edited by V. Kohonen and N. E. Enkvist, 1–27. Turku, Finland: Suomen Sovelletun Kielitieteen Yhdistyksen (Afinla) Julkaisuja, 22, 1978.

———. "Contrastive Linguistics and Text Linguistics." In *Contrastive Linguistics: Prospects and Problems*, edited by J. Fisiak, 45–67. The Hague: Mouton, 1984.

———. "Introduction: Coherence, Composition, and Text Linguistics." In *Coherence and Composition: A Symposium*, edited by N. E. Enkvist, 11–26. Åbo, Finland: Research Institute of the Åbo Akademi Foundation, 1985a.

———. *Text Linguistics and Written Composition*. Special issue, *Text 5* (1985b): 4.

———. "Text Linguistics for an Applier: An Introduction." In *Writing Across Languages: Analysis of L2 Text*, edited by U. Connor and R. B. Kaplan, 19–43. Reading, MA: Addison-Wesley. 1987.

———. "Seven Problems in the Study of Coherence and Interpretability." In *Coherence in Writing: Research and Pedagogical Perspectives*, edited by U. Connor and A. M. Johns, 23–43. Arlington, VA: TESOL, 1990.

Evensen, L. S., ed. *Nordic Research in Text Linguistics and Discourse Analysis*. Trondheim, Norway: University of Trondheim, Tapir, 1986.

Evensen, L. S. "Contrastive Rhetoric and Developing Discourse Strategies." Paper presented at the 21st International TESOL Conference, Miami, Florida, April 1987.

———. "Pointers to Superstructure in Student Writing." In *Coherence in Writing: Research and Pedagogical Perspectives*, edited by U. Connor and A. M. Johns, 169–186. Arlington, VA: TESOL, 1990.

Fagan, E. R., and P. Cheong. "Contrastive Rhetoric: Pedagogical Implication for the ESL Teacher in Singapore." *RELC: A Journal of Language Teaching and Research in Southeast Asia* 18, no. 1 (1987): 19–31.

Fairclough, N. *Language and Power*. London: Longman, 1989.

Fishman, J. "The Sociology of Language: Yesterday, Today and Tomorrow." In

Current Issues in Linguistic Theory, edited by R. W. Cole, 51–75. Bloomington, IN: Indiana University Press, 1977.

Fisiak, J. *Contrastive Linguistics and the Language Teacher.* New York: Pergamon, 1981.

Flower, L. S., and J. R. Hayes. "A Cognitive Process Theory of Writing." *College Composition and Communication* 32, no. 4 (1981): 365–387.

Fogarty, D., *Roots for a New Rhetoric.* New York: Russell and Russell, 1959.

Folman, S., and U. Connor. "Intercultural Rhetorical Differences in Composing a Research Paper." Paper presented at the International Teachers of English to Speakers of Other Languages Conference, Vancouver, British Columbia, March 1992.

Folman, S., and G. Sarig. "Intercultural Rhetorical Differences in Meaning Construction." *Communication and Cognition* 23, no. 1 (1990): 45–92.

Freire, P. *Pedagogy of the Oppressed.* New York: The Seabury Press, 1970.

Fries, C. *Teaching and Learning English as a Foreign Language.* Ann Arbor, MI: University of Michigan Press, 1945.

Geertz, C. *Local Knowledge: Further Essays in Interpretive Anthropology.* New York: Basic Books, 1983.

Gentzler, E. *Contemporary Translation Theories.* New York: Routledge, 1993.

Glenn, E. S., and C. G. Glenn. *Man and Mankind: Conflict and Communication Between Cultures.* Norwood, NJ: Ablex, 1981.

Goldstein, L. M., and S. M. Conrad. "Student Input and Negotiation of Meaning in ESL Writing Conferences." *TESOL Quarterly* 24, no. 3 (1990): 443–460.

Goodenough, W. H. "Cultural Anthropology and Linguistics." In *Language in Culture and Society: A Reader in Linguistics and Anthropology,* edited by D. Hymes, 36–39. New York: Harper & Row, 1964.

Goody, J., and I. Watt. "The Consequences of Literacy." In *Literacy in Traditional Societies,* edited by J. Goody, 27–68. New York: Cambridge University Press, 1968.

Gorman, T. P., A. C. Purves, and R. E. Degenhart, eds. *The IEA Study of Written Composition I: The International Writing Tasks and Scoring Scales.* New York, Pergamon Press, 1988.

Grabe, W. "Contrastive Rhetoric and Text-Type Research." In *Writing Across Languages: Analysis of L2 Text,* edited by U. Connor and R. B. Kaplan, 115–137. Reading, MA: Addison-Wesley, 1987.

———. *Annual Review of Applied Linguistics* 11. New York: Cambridge University Press, 1990.

Grabe, W., and D. Biber. "Freshman Student Writing and the Contrastive Rhetoric Hypothesis." Paper presented at the Second Language Research Forum, University of Southern California, 1987.

Grabe, W., and R. B. Kaplan. "Writing in a Second Language: Contrastive Rhetoric." In *Richness in Writing: Empowering ESL Students,* edited by D. M. Johnson and D. H. Roen, 263–283. New York: Longman, 1989.

Granger, S. "The International Corpus of Learner English." In *English Language Corpora: Design, Analysis, and Exploitation,* papers from the Thirteenth International Conference on English Language Research Computerized Corpora, Nijmegen, 1992, edited by J. Aarts, P. de Haas, and N. Oostdijk, 57–71. Amsterdam: Rodopi, 1993.

Gubb, J., T. P. Gorman, and E. Price. *The Study of Written Composition: A Report of the IEA Study of Written Composition in England and Wales.* Oxford: NFER Nelson, 1987.

Gunnarsson, B.L. *Research on Language for Specific Purposes in the Past and in the Future.* Forskningsgruppen för Text och Fackspråksstudier. NR 8. Uppsala: Uppsala Universitet, 1993.

Halliday, M. A. K. *Explorations in the Functions of Language.* London: Edward Arnold, 1973.

Halliday, M. A. K., and R. Hasan. *Cohesion in English.* London: Longman, 1976.

Hayes, J. R., R. E. Young, M. L. Matchett, M. McCaffrey, C. Hajduk, and T. Hajduk, eds. *Reading Empirical Research Studies: The Rhetoric of Research.* Hillsdale, NJ: Erlbaum, 1992.

Hazen, M. D. "The Universality of Logic Processes in Japanese Argument." In *Argumentation: Analysis and Practices,* edited by F. H. Van Eemeren, R. Grootendorst, J. A. Blair, and C. A. Willard, 115–126. Dordrecht, Holland: Foris, 1987.

Heath, S. B. *Ways with Words: Language, Life, and Work in Communities and Classrooms.* New York: Cambridge University Press, 1983.

Herrington, A. J. "Writing in Academic Settings: A Study of the Contexts for Writing in Two College Chemical Engineering Courses." *Research in the Teaching of English* 19 (1985): 331–361.

———. "Teaching, Writing, and Learning: A Naturalistic Study of Writing in an Undergraduate Literature Course." In *Advances in Writing Research, vol. 2: Writing in Academic Disciplines,* edited by D. A. Jolliffe, 133–166. Norwood, NJ: Ablex, 1988.

Herzberg, B. "The Politics of Discourse Communities." Paper presented at the College Composition and Communication Conference, New Orleans, Louisiana, March 1986.

Hillocks, G., Jr. *Research on Written Composition: New Directions for Teaching.* Urbana, IL: National Council of Teachers of English, 1986.

Hinds, J. "Japanese Expository Prose." *Papers in Linguistics* 13 (1980): 117–158.

———. "Contrastive Rhetoric: Japanese and English. *Text* 3, no. 2 (1983a): 183–195.

———. "Linguistics in Written Discourse in Particular Languages: Contrastive Studies: English and Japanese." In *Annual Review of Applied Linguistics* III, edited by R. B. Kaplan, 78–84. Rowley, MA: Newbury House, 1983b.

———. "Retention of Information Using a Japanese Style of Presentation." *Studies in Linguistics* 8 (1984): 45–69.

———. "Reader Versus Writer Responsibility: A New Typology." In *Writing Across Languages: Analysis of L2 Text,* edited by U. Connor and R. B. Kaplan, 141–152. Reading, MA: Addison-Wesley, 1987.

———. "Inductive, Deductive, Quasi-Inductive: Expository Writing in Japanese, Korean, Chinese, and Thai." In *Coherence in Writing: Research and Pedagogical Perspectives,* edited by U. Connor and A. M. Johns, 87–110. Alexandria, VA: TESOL, 1990.

Hirose, K., and M. Sasaki. "Explanatory Variables for Japanese Students' Expository Writing in English: An Explanatory Study," *Journal of Second Language Writing,* 3, no. 3 (1994): 203–230.

Hoey, M. *Patterns of Lexis in Text.* Oxford: Oxford University Press, 1991.

———. *On the Surface of Discourse.* London: George Allen and Unwin, 1983.

———. "Overlapping Patterns of Discourse Organization and Their Implications for Clause Relational Analysis in Problem-Solution Texts." In *Studying Writing: Linguistic Approaches,* edited by C. R. Cooper and S. Greenbaum, 187–214. Newbury Park, CA: Sage, 1986.

Hoffman, E. *Lost in Translation. A Life in a New Language.* New York: Penguin, 1989.

Hofstede, G. *Culture's Consequences: International Differences in Work-Related Values.* Beverly Hills, CA: Sage, 1980.

Holes, C. "Textual Approximation in the Teaching of Academic Writing to Arab Students: A Contrastive Approach." In *English for Specific Purposes in the Arab World,* edited by J. Swales and H. Mustafa, 228–242. Birmingham, U.K.: The Language Studies Unit, University of Aston, 1984.

Holmes, J. S. *The Name and Nature of Translation Studies.* 3d International Congress of Applied Linguistics: Abstracts. Copenhagen, 1972.

———. *The Name and Nature of Translation Studies.* Amsterdam: University of Amsterdam, Department of General Studies, 1975.

Hong Chua, S., and P. Ghim Lian Chew. "English International – A Future Theme in Native and Non-Native Classrooms." *English International* 1, no. 1 (1993): 49–55.

Horner, W. B. "The Eighteenth Century." In *The Present State of Scholarship in Historical and Contemporary Rhetoric,* edited by W. B. Horner, 101–127. Columbia, MO: University of Missouri Press, 1983.

Horowitz, D. "What Professors Actually Require: Academic Tasks for the ESL Classroom." *TESOL Quarterly* 20, no. 3 (1986a): 445–462.

———. "Process, Not Product: Less Than Meets the Eye." *TESOL Quarterly* 20, no. 1 (1986b): 141–144.

Houghton, D., and M. P. Hoey. Linguistics and Written Discourse: Contrastive Rhetorics." In *Annual Review of Applied Linguistics* III, edited by R. B. Kaplan, 2–22. Rowley, MA: Newbury House, 1983.

House, J. *A Model for Translation Quality Assessment.* Tübingen, Germany: Gunter Narr Verlag, 1977.

Hull, G., M. Rose, K. L. Fraser, and M. Castellano. "Remediation as a Social Construct: Perspectives from an Analysis of Classroom Discourse." *College Composition and Communication* 42, no. 3 (1991): 299–329.

Hunt, E., and F. Agnoli. "The Whorfian Hypothesis: A Cognitive Psychology Perspective." *Psychological Review* 98, no. 3 (1991): 377–389.

Hunt, K. W. 1970. *Syntactic Maturity in Schoolchildren and Adults: Monographs of the Society for Research in Child Development,* vol. 35, no. 1. Chicago: University of Chicago Press, 1970.

Hymes, D., ed. *Language in Culture and Society: A Reader in Linguisitics and Anthropology.* New York: Harper & Row, 1964.

Indrasuta, C. "Narrative Styles in the Writing of Thai and American Students." In *Writing Across Languages and Cultures. Issues in Contrastive Rhetoric,* edited by A. C. Purves, 206–226. Newbury Park, CA: Sage, 1988.

Ingberg, M. "Finland-Swedish Paragraph Patterns in EFL Compositions." In *Proceedings from the Third Nordic Conference for English Studies,* edited by I. Lindblad and M. Ljung, 417–426. Stockholm: Almquist and Wiksell International, 1987.

Jenkins, S., and J. Hinds. "Business Letter Writing: English, French, and Japanese." *TESOL Quarterly* 21, no. 2 (1987): 327–354.

Johns, A. M. "Textual Cohesion and the Chinese Speaker of English." *Language Learning and Communication* 3, no. 1 (1984): 69–74.

———. "L1 Composition Theories: Implications for Developing Theories of L2 Composition." In *Second Language Writing: Research Insights for the Classroom,* edited by Barbara Kroll, 24–36. New York: Cambridge University Press, 1990.

———. "Interpreting an English Competency Examination: The Frustrations of an ESL Science Student." *Written Communication* 8, no. 3 (1991): 379–401.

———. "Written Argumentation for Real Audiences: Suggestions for Teacher Research and Classroom Practice." *TESOL Quarterly* 27, no. 1 (1993): 75–90.

Johnson, D. M. *Approaches to Research in Second Language Learning.* New York: Longman, 1992.

Johnstone, B. "Arguments with Khomeni: Rhetorical Situation and Persuasive Style in Cross-Cultural Perspective." *Text* 6, no. 2 (1986): 171–187.

Kachru, B. B., ed. *The Other Tongue. English Across Cultures.* Urbana, IL: University of Illinois Press, 1984.

Kádár-Fülop, J. "Culture, Writing, and Curriculum." In *Writing Across Languages and Cultures. Issues in Contrastive Rhetoric,* edited by A. C. Purves, 25–50. Newbury Park, CA: Sage, 1988.

———. *Hogyan Crnak a Tizenevesek.* Budapest: Akademiai Kiado. 1990.

Kaplan, R. B. "Cultural Thought Patterns in Intercultural Education." *Language Learning* 16 (1966): 1–20.

———. *The Anatomy of Rhetoric: Prolegomena to a Functional Theory of Rhetoric.* Philadelphia: Center for Curriculum Development, 1972.

———. "Contrastive Rhetorics: Some Implications for the Writing Process." In *Learning to Write: First Language/Second Language,* edited by A. Freedman, I. Pringle, and J. Yalden, 139–161. New York: Longman, 1983a.

———, ed. *Annual Review of Applied Linguistics* III. Rowley, MA: Newbury House, 1983b.

———. "Cultural Thought Patterns Revisited." In *Writing Across Languages: Analysis of L2 Text,* edited by U. Connor and R. B. Kaplan, 9–21. Reading, MA: Addison-Wesley, 1987.

———. "Contrastive Rhetoric and Second Language Learning: Notes Toward a Theory of Contrastive Rhetoric." In *Writing Across Languages and Cultures. Issues in Contrastive Rhetoric,* edited by A. C. Purves, 275–304. Newbury Park, CA: Sage, 1988.

Karbach, J. "Using Toulmin's Model of Argumentation." *Journal of Teaching Writing* 6, no. 1 (1987): 81–91.

Kemppinen, A. "Translating for Popular Literature with Special Reference to Harlequin Books and Their Finnish Translations." In *Empirical Studies in Translation and Linguistics,* edited by S. Tirkkonen-Condit and S.

Condit, 113–140. Joensuu, Finland: University of Joensuu, Faculty of Arts, 1988.

Kinneavy, J. L. *A Theory of Discourse.* Englewood Cliffs, NJ: Prentice-Hall, 1971.

Kirsch, G., and P. A. Sullivan, eds. *Methods and Methodology in Composition Research.* Carbondale, IL: Southern Illinois University Press, 1992.

Kobayashi, H. "Rhetorical Patterns in English and Japanese." *TESOL Quarterly* 18, no. 4 (1984): 737–738.

Krapels, A. R. "An Overview of Second Language Writing Process Research." In *Second Language Writing. Research Insights for the Classroom,* edited by B. Kroll, 37–56. New York: Cambridge University Press, 1990.

Krashen, S. "The Monitor Model for Adult Second Language Performance." In *Viewpoints on English as a Second Language,* edited by M. K. Burt, H. C. Dulay, and M. Finocchiaro, 152–161. New York: Regents Publishing, 1977.

Kroll, B., ed. *Second Language Writing: Research Insights for the Classroom.* New York: Cambridge University Press, 1990.

Krzeszowski, T. *Contrasting Languages: The Scope of Contrastive Linguistics.* Berlin: Mouton De Gruyter, 1990.

Kubota, R. "Contrastive Rhetoric of Japanese and English: A Critical Approach." Ph.D. dissertation, Department of Education, University of Toronto, 1992.

Kuhn, T. S. *The Structure of Scientific Revolutions.* 2d ed. Chicago: University of Chicago Press, 1970.

Labov, W., and J. Waletsky. "Narrative Analysis: Oral Versions of Personal Experience." In *Essays on the Verbal and Visual Arts: Proceedings of the 1966 Annual Spring Meeting of the American Ethnological Society,* edited by J. Helm, 12–14. Seattle, WA: University of Washington Press, 1967.

Lado, R. *Linguistics Across Cultures.* Ann Arbor, MI: University of Michigan Press, 1957.

Lamb, H. F. *Writing Performance in New Zealand Schools: A Report on the IEA Study of Written Composition in New Zealand.* Wellington, New Zealand: Department of Education, 1987.

Lauer, J. M., and J. W. Asher. *Composition Research: Empirical Designs.* New York: Oxford University Press, 1988.

Lautamatti, L. "Observations on the Development of the Topic in Simplified Discourse." In *Text Linguistics, Cognitive Learning and Language Teaching,* edited by V. Kohonen and N. E. Enkvist, 71–104. Suomen Sovelletun Kielitieteen Yhdistyksen Julkaisuja, no. 22. Turku, Finland: Afinla, 1978.

———. "Observations in the Development of the Topic in Simplified Discourse." In *Writing Across Languages: Analysis of L2 Text,* edited by U. Connor and R. B. Kaplan, 87–114. Reading, MA: Addison-Wesley, 1987.

Lehmann, R. H., and W. Hartmann. *The Hamburg Study of Achievement in Written Composition: National Report for the IEA International Study of Achievement in Written Communication, Part I: Method and Findings.* Hamburg: University of Hamburg, 1987.

Lehtonen, J., and K. Sajavaara. "The Silent Finn." In *Perspectives on Silence,* edited by D. Tannen and M. Saville-Troike, 193–201. Norwood, NJ: Ablex, 1985.

Leki, I. "Twenty-Five Years of Contrastive Rhetoric: Text Analysis and Writing Pedagogies." *TESOL Quarterly* 25, no. 1 (1991): 123–143.

————. *Understanding ESL Writers. A Guide for Teachers.* Portsmouth, NH: Boynton/Cook, 1992.

Li, X-M. "A Celebration of Tradition or of Self? – An Ethnographic Study of Teachers' Comments on Student Writing in America and in China. Ph.D. dissertation, University of New Hampshire, 1992.

Liebman, J. D. "Toward a New Contrastive Rhetoric: Differences Between Arabic and Japanese Rhetorical Instruction." *Journal of Second Language Writing* 1, no. 2 (1992): 141–166.

Lifqvist, G. *The IEA Study of Written Composition in Sweden. Studia Psychologica et Paedagogica – Series Altera.* Lund, Sweden: Student Litteratur, 1990.

Limaye, M., and D. A. Victor. "Cross-Cultural Business Communication Research: State of the Art and Hypotheses for the 1990s." *Journal of Business Communication* 28, no. 3 (1991): 277–299.

Lindeberg, A. C. "Cohesion, Coherence, and Coherence Patterns in Expository and Argumentative Student Essays in EFL: An Exploratory Study." Licenciate thesis, Department of English, Åbo Akademi University, Turku, Finland, 1988.

Linnarud, M. "Lexis and Lexical Cohesion." *Nordwrite Reports I. Trondheim Papers in Applied Linguistics,* edited by L. S. Evensen, 11–25. Trondheim, Norway: University of Trondheim, 1986.

Lopez, G. S. "Article Introductions in Spanish: A Study in Comparative Rhetoric." Unpublished Master of Science dissertation, Birmingham, UK: The Language Studies Unit, University of Aston, 1982.

Lucisano, P. *Indagine Sulla Produzione Scritta Italia. Ricerca Educativa.* 5: 2–3. Rome: Centro Europeo Dell' Educazione, 1988.

Lux, P. "Discourse Styles of Anglo and Latin American College Student Writers." Ph.D. dissertation, Arizona State University, 1991.

Lux, P., and W. Grabe. "Multivariate Approaches to Contrastive Rhetoric." *Lenguas Modernas* 18 (1991): 133–160.

Maier, P. "Politeness Strategies in Business Letters by Native and Non-Native English Speakers." *English for Specific Purposes* 11, no. 3 (1992): 189–205.

Mandler, J. M., and N. S. Johnson. "Remembrance of Things Parsed: Story Structure and Recall." *Cognitive Psychology* 9 (1977): 111–151.

Markkanen, R. "The Problem of Tertium Comparationis in Cross-Language Discourse Analysis." In *Proceedings from the 2nd Finnish Seminar on Discourse Analysis,* Oulu, September 27–28, 1988, edited by H. Nyyssönen, L. Kuure, E. Kärkkäinen, and P. Raudaskoski. Oulu, Finland: Publications of the Department of English 9. University of Oulu, 1990.

Markkanen, R., M. S. Steffensen, and A. Crismore. "Quantitative Contrastive Study of Metadiscourse: Problems in Design and Analysis of Data." In *Papers and Studies in Contrastive Linguistics,* vol. 23, edited by J. Fisiak, 137–151. Poznan, Poland: Adam Mickiewicz University Press, 1993.

Martin, J. E. *Toward a Theory of Text for Contrastive Rhetoric: An Introduction to Issues of Text for Students and Practitioners of Contrastive Rhetoric.* New York: Peter Lang, 1992.

Martin, J. R. "Genre and Literacy-Modeling Context in Educational Linguistics." *Annual Review of Applied Linguistics* 13 (1993): 141–172.

Martin, J. R., and J. Rothery. "What a Functional Approach Can Show Teachers." In *Functional Approaches to Writing: Research Perspectives,* edited by B. Couture, 241–265. Norwood, NJ: Ablex, 1986.

Matalene, C. "Contrastive Rhetoric: An American Writing Teacher in China." *College English* 47, no. 8 (1985): 789–808.

Mauranen, A. "Reference in Academic Rhetoric: A Contrastive Study of Finnish and English Writing." In *Nordic Research on Text and Discourse. Nordtext Symposium 1990,* edited by A. C. Lindeberg, N. E. Enkvist, and K. Wikberg, 237–250. Åbo, Finland: Åbo Akademi Press, 1992.

———. "Contrastive ESP Rhetoric: Metatext in Finnish-English Economics Texts." *English for Specific Purposes* 12 (1993): 3–22.

———. *Cultural Differences in Academic Rhetoric.* Frankfurt am Main: Peter Lang, 1993.

McKay, S. L. "Examining L2 Composition Ideology: A Look at Literacy." *Journal of Second Language Writing* 2, no. 1 (1993a): 65–81.

———. *Agendas for Second Language Literacy.* New York: Cambridge University Press, 1993b.

Meyer, B. J. F. *The Organization of Prose and its Effects on Memory.* Amsterdam: North Holland, 1975.

Mohan, B. A., and W. A-Y Lo. "Academic Writing and Chinese Students: Transfer and Developmental Factors." *TESOL Quarterly* 19, no. 3 (1985): 515–534.

Montaño-Harmon, M. "Discourse Features in the Compositions of Mexican, English-as-a-Second-Language, Mexican/American Chicano, and Anglo High School Students: Considerations for the Formulation of Educational Policies." Ph.D. dissertation, University of Southern California, 1988.

———. "Discourse Features of Written Mexican Spanish: Current Research in Contrastive Rhetoric and its Implications." *Hispania* 74 (1991): 417–425.

Moran, M. H., and M. G. Moran. "Business Letters, Memoranda, and Résumés." In *Research in Technical Communication,* edited by M. G. Moran and D. Journet, 313–352. Westport, CT: Greenwood Press, 1985.

Muramatsu, T., S. Higuchi, K. Shigemori, M. Saito, M. Sasao, S. Harada, Y. Shigeta, K. Yamada, H. Muraoka, S. Takagi, K. Maruyama, and H. Kono. "Ethanol Patch Test – A Simple and Sensitive Method for Identifying ALDH Phenotype." *Alcoholism: Clinical and Experimental Research* 13, no. 2 (1989): 229.

Murray, D. "The Interior View: One Writer's Philosophy of Composition." *College Composition and Communication* 21 (1970): 21–26.

Myers, G. "The Social Construction of Two Biologists' Proposals." *Written Communication* 2, no. 3 (1985): 219–245.

———. *Writing Biology. Texts in the Social Construction of Scientific Knowledge.* Madison, WI: University of Wisconsin Press, 1990.

Najjar, H. Y. "Arabic as a Research Language: The Case of the Agricultural Sciences." Unpublished Ph.D. dissertation, University of Michigan, 1990.

Nelson, G. L., and J. G. Carson, with N. Danison and L. Gajdusek. "Social Dimensions of Second-Language Writing Instruction: Peer Response Groups as Cultural Context." In *Composing Social Identity in Written Language,* edited by D. L. Rubin, 89–112. Hillsdale, N.J.: Erlbaum, 1995.

Nelson, G. L., and J. M. Murphy. "An ESL Writing Group: Task and Social Dimensions." *Journal of Second Language Writing* 1, no. 3 (1992): 171–194.

Newmark, P. *Approaches to Translation.* Oxford: Pergamon Press, 1981.

Nida, E. A. *Toward a Science of Translating.* Leiden: E. J. Brill, 1964.

North, S. M. *The Making of Knowledge in Composition. Portrait of an Emerging Field.* Upper Montclair, NJ: Boynton/Cook, 1987.

Nozaki, K. "Stilted English: Nihonjin Eigo no Sutairu" ("Stilted English: The Style of English Used by the Japanese)." *Gendai Eigo Kyoiku* (Modern English Teaching) 25, no. 5 (1988): 12–13.

Nystrand, M. "Rhetoric's Audience and Linguistics' Speech Community: Implications for Understanding Writing, Reading, and Text." In *What Writers Know: The Language, Process, and Structure of Written Discourse,* edited by M. Nystrand, 1–28. New York: Academic Press, 1982.

———. *The Structure of Written Communication. Studies in Reciprocity Between Writers and Readers.* Orlando, FL: Academic Press, 1986.

———. "A Social-Interactive Model of Writing. *Written Communication* 6, no. 1 (1989): 66–85.

Odell, L., and D. Goswami, eds. *Writing in Nonacademic Settings.* New York: Guilford Press, 1985.

Odlin, T. *Language Transfer.* Cambridge: Cambridge University Press, 1989.

Oi, K., and T. Sato. "Cross-cultural Rhetorical Differences in Letter Writing: Refusal Letter and Application Letter." *JACET Bulletin* 21 (1990): 117–136.

Ong, W. "Foreword." In *The Present State of Scholarship in Historical and Contemporary Rhetoric,* edited by W. B. Horner, 1–9. Columbia, MO: University of Missouri Press, 1983.

Ostler, S. E. "English in Parallels: A Comparison of English and Arabic Prose." In *Writing Across Languages: Analysis of L2 Text,* edited by U. Connor and R. B. Kaplan, 169–185. Reading, MA: Addison-Wesley, 1987.

Parkhurst, C. "The Composition Process of Science Writers." *English for Specific Purposes* 9, no. 2 (1990): 169–180.

Perelman, C. H. *The Realm of Rhetoric,* translated by W. Kluback. Notre Dame, IN: University of Notre Dame Press, 1982.

Perelman, C. H., and L. Olbrechts-Tyteca. *The New Rhetoric: A Treatise on Argumentation,* translated by J. Wilkinson and P. Weaver. Notre Dame, IN: University of Notre Dame Press, 1969.

Péry-Woodley, M. P. "Contrasting Discourses: Constrastive Analysis and a Discourse Approach to Writing." *Language Teaching* 23, no. 3 (1990): 143–151.

Pinker, S. *The Language Instinct: How the Mind Creates Language.* New York: William Morrow, 1994.

Pitkin, W. L. "Discourse Blocs." *College Composition and Communication* 20, no. 2 (1969): 138–148.

Pochhacker, F. "Beyond Equivalence: Recent Developments in Translation Theory." In *American Translators' Association Conference 1989,* edited by D. Lindberg Hammond, 563–572. Medford, NJ: Learned Information, 1989.

Prior, P. "Contextualizing Writing and Response in a Graduate Seminar." *Written Communication* 8 (1991): 267–31.

————. "Redefining the Task: An Ethnographic Examination of Writing and Response in Six Graduate Seminars." In *Academic Writing in a Second Language: Essays on Research and Pedagogy,* edited by D. Belcher and G. Braine 47–82. Norwood, NJ: Ablex, 1995.

Purves, A. C. "Introduction." In *Writing Across Languages and Cultures: Issues in Contrastive Rhetoric,* edited by A. C. Purves, 9–21. Newbury Park, CA: Sage, 1988.

————. "Reflections on Research and Assessment in Written Composition." *Research in the Teaching of English* 26, no. 1 (1992): 108–122.

Purves, A. C., and G. Hawisher. "Writers, Judges, and Text Models." In *Developing Discourse Practices in Adolescence and Adulthood,* edited by R. Beach and S. Hynds, 183–199. Norwood, NJ: Ablex, 1990.

Purves, A. C., and W. C. Purves. "Viewpoints: Cultures, Text Models, and the Activity of Writing." *Research in the Teaching of English* 20, no. 2 (1986): 174–197.

Raimes, A. "What Unskilled Writers Do as They Write: A Classroom Study of Composing." *TESOL Quarterly* 19, no. 2 (1985): 229–258.

————. "Language Proficiency, Writing Ability, and Composing Strategies: A Study of ESL College Student Writers." *Language Learning* 37, no. 3 (1987): 439–468.

————. "Out of the Woods: Emerging Traditions in the Teaching of Writing." *TESOL Quarterly* 25, no. 3 (1991a): 407–430.

————. "Instructional Balance: From Theories to Practices in the Teaching of Writing." In *Linguistics and Language Pedagogy. Georgetown University Round Table on Languages and Linguistics,* edited by J. E. Alatis, 238–249. Washington, D.C.: Georgetown University Press, 1991b.

Reid, J. "Comments on Vivian Zamel's 'The Composing Processes of Advanced ESL Students: Six Case Studies.'" *TESOL Quarterly* 18, no. 1 (1984a):149–153.

————. "The Radical Outliner and the Radical Brainstormer: A Perspective on Composing Processes." *TESOL Quarterly* 18, no. 3 (1984b): 529–533.

————. "Quantitative Differences in English Prose Written by Arabic, Chinese, Spanish, and English Students." Ph.D. dissertation, Colorado State University, 1988.

————. "A Computer Text Analysis of Four Cohesion Devices in English Discourse by Native and Nonnative Writers." *Journal of Second Language Writing* 1, no. 2 (1992): 79–108.

————. *Teaching ESL Writing.* Englewood Cliffs, NJ: Prentice Hall, 1993.

Reppen, R., and W. Grabe. "Spanish Transfer Effects in the English Writing of Elementary School Children." *Lenguas Modernas* 20 (1993): 113–128.

Ringbom, H., ed. *Near-native Proficiency in English.* Åbo, Finland: English Department Publications, 1993.

Rottenberg, A. T. *Elements of Argument: A Text and Reader.* New York: St. Martin's Press, 1985.

Rutherford, W. "Markedness in Second Language Acquisition." *Language Learning* 32 (1982): 85–108.

Sa'adeddin, M. A. "Text Development and Arabic-English Negative Interference." *Applied Linguistics* 10, no. 1 (1989): 36–51.

Saisho, F. *Nihongo to Eigo: Hasso to Hyogen no Hikaku* (Japanese and English: A Comparison of Thoughts and Expressions). Tokyo: Kenkyusha, 1975.

Sajavaara, K., and J. Lehtonen, eds. "Prisoners of Code-Centered Privacy: Reflections on Contrastive Analysis and Related Disciplines." In *Papers in Discourse and Contrastive Discourse Analysis*. Jyväskylä Contrastive Studies 5, Reports from the Department of English, Jyväskylä: University of Jyväskylä, 7–26, 1980.

Salomon, G. "Transcending the Qualitative-Quantitative Debate: The Analytic and Systemic Approaches to Educational Research." *Educational Researcher* 20, no. 6 (1991): 10–18.

Santana-Seda, O. "A Contrastive Study in Rhetoric: An Analysis of the Organization of English and Spanish Paragraphs Written by Native Speakers of Each Language." Ph.D. dissertation, New York University, 1970.

Santiago, R. L. "A Contrastive Analysis of Some Rhetorical Aspects in the Writing in Spanish and English of Spanish Speaking College Students in Puerto Rico." Ph.D. dissertation, New York University, 1970.

Santos, T. "Ideology in Composition: L1 and ESL." *Journal of Second Language Writing* 1 (1992): 1–16.

Sapir, E. "Language." In *Selected Writings of Edward Sapir in Language, Culture, and Personality,* edited by D. G. Mandelbaum, 7-32. Berkeley: University of California Press, 1912, 1951.

Scarcella, R. "How Writers Orient Their Readers in Expository Essays: A Comparative Study of Native and Non-Native English Writers." *TESOL Quarterly* 18, no. 14 (1984a): 671–688.

———. "Cohesion in the Writing Development of Native and Non-Native English Speakers. Ph.D. dissertation, University of Southern California, 1984b.

Schneider, M., and U. Connor. "Analyzing Topical Structure in ESL Essays: Not All Topics Are Equal." *Studies in Second Language Acquisition* 12 (1991): 411–427.

Scollon, R. "Eight Legs and One Elbow. Stance and Structure in Chinese English Compositions." Paper presented at International Reading Association, Second North American Conference on Adult and Adolescent Literacy, Banff, March 21, 1991.

Scollon, R., and S. B. K. Scollon. *Narrative, Literacy, and Face in Interethnic Communication.* Norwood, NJ: Ablex, 1981.

Scribner, S., and M. Cole. *The Psychology of Literacy.* Cambridge, MA: Harvard University Press, 1981.

Selinker, L. "Interlanguage." *IRAL: International Review of Applied Linguistics* 10 (1972): 209–231.

Selinker, L., M. Swain, and G. Dumas. "The Interlanguage Hypotheses Extended to Children." *Language Learning* 25 (1975): 139–155.

Severino, C., J. Guerra, and J. Butler, eds. *Writing in Multicultural Settings.* New York: Modern Language Association, in press.

Shen, F. "The Classroom and the Wider Culture: Identity as a Key to Learning English Composition." *College Composition and Communication* 40, no. 4 (1989): 459–466.

Silva, T. "Toward an Understanding of the Distinct Nature of L2 Writing: The ESL Research and its Implications." *TESOL Quarterly* 27, no. 4 (1993): 657–677.

Söter, A. "The Second Language Learner and Cultural Transfer in Narration." In *Writing Across Languages and Cultures. Issues in Contrastive Rhetoric,* edited by A. C. Purves, 177–205. Newbury Park, CA: Sage, 1988.

Spack, R. "Invention Strategies and the ESL College Composition Student." *TESOL Quarterly* 18 (1984): 649–670.

Strevens, P. "English as an International Language." *English Teaching Forum* 25, no. 4 (1987): 56–63.

Stygall, G. "Toulmin and the Ethics of Argument Fields: Teaching Writing and Argument." *Journal of Teaching Writing* 6, no. 1 (1987): 93–107.

Svartvik, J., N. Blake, and G. Toury. *Peer Review of the Teaching of English Studies in Finnish Universities.* Helsinki: University of Helsinki, 1994.

Swales, J. *Aspects of Article Introductions.* Birmingham, UK: The Language Studies Unit, University of Aston, 1981.

———. "Nonnative Speaker Graduate Engineering Students and Their Introductions: Global Coherence and Local Management." In *Coherence in Writing: Research and Pedagogical Perspectives,* edited by U. Connor and A. M. Johns, 187–208. Arlington, VA: TESOL, 1990a.

———. *Genre Analysis: English in Academic and Research Settings.* New York: Cambridge University Press, 1990b.

Swales, J., and H. Mustafa, eds. *English for Specific Purposes in the Arab World.* Birmingham, UK: The Language Studies Unit, University of Aston, 1984.

Takala, S. "The Domain of Writing." In *On the Specification of the Domain of Writing,* edited by S. Takala and A. Vähäpassi, 1–61. Jyväskylä, Finland: Institute for Educational Research Bulletin, University of Jyväskylä, 1983.

———. "Origins of the International Study of Writing." In *The IEA Study of Written Composition I: The International Writing Tasks and Scoring Scales,* edited by T. P. Gorman, A. C. Purves, and R. E. Degenhart, 3–14. New York: Pergamon Press, 1988.

Taylor, G., and T. Chen. "Linguistic, Cultural, and Subcultural Issues in Contrastive Discourse Analysis: Anglo-American and Chinese Scientific Texts." *Applied Linguistics* 12, no. 3 (1991): 319–336.

Tierney, R. J., and J. H. Mosenthal. "Cohesion and Textual Coherence." *Research in the Teaching of English* 17 (1983): 215–229.

Tirkkonen-Condit, S. "Argumentative Text Structure and Translation." *Studia Philologica Jyväskyläensia* vol. 18. Jyväskylä, Finland: Kirjapaino Oy, Sisäsuomi, 1985.

———. "Text Type Markers and Translation Equivalence." In *Interlingual and Intercultural Communication,* edited by J. House and S. Blum-Kulka, 95–114. Tübingen, Germany: Gunter Narr Verlag, 1986.

———. "Editorials as Argumentative Dialogues: Explicit vs. Implicit Expression of Disagreement in Finnish, English, and American Newspaper Editorials." In *LSP and Theory of Translation, Papers from Vakki Seminar VIII,* 168–175. Vaasa: University of Vaasa, School of Modern Languages, 1988.

———. "Theory and Methodology in Translation Research." In *Empirical Studies in Translation and Linguistics,* edited by S. Tirkkonen-Condit and S. Condit, 3–18, Studies in Language, 17. Joensuu, Finland: University of Joensuu, Faculty of Arts, 1989.

Tirkkonen-Condit, S., and L. Lieflander-Koistinen. "Argumentation in Finnish Versus English and German Editorials." In *Text-Interpretation-*

Argumentation, edited by M. Kusch and H. Schröder, 173–181. Hamburg, Germany: Helmut Buske Verlag, 1989.

Toulmin, S. *The Uses of Argument.* Cambridge, Cambridge University Press, 1958.

Toulmin, S., R. Rieke, and A. Janik. *An Introduction to Reasoning.* New York: Macmillan, 1979.

Toury, G. *In Search of a Theory of Translation.* Tel Aviv: Porteer Institute for Poetics and Semiotics, 1980.

———. "Monitoring Discourse Transfer: A Test-Case for a Developmental Model of Translation." In *Interlingual and Intercultural Communication. Discourse and Cognition and Second-Language Acquisition Studies,* edited by J. House and S. Blum-Kulka, 79–94. Tübingen, Germany: Gunther Narr Verlag, 1986.

———. "What Are Descriptive Studies into Translation Likely to Yield Apart from Isolated Descriptions?" In *Translation Studies: The State of the Art,* edited by K. Van Leuven-Zwart and T. Naaijkens, 179–192. Amsterdam: Rodopi, 1991.

Toury, G., and J. Laffling. "Translation of Literary Texts vs. Literary Translation: A Distinction Reconsidered." In *Recent Trends in Empirical Translation Research,* edited by S. Tirkkonen-Condit. Studies in Language no. 28. University of Joensuu, Faculty of Arts: Joensuu, 1993.

Triandis, H. C. *Some Dimensions of Intercultural Variation and Their Implications for Interpersonal Behavior.* (Manuscript). University of Illinois at Urbana-Champaign, 1981.

Trimbur, J. "Consensus and Difference in Collaborative Learning." *College English* 51 (1989): 602–616.

Tsao, F. F. "Linguistics and Written Discourse in Particular Languages: English and Mandarin." In *Annual Review of Applied Linguistics III,* edited by R. B. Kaplan, 99–117. Rowley, MA: Newbury House, 1983.

Tu, W-M. *Confucian Thought: Selfhood as Creative Transformation.* Albany, NY: State University of New York Press, 1985.

Vähäpassi, A. "The Domain of School Writing and Development of the Writing Tasks." In *The IEA Study of Written Composition I: The International Writing Tasks and Scoring Scales,* edited by T. P. Gorman, A. C. Purves, and R. E. Degenhart, 15–40. New York: Pergamon Press, 1988.

———. "The Problem of Selection of Writing Tasks in Cross-Cultural Study." In *Writing Across Languages and Cultures: Issues in Contrastive Rhetoric,* edited by A. C. Purves, 51–78. Newbury Park, CA: Sage, 1998b.

Van Dijk, T. A. *Some Aspects of Text Grammars.* The Hague: Mouton, 1972.

———. *Macrostructures: An Interdisciplinary Study of Global Structures in Discourse, Interaction, and Cognition.* Hilldale, NJ: Erlbaum, 1980.

———. *Handbook of Discourse Analysis.* vols. 1–4. New York: Academic Press, 1985a.

———. "Introduction: Discourse Analysis as a New Cross-Discipline." In *Handbook of Discourse Analysis,* edited by T. A. Van Dijk, 1–10. New York: Academic Press, 1985b.

Vande Kopple, W. J. "Some Exploratory Discourse on Metadiscourse." *College Composition and Communication* 36 (1985): 82–93.

———. "Given and New Information and Some Aspects of the Structures, Semantics, and Pragmatics of Written Texts." In *Studying Writing: Linguistic Approaches,* vol. 1, edited by C. R. Cooper and S. Greenbaum, 72–111. Newbury Park, CA: Sage, 1986.

Ventola, E., and A. Mauranen. "Non-Native Writing and Native Revising of Scientific Articles." In *Functional and Systemic Linguistics: Approaches and Uses,* edited by E. Ventola, 457–492. Berlin: Mouton De Gruyter, 1991.

Virtanen, T. "On the Definitions of Text and Discourse." *Folia Linguistica* 24, no. 3–4 (1990): 447–455.

———. *Discourse Functions of Adverbial Placement in English. Clause-Initial Adverbials of Time and Place in Narratives and Procedural Place Descriptions.* Åbo, Finland: Åbo Akademi, 1992.

Watson-Gegeo, K. A. "Ethnography in ESL: Defining the Essentials." *TESOL Quarterly* 22, no. 4 (1988): 575–592.

Weissberg, R., and S. Buker. *Writing Up Research.* Englewood Cliffs, NJ: Prentice Hall, 1990.

Werlich, E. *A Text Grammar of English.* Heidelberg: Quelle and Meyer, 1976.

Whorf, B. *Language, Thought and Reality. Selected Writings of Benjamin Lee Whorf,* edited by J. B. Carroll. Cambridge, MA: MIT Press, 1956.

Wikborg, E. "Types of Coherence Breaks in Swedish Student Writing: Misleading Paragraph Divisions." In *Coherence in Writing: Research and Pedagogical Perspectives,* edited by U. Connor and A. M. Johns, 131–150. Arlington, VA: TESOL, 1990.

Williams, H. P. "A Problem of Cohesion." In *English for Specific Purposes in the Arab World,* edited by J. Swales and H. Mustafa, 118–128. Birmingham, UK: The Language Studies Unit, University of Aston, 1984.

Witte, S. P. "Topical Structure and Revision: An Exploratory Study." *College Composition and Communication* 34, no. 3 (1983a): 313–341.

———. "Topical Structure and Writing Quality: Some Possible Text-Based Explanations of Readers' Judgements of Students' Writing." *Visible Language* 17 (1983b): 177–205.

———. "Toward a Constructivist Semiotic of Writing." *Written Communication* 9, no. 2 (1992): 237–308.

Witte, S. P., and L. Faigley. "Coherence, Cohesion, and Writing Quality." *College Composition and Communication* 32, no. 2 (1981): 189–204.

Yli-Jokipii, H. "Running Against Time and Technology: Problems in Empirical Research into Written Business Communication." In *Communication and Discourse Across Cultures and Languages,* edited by K. Sajavaara, D. March, and T. Keto, 59–72. Afinla Series, no. 49. Jyväskylä, Finland: Kopi-Jyvä Oy, 1991.

———. "Requests in Professional Discourse: A Cross-Cultural Study of British, American, and Finnish Business Writing. Ph.D. dissertation, Department of English, University of Turku. Finland. Annales Academiae Scientiarum Fennicae. Dissertationes Humanarum Litterarum 71. Suomalainen Tiedeakatemia, Helsinki, 1994.

Zak, H., and T. Dudley-Evans. "Features of Word Omission and Abbreviation in Telexes." *ESP Journal* 5 no. 1 (1986): 59–71.

Zamel, V. "Teaching Composition in the ESL Classroom: What We Can Learn from Research in the Teaching of English." *TESOL Quarterly* 10 (1976): 67–76.

————. "In Search of the Key: Research and Practice in Composition." In *On TESOL '83,* edited by J. Handscombe, R. A. Orem, and B. P. Taylor, 195–207. Washington, D.C.: TESOL, 1984.

————. "Recent Research on Writing Pedagogy. *TESOL Quarterly* 21, no. 4 (1987): 697–715.

Author index

In all cases of work involving co-authors, only the name of the first author of the work appears in this index.

Al-Jubouri, A., 35
Allaei, S., 23, 161, 168
Altehenger-Smith, S., 17
Aristotle, 31, 62, 64, 65, 127

Bailey, N., 13
Bain, A., 65
Ballard, B., 171
Bar-Lev, Z., 36
Bazerman, C, 77
Belcher, D., 78, 143, 171
Bereiter, C., 154, 155, 156
Berkenkotter, C., 77, 126, 128, 129, 145, 173
Berlin, J., 25, 59, 60, 62, 64
Bhatia, V., 127, 136, 137
Biber, D., 16, 94, 126, 143, 158, 159, 160, 164
Bickner, R., 91, 92, 131
Bizzell, P., 76, 77
Bloom, A., 29
Bloom, L., 61
Bloomfield, L., 31
Blum-Kulka, S., 163
Bolivar, A., 145
Briggs, C., 127, 128
Brown, G., 19
Bruffee, K., 61

Cai, G., 37, 38, 39
Cameron, D., 173
Campbell, G., 65
Carlson, S., 171

Carson, J., 21, 22, 24, 114, 115, 161, 168
Casanave, C, 78, 145, 173
Cerniglia, C., 87
Chesterman, A., 118
Choi, Y., 46
Chomsky, N, 30, 80, 158
Christensen, F., 32
Clancy, P., 113
Clark, H., 29
Clyne, M., 20, 46, 95, 164
Čmejrková, S., 53, 54
Confucius, 38, 39, 73
Connor, U., 19, 20, 24, 32, 33, 45, 46, 52, 65, 66, 70, 71, 84, 87, 89, 91, 92, 94, 96, 97, 98, 113, 114, 131, 132, 137, 138, 140, 141, 144, 145, 148, 155, 156, 159, 160, 161, 162, 164, 165, 173
Connors, R., 63, 64
Corbett, E., 61, 65
Corder, S., 12, 13
Crismore, A., 47, 48, 49, 92, 94, 131, 156, 163, 164
Croft, K., 30

Dantas-Whitney, M., 143, 159
de Beaugrande, R., 20, 82
Devahastin, W., 113
Dressler, W., 81
Dulay, H., 13, 15

Edmondson, W., 19
Eggington, W., 20, 25, 45, 46, 93, 95, 156, 161, 164

Elbow, P., 61, 71, 73
Emig, J., 61, 74
Enkvist, N., 19, 82, 89, 90, 91
Evensen, L., 90, 91, 92

Fagan, E., 39
Fairclough, N., 173
Fallaci, O., 36
Fillmore, 83
Fishman, J., 29
Fisiak, J., 54
Flower, L., 18, 75
Fogarty, D., 66
Folman, S., 21, 22, 114, 132, 172
Freire, P., 26
Fries, C., 13

Gentzler, E., 117
Glenn, E., 101, 102, 107
Goldstein, L., 24
Goodenough, W., 101
Goody, J., 104
Gorman, T., 21, 107, 108
Grabe, W., 155, 158, 160, 166, 167
Granger, S., 173
Gubb, J., 113
Gunnarsson, B., 136

Halliday, M., 80, 81, 82, 83, 84, 87,
    90, 94
Hayes, J., 153
Hazen, M., 140
Heath, S., 21, 76, 105, 106
Herrington, A., 78
Herzberg, B., 76
Hillocks, G., 75
Hinds, J., 15, 16, 19, 20, 41, 42, 43,
    44, 46, 52, 71, 95, 98, 138, 156,
    158, 161, 163
Hirose, K., 44
Hoey, M., 19, 87
Hoffman, E., 4
Hofstede, G., 101, 102, 103, 107
Holes, C., 35, 36
Holmes, J., 118, 123
Hong Chua, S, 17
Horner, W., 63
Horowitz, D., 70
House, J., 119, 121
Hull, G., 23, 169
Hunt, E., 10, 29

Hunt, K., 91
Hymes, D., 80

Indrasuta, C., 92, 93, 97
Ingberg, M., 91, 92

Jenkins, S., 45, 138, 140
Johns, A., 84, 134, 135, 148, 156,
    161
Johnson, D., 153, 165
Johnstone, B., 36

Kachru, B., 17, 173
Kádár-Fülop, J., 108, 109, 112
Kaplan, R., 5, 6, 7, 8, 9, 10, 15, 16,
    28, 30, 31, 32, 34, 35, 37, 38,
    39, 40, 42, 50, 52, 54, 70, 91,
    93, 97, 100, 104, 123, 129, 155,
    156, 157, 158, 166, 167
Karbach, J., 69
Kemppinen, A., 119, 120
Khomeini, A., 36
Kinneavy, J., 11, 32, 65, 70, 126
Kirsch, G., 153
Kobayashi, H., 43
Krapels, A., 75, 76
Krashen, S., 12, 13
Kroll, B., 85
Kreszowski, T., 163
Kubota, R., 25, 43
Kuhn, T., 6, 18

Labov, W., 85
Lado, R., 13
Lamb, H., 112
Lauer, J., 65, 97, 153, 154, 155, 156,
    165
Lautamatti, L., 84, 89, 97
Lehmann, R., 113
Lehtonen, J., 47, 74, 143
Leki, I., 18, 62, 155, 156, 167
Li, X-M., 106, 173
Liebman, J., 31, 114, 115, 156, 160,
    161, 173
Lifqvist, G., 112
Limaye, M., 138
Lindeberg, A., 51, 90
Linnarud, M., 90
Lopez, G., 134
Lucisano, P., 112
Lux, P., 53, 143

Maier, P., 138, 141
Mandler, J., 87
Markkanen, R., 47, 51, 95, 155
Martin, J.E., 20
Martin, J.R., 87, 88
Matalene, C., 16, 38, 39, 40
Mauranen, A., 24, 49, 50, 63, 74,
    96, 97, 98, 155
McKay, S., 26
Melis, I., 144, 146
Meyer, B., 87, 93
Mohan, B., 16, 37, 164
Montaño-Harmon, M., 53
Moran, M., 137
Muramatsu, T., 133
Murray, D., 61, 71
Myers, G., 77, 134, 135, 165

Najjar, H., 134
Nelson, G., 102, 156, 161, 174
Newmark, P., 119
Nida, E., 121
North, S., 59
Nozaki, K., 44
Nystrand, M., 18, 76

Odell, L., 76, 137
Odlin, T., 13
Oi, K., 44
Ong, W., 62, 63
Ostler, S., 24, 32, 34, 35, 92, 93,
    156, 158

Parkhurst, C., 148
Perelman, C., 6, 66, 69, 70
Perý-Woodley, M. P., 5, 6
Pinker, S., 29
Pitkin, W., 32
Pochhacker, F., 118, 119
Prior, P., 78, 145
Purves, A., 7, 21, 52, 66, 108, 111,
    112, 155, 156, 157, 163, 170

Raimes, A., 16, 18, 69, 72, 75
Reid, J., 52, 62, 72, 92, 94, 99, 156,
    160
Reppen, R., 53
Ringbom, H., 173
Rottenberg, A., 68
Rutherford, W., 13

Saisho, F., 44
Sajavaara, K., 14, 47
Salomon, G., 162
Sa'adeddin, M., 36
Santana-Seda, O., 52
Santiago, R., 52
Santos, T., 25
Sapir, E., 10, 28, 29
Scarcella, R., 83, 92, 93
Schneider, M., 85, 86, 97
Scollon , R., 23, 38, 73
Scribner, S., 21, 103, 104, 105
Selinker, L, 13
Severino, C., 169
Shen, F., 73
Silva, T., 34
Söter, A., 20, 70, 92, 93, 110, 130
Spack, R., 72
Spove, S., 144, 146
Strevens, P., 17
Stygall, G., 69
Svartvik, J., 118
Swales, J., 11, 15, 24, 35, 40, 76, 77,
    78, 99, 126, 127, 129, 132, 134,
    135, 145, 148, 165, 173

Takala, S., 108, 129, 130
Taylor, G., 40, 41, 134, 165
Tierney, R., 83
Tirkkonen-Condit, S., 46, 87, 89, 94,
    119, 120
Toulmin, S., 66, 67, 68, 94, 96, 131,
    140
Toury, G., 117, 118, 120, 121, 122,
    123
Triandis, H., 102, 103, 107
Trimbur, J., 25
Tsao, F., 39

Vähäpassi, A., 108, 109, 110, 111
Van Dijk, T., 11, 80, 81, 82, 85
Vande Kopple, W., 48, 49, 51, 95
Ventola, E., 34, 49, 96, 97, 98, 122,
    125, 164, 169, 172
Virtanen, T., 11, 19

Watson-Gegeo, K., 131
Weissberg, R., 132
Werlich, E., 108, 109
Whitman, W., 73

Whorf, B., 28, 29, 30, 32, 43, 52
Wikborg, E., 90
Williams, H., 35
Witte, S., 76, 82, 83, 85, 97

Yli-Jokipii, H., 137, 142

Zak, H., 137
Zamel, V., 72

Subject index

academic writing, 50–52, 96, 132–5
acceptability of texts, 121–3, 173
  see also translation theory
adequacy of texts, 121–3, 173
  see also translation theory
Aristotelean rhetoric, 10, 31–2, 62–6
  see also composition pedagogy;
    rhetoric
argumentative writing, 24, 36, 46,
  66–70, 79, 88–9, 92, 94, 99,
  108, 126, 131, 134, 149, 165,
  171
audience, 69–70

Biber's multifeature/multidimensional
  text analysis, 94, 143, 158–60,
  164
business letters, 138–40
business writing, 96, 137–43

classroom-based studies, 23–4, 167–
  9, 173–4
  see also case studies and ethnogra-
    phies under research design;
    process-based writing
coherence, 84–7
cohesion, 83–4
collaborative writing groups, 23–4,
  114, 168–9, 173
composition pedagogy, 59–79
  rhetorical approach, 61–70
  expressionist approach, 71–4
  cognitive approach, 74–6
  social constructivist approach, 76–
    9
  see also Aristotelean rhetoric; new
    rhetoric; rhetoric

conferencing, 24
contrastive analysis, 12–15
contrastive rhetoric
  definition, 5
  extended, new definition, 8–11
  methods of research, 153–65
  paradigm shift, 18–9
  implications for teaching, 166–70
  implications for testing, 170–2
  future research directions, 172–4
contrastive rhetoric studies by
    language
  Arabic, 34–7
  Chinese, 37–41
  Finnish, 47–52
  German, 46–7
  Japanese, 41–5
  Korean, 45–6
  Spanish, 52–3
  Czech, 53–4
corpus research, 173
  see also Biber's multifeature/
    multidimensional analysis
creating research space (CARS)
    model, 132–4
  see also genre; move analysis
critical pedagogy, see ideology
culture, definition, 101

discourse
  aims, 65
  modes, 65
  see also Kinneavy's theory of
    discourse
discourse analysis, 19–20, 80–1
  see also text linguistics
discourse bloc, 32–3
discourse community, 76–9
discourse type, 10

editorials, 143–4
eight-legged essay, 37, 39, 41, 129
Enkvist's theory of texts, 90–1
error analysis, 12–14
ethnocentrism, 16, 162–3
Euro-English, 17
expository writing, 15, 24, 43, 65, 92, 108, 132

gender bias, 173
genre, 11, 99, 126–49, 164–5, 169–70, 172–3
   Bakhtin's definition, 128
   Berkenkotter and Huckin's definition, 128
   Bhatia's definition, 127
   Swales's definition, 126–7
genre analysis, 24–5, 132–4
   see also CARS model; move analysis
grant proposals, 134–5
Gunnarsson's model of professional discourse, 136

Hofstede's cross-cultural value dimensions, 101–103

ideology, 25–6
   see also international Englishes; norms
interlanguage, 12–14
The International Association for the Evaluation of Educational Achievement (IEA) Study of Written Communication, 21, 107–13, 131, 163, 170–1
international Englishes, 16–17, 173
   see also norms
interrater reliability, 165

Kaplan's model of contrastive rhetoric
   first work, 15–16
   theoretical premise, 30–2
   text analysis, 32–3
   further developments, 156–7
Kinneavy's theory of discourse, 11, 32, 65
ki-shoo-Ten-ketsu pattern, 41–2, 45, 95

learning academic writing, 77–9, 145–9, 171
   see also social constructivist approach
linguistic relativity
   see Sapir-Whorf hypothesis
literacy, 20–1, 98–114, 173
   see also writing as a cultural activity

metadiscourse, 47–8, 50–1, 94–5
metatext, *see* metadiscourse
methods of contrastive rhetoric research, 153–65
   see also research design
move analysis, 40–1, 132–4

narrative writing, 43, 65, 74, 87–8, 92–3, 99, 108, 112, 126, 131–2, 149, 171
new rhetoric, 6–7, 66–70
   see also Perelman's new rhetoric; Toulmin's rhetoric
NORDTEXT and NORDWRITE projects, 89–90, 169
norms of writing, 170, 173
   see also international Englishes

orality vs. literacy, 103–5
organization of prose
   deductive, 20, 42, 50, 91
   inductive, 20, 42–3, 50, 52, 91
   quasi-inductive, 20, 42

Perelman's new rhetoric, 6, 67, 69–70
persuasive appeals, 64
persuasive writing, 24, 47, 64–5, 70, 79, 97, 108, 127, 132, 134
political discourse, 145
process-based writing, 167–9
   see also expressionist approach under composition pedagogy
professional writing, 135–7
promotional writing, 136–7

qualitative vs. quantitative research, 162

reader-responsible text, 20, 42, 51–2, 71

research article, 132–4
research design, 153–65
  case study, 154, 156, 161, 173
  ethnography, 154, 156, 161
  prediction and classification, 154,
    156, 160
  quantitative research, 154, 156,
    157–60
  reflective inquiry, 155–7
  survey, 154, 156, 160–1
  true and quasi experiments, 154,
    160–1
resume, 144–5, 172
rhetoric
  Aristotelean, 10, 31–2, 62–6
  definitions, 10, 60–3
  classical, 62–3
  see also new rhetoric; Perelman's
    new rhetoric; Toulmin's rhetoric

Sapir-Whorf hypothesis, 9–10, 28–
  30, 43
school writing, 129–32
script, *see* writing system
social construction of meaning
  see learning academic writing; so-
    cial constructivist approach un-
    der composition pedagogy
superstructures of text, 87–9
  macrostructures, 87
  problem-solution, 87, 89
  rhetorical predicates, 87

story grammar, 87
superstructure of argument, 87,
  89

Takala's model of writing, 129–30
teacher-student conferencing, 24
tertium comparationis, 163–4, 172
testing of writing, 170–2
text linguistics, 9–11, 19–20, 167
  definitions, 19–20, 80–1
  review of contrastive studies, 80–
    99
  schools of thought of text linguis-
    tics, 81–2
  Prague school, 81–2
  New school, 82–3
  Systemic, 82
  see also discourse analysis
topical structure analysis, 84–7, 97
transfer, 16, 120–1, 123
translation theory, 9, 11, 117–25
  see also acceptability; adequacy
Toulmin's rhetoric, 66–69
translator/editor, 123–5

Vähäpassi's model of school writing,
  109–110

writer-responsible text, 20, 42, 51–2
writing as a cultural activity, 20–1,
  100–16, 173
writing systems, 22, 103–5